Social Media Marketing FOR DUMMIES®
2ND EDITION

by Shiv Singh and Stephanie Diamond

WILEY

John Wiley & Sons, Inc.

Social Media Marketing For Dummies®, 2nd Edition

Published by
John Wiley & Sons, Inc.
111 River Street
Hoboken, NJ 07030-5774

www.wiley.com

For general information on our other products and services, please contact our Customer Care Department within the U.S. at 877-762-2974, outside the U.S. at 317-572-3993, or fax 317-572-4002.

For technical support, please visit www.wiley.com/techsupport.

Wiley publishes in a variety of print and electronic formats and by print-on-demand. Some material included with standard print versions of this book may not be included in e-books or in print-on-demand. If this book refers to media such as a CD or DVD that is not included in the version you purchased, you may download this material at http://booksupport.wiley.com. For more information about Wiley products, visit www.wiley.com.

Library of Congress Control Number: 2012933918

ISBN 978-1-118-06514-3 (pbk); ISBN 978-1-118-22235-5 (ebk); ISBN 978-1-118-23630-7 (ebk); ISBN 978-1-118-26101-9 (ebk)

Manufactured in the United States of America

10 9 8 7 6 5 4 3 2

WILEY

About the Authors

Shiv Singh is global head of digital for PepsiCo Beverages. Previously, he worked with Razorfish. Shiv has been published widely, and he has spoken at conferences such as South by Southwest Interactive, the Direct Marketing Association's Leader's Forum, OMMA Global, O'Reilly Graphing Social Patterns, the ARF Annual Summit, and the Social Ad Summit. He has also been quoted in the *Wall Street Journal* and by Reuters, Associated Press, *Adweek*, *Ad Age*, and several other noted publications discussing digital strategy and social influence marketing.

Stephanie Diamond is a thought leader and management marketing professional with years of experience building profits in more than 75 different industries. She has worked with solopreneurs, small business owners, and multibillion dollar corporations.

She worked for eight years as a Marketing Director at AOL. When she joined, there were less than 1 million subscribers. When she left in 2002, there were 36 million. She had a front row seat to learn how and why people buy online. While at AOL, she developed, from scratch, a highly successful line of multimedia products that brought in an annual $40 million dollars in incremental revenue.

In 2002, she founded Digital Media Works, Inc. (`MarketingMessage Mindset.com`), an online marketing company that helps business owners discover the hidden profits in their business. She is passionate about guiding online companies to successfully generate more revenue and use social media to its full advantage.

As a strategic thinker, Stephanie uses all the current visual thinking techniques and brain research to help companies to get to the essence of their brand. She continues this work today with her proprietary system to help online business owners discover how social media can generate profits. You can read her blog at `www.MarketingMessageBlog.com`.

Stephanie's other books include *Prezi For Dummies* and *Dragon Naturally Speaking For Dummies*.

Stephanie received a BA in Psychology from Hofstra University and an MSW and MPH from the University of Hawaii. She lives in New York with her husband and Maltese named Colby.

Dedication

To Barry, who makes all things possible. To my family, for their love and support.

— Stephanie Diamond

Authors' Acknowledgments

It has been my distinct privilege to write this book. I want to offer great thanks to my wonderful co-author Shiv Singh for his brilliance and Wiley Publishing, Inc. for letting me write this book for their audience of smart readers.

The following people were especially important in creating this book, and I offer very sincere thanks to the great creative group at Wiley: executive editor Steve Hayes, project editor Linda Morris, and technical editor Michelle Oxman. They made this project great fun to work on! I also want to thank Matt Wagner, my agent at Fresh Books, for his continued hard work and support on my behalf.

Finally, thanks to you for choosing this book to learn about social media marketing. I wish you enormous joy on your exciting journey into social media.

— Stephanie Diamond

I've always wanted to write, a desire that was constantly fueled by my parents, who encouraged me to write first by keeping a diary, and then exploring poetry and fiction, and finally, nonfiction as I grew older. And the same goes for my brother, who fueled the interested by patiently reading drafts of whatever I've written and providing valuable feedback. Many teachers in school pushed me along in a similar fashion. Without all the continuous encouragement from my childhood days to put pen to paper, no book would have ever been written.

This specific book would have never been completed had it not been for my wife, who sacrificed what should have been many a family weekend to let me sit at my desk and churn out chapter after chapter. Her encouragement, which often took the form of incentivizing me with the lure of a nice wine if I finished a chapter before an agreed-upon deadline, made all the difference, especially at a time when I was juggling a day job, a night job in the form of a wine magazine I copublish, and the birth of a son who thankfully started sleeping through the night rather quickly.

Finally, the editors at Wiley deserve acknowledgment. Especially Steve Hayes, who first saw the opportunity and reached out to me, and then coaxed each chapter out of me while providing incredibly valuable guidance to a first-time author. Their patience, especially with the timeline as I struggled to deliver chapters on time, made the mammoth task all the easier.

— Shiv Singh

Publisher's Acknowledgments

We're proud of this book; please send us your comments at http://dummies.custhelp.com. For other comments, please contact our Customer Care Department within the U.S. at 877-762-2974, outside the U.S. at 317-572-3993, or fax 317-572-4002.

Some of the people who helped bring this book to market include the following:

Acquisitions and Editorial

Project Editor: Linda Morris

Executive Editor: Steve Hayes

Copy Editor: Linda Morris

Technical Editor: Michelle Oxman

Editorial Manager: Jodi Jensen

Editorial Assistant: Amanda Graham

Sr. Editorial Assistant: Cherie Case

Cover Photo: ©iStockphoto.com / pagadesign

Cartoons: Rich Tennant (www.the5thwave.com)

Composition Services

Senior Project Coordinator: Kristie Rees

Layout and Graphics: Corrie Niehaus, Mark Pinto, Lavonne Roberts, Christin Swinford

Proofreaders: John Greenough, Kathy Simpson

Indexer: BIM Indexing & Proofreading Services

Publishing and Editorial for Technology Dummies

Richard Swadley, Vice President and Executive Group Publisher

Andy Cummings, Vice President and Publisher

Mary Bednarek, Executive Acquisitions Director

Mary C. Corder, Editorial Director

Publishing for Consumer Dummies

Kathleen Nebenhaus, Vice President and Executive Publisher

Composition Services

Debbie Stailey, Director of Composition Services

Contents at a Glance

Table of Contents

Introduction

● ●

On August 23, 1999, Blogger launched as one of the earliest dedicated blog-publishing tools. At that time, social media was considered a niche activity on the fringes of the Internet. But today, Blogger is the seventh-most-popular site on the Internet, hosting millions of blogs. In a span of seven years, Facebook has grown to more than 800 million users, and Wikipedia, for all practical purposes, has replaced Britannica as an encyclopedia. Social media is the most important phenomena transforming the Internet.

There is more to it than the phenomena, though. It also presents unique marketing opportunities, which force marketers to revisit the core guiding principles of marketing while providing new ways to reach social influencers and allow for people to influence each other and do the marketing for the brand. Social media marketing (SMM) forces companies to rethink how they market online, to whom they market, and how to structure their own organizations to support these new marketing opportunities. For anyone involved with social media marketing — and Internet marketing, more broadly — this is indeed an exciting time.

Social Media Marketing For Dummies, 2nd Edition, is written to help you make sense of the madness. Because it's such a hot topic, the press and the experts alike are quick to frighten marketers, like you, and introduce new terminology that confuses rather than enlightens. This book cuts through all that noise and simply explains what social media marketing is and how you can harness it to achieve your objectives as a marketer. It also aims to help you prioritize what's important and what isn't.

About This Book

The social media marketing space is changing rapidly, so by very definition, this book can't be completely comprehensive. It does, however, aim to distill the core concepts, trends, tips, and recommendations down to bite-sized, easy-to-digest nuggets. As social media marketing touches all parts of marketing and all parts of the Internet, too (from traditional websites to social platforms to the mobile web), based on your own experiences, you'll find some sections more valuable than others.

As you read this book, keep in mind that the way people influence each other online and impact purchasing and brand affinity decisions is similar to the way they've done for thousands of years in the real world. The technology is finally catching up, and social media marketing is fundamentally about allowing and encouraging that behavior to happen in a brand-positive manner online, too.

This book helps you understand why social media matters to marketers and how you can harness it to directly impact your own marketing efforts in meaningful ways. Targeted at both marketers in large organizations and those of you who work in small businesses or run small businesses, it includes advice for every business scenario.

Conventions Used in This Book

To make the book easier to read, I use the following conventions:

- ✔ Social media marketing is sometimes abbreviated SMM.
- ✔ When you see URLs (web addresses) appearing within a paragraph, caption, or table, they look like this: www.dummies.com.

Foolish Assumptions

In writing this book, we imagined someone pulling a copy off a bookshelf in a Barnes and Noble and scanning it to see whether it's a valuable guide. And we wondered what that person would need to know to find this book interesting. Here are some of the assumptions we came up with about you:

- ✔ You have a computer with Internet access.
- ✔ You've visited a social media site like Facebook or Twitter.
- ✔ You're working in marketing or want to join the marketing field.
- ✔ You have customers or prospective customers who use the web frequently.
- ✔ You sell a product or service that you can market online.
- ✔ You're curious about social media and whether it changes marketing.

How This Book Is Organized

This is book is divided into five distinct parts. As you progress through the chapters, you'll move from learning the fundamentals of social media marketing to practical strategies for implementing SMM programs and campaigns for your brand.

Rather than have separate chapters for marketers at small businesses versus large corporations, each chapter addresses the circumstances of both using the differences between the two to explain the core concepts more strongly.

And unlike most books that deal with social media marketing, this book looks at every dimension of the field holistically, with chapters dedicated to using SMM techniques on your website, in marketing campaigns, on mobile devices, and behind your company's firewall.

Part I: Getting Social with Your Marketing

A common misconception about social media marketing is that it's fundamentally about marketing on social platforms such as Facebook, Twitter, LinkedIn, and YouTube. But that's not the case, and Part I lays out the landscape of SMM, places it in the context of other forms of marketing, and then walks you through different stages of the marketing funnel.

With important information about how to find competitors, this section also explains why SMM matters.

Part II: Practicing SMM on the Social Web

Part II is very much the practitioner's part, explaining the nuts and bolts of SMM campaigns, including planning for them, managing participation, seeding viral video clips, and tips and tricks for turning a crisis to your advantage.

The chapters in this section also detail how, exactly, you can market on the mainstream and niche social platforms, what each platform allows you to do, and the best way to manage your influencers.

Part III: Reaching Your Audience via Mainstream Social Platforms

When you're ready to start your campaign, Part III helps you choose the SMM platforms that will work best for you. We look at several of the major platforms — Facebook, Twitter, LinkedIn, Google+, and foursquare — to understand who uses them and how to maximize your efforts with them.

We also cover niche networks and look at how to reach your key influencers. In addition, we look at best practices for SMM campaigns.

Part IV: Old Marketing Is New Again with SMM

In Part IV, you learn how to transform your own website to allow for social media marketing. We also explain what it means to be an authentic and engaged advertiser — in other words, how to take your existing advertising efforts social and get more mileage out of them.

The chapters on mobile marketing and employee influence explain how you can encourage your employees to road test your SMM efforts. We also emphasize that you can't ignore the mobile web today. The chapter on metrics explains how you can easily measure all your SMM efforts. In the chapter on social media governance, we demonstrate models you can use along with policies you can employ. Finally, the chapter on real-time marketing looks at how to make use of ongoing feedback from customers to improve your marketing efforts.

Part V: The Part of Tens

And lastly, the Part of Tens, as with all *For Dummies* books, lists ten key SMM best practices that you must absolutely pay attention to. Also included are ten common mistakes — mistakes made by the best of us who have been practicing SMM time and again. Also included are the ten must-read blogs that will keep you updated with the world of SMM and digital marketing more broadly. The section ends with the top ten SMM tools to try.

Icons Used in This Book

In the margins of the book, you'll find these icons helping you out:

Whenever we provide a hint that makes an aspect of social influence marketing easier, we mark it with a Tip icon.

The Remember icon marks paragraphs that contain a friendly reminder.

Heed the paragraphs marked with the Warning icon to avoid potential disaster.

Whenever we get technically inclined, we mark the paragraph with a Technical Stuff icon. If you're not technically inclined, you can skip these nuggets of info.

Where to Go from Here

The book is designed such that you can quickly jump to a specific chapter or section that most interests you in a particular moment. You don't have to start with the first chapter — although if you're new to social media marketing, we recommend that you do so. Understanding the foundation of social media marketing (which we explain in the early chapters) helps you better apply the techniques that you learn in the later ones to the specifics of your business.

Occasionally, we have updates to our technology books. If this book does have technical updates, they will be posted at dummies.com/go/social mediamarketingfdupdates.

Part I
Getting Social with Your Marketing

The 5th Wave   By Rich Tennant

"Jim and I do a lot of business together on Facebook. By the way, Jim, did you get the sales spreadsheet and little blue pony I sent you?"

In this part . . .

Part I lays out the landscape of SMM, places it in the context of other forms of marketing, and then walks you through different stages of the marketing funnel.

Chapter 1 discusses the fundamentals of social influence marketing: what it is, how it works, and what it means in the context of your other marketing efforts. In Chapter 2, we highlight some of the key social media statistics so that you have a sense of what to expect when you do your own competitive research. In Chapter 3, we explain how you need to think about the big idea a little differently than you do with traditional marketing as you deploy social media marketing to meet your marketing and business objectives.

Chapter 1

Understanding Social Media Marketing

*W*hen marketing online, you design websites, run display advertising, publish content to YouTube, and push your website listings higher up in the search engine rankings to promote and sell products. It's easy to forget how people actually buy. It's easy to assume that the potential customers are lonely people crouched over their computers late at night choosing what products to add to a shopping cart — isolated from the real world and their family and friends.

But in reality, that's not how people buy online today. It might have been the case in the early days of the web, when the people spending time online were the early adopters and the mavericks, the ones willing to take the risk of putting their credit card numbers into a computer hoping for accurate charges and secure transactions. In those days, few people bought online, and the ones who did were on the fringes of mainstream society.

Those days are over now. With more than 260 million people using the web on a regular basis in the United States alone, using the Internet has become a mainstream social activity. Consumers approach purchasing online differently, too, and as a result, you need to approach your marketing online differently as well. Your approach must incorporate influence and the different roles that people play in the realm of social media.

This chapter discusses the fundamentals of social media marketing: what it is, how it works, who the players are, and what it means in the context of your other marketing efforts.

Defining Social Media Marketing

A discussion of any subject needs to begin with a definition, and so here's the one for social media marketing: *Social media marketing* is a technique that employs *social media* (content created by everyday people using highly accessible and scalable technologies such as blogs, message boards, podcasts, microblogs, bookmarks, social networks, communities, wikis, and vlogs).

Social media (which was probably one of the most-hyped buzzwords of the last few years) refers to content created and consumed by regular people for each other. It includes the comments a person adds at the end of an article on a website, the family photographs he uploads to a photo-sharing site, the conversations he has with friends in a social network, and the blog posts that he publishes or comments on. That's social media, and it's making everyone in the world a content publisher and arbitrator. It's democratizing the web. WordPress (www.wordpress.com), shown in Figure 1-1, is the most popular blogging platform. It allows you to launch your own blog in a matter of minutes.

Figure 1-1: WordPress. com — just one example of many blog and social media platforms.

Learning about the Roles People Play

To look at the framework of social media marketing, we need to look at the different roles played by those engaged in social media. They are as follows:

✓ **Marketers:** They share content online to achieve an organization's marketing and business needs. Today's marketer looks nothing like the marketers of the twentieth century. Customers now own the brand conversation. The opportunity to interrupt and annoy has dwindled. Customers now meet businesses on their own terms. In the following section, we discuss the new role that marketers have to play.

✓ **Influencers:** Several types of influencers contribute to the decisions customers make. They may be everyday people who influence the consumer as he makes a purchasing decision. Depending on the decision, the social influencers may be a wife (or husband), friends, peers at work, or even someone the consumer has never even met in real life. Simply put, the people who influence a brand affinity and purchasing decision are the social influencers. They may do this directly by rating products and commenting or by publishing opinions and participating in conversations across the web. Anyone can be a social influencer, influencing someone else's brand affinity and purchasing decisions, and you, the reader, are probably one, too, without realizing it. We discuss the specific types of influencers in the section "Understanding the role of the influencer."

It isn't enough to market to the consumer anymore; as a marketer, you have to market to your potential customers' social influencers as well so that they in turn influence either overtly or just by what they publish and share online. And that's what social media marketing is about.

Changing role of the social media marketer

Anyone who has worked in online marketing for a while has watched amazing changes take place. Starting in 1994, Stephanie watched AOL and other online services help start a social media revolution that continues to change the world. Many marketers are looking for a specific set of rules to follow to be successful. We can assure you, there aren't any, but there are some guidelines. Following are some of the things that social media marketers must do if they want their company to compete successfully in the new social marketplace:

✓ **Become the top persuader.**

When you lead a SMM team, you need to understand that persuasion is your most important tool. You persuade your team that you can help them achieve success, and you persuade your customer to buy your product. Throughout this book, we discuss the role that influence plays in social media. Before you influence, you need to figure out the persuasive message that will sell. When you do that, you can unleash the groups that influence your customers.

✔ **Utilize a variety of distribution channels.**

The key mistake that some new social media marketers make is to focus solely on social media platforms to carry their message. This does half the job. It gets people's attention: It just doesn't get them to the sale. For example, imagine that you have just tweeted about a solution for stain removal. Unless you provide a link to your product and a place for discussion and reviews, you have a missed opportunity. Draw a map of all your channels (blog, website, newsletter, and so on), and use it whenever you plan a new campaign. You need a link to all your venues.

✔ **Reinvent your strategy to emphasize value.**

Value is a secret weapon in this economy. When you boil away all the other ingredients of a product sale, you uncover value. This is a tricky concept because value is in the eye of the beholder. Understanding what imparts that value should underlie your entire marketing strategy. Think about your current SMM campaign. Are you focusing on features and benefits or how the product makes your customer feel? For example, some companies focus on making people feel smart and sexy when they buy a certain model car. By the same token, others may focus on models that emphasize safety and responsibility. If you understand the value, you can establish a bond with your buyer.

✔ **Market to inspire.**

The globalization of our world via the Internet has given us a window into the lives of others. It's hard to ignore the poverty and disease that plague the world's population. Many companies are seizing the opportunity to use their businesses to help make an impact. SMM encourages the connection we share with others. Think about how your business can participate. In 2009, Everywhere, an online media company, launched a campaign using social media. For every tweet containing the #BeatCancer hashtag, eBay, PayPal, and Miller Coors donated one cent to cancer research. The campaign raised $70,000 in a 24-hour period, demonstrating that very little effort on the part of a tweeter can have a big impact on society.

✔ **Create and curate content.**

Engaging content is a big part of any SMM campaign. You need an editorial calendar that lays out your topics, creation tools, and deadlines. You also need to focus on curating content already published on the web. Becoming a trusted source of information is key to getting your customers to visit often.

✔ **Know when to resist the next shiny object.**

As you well know, new web tools pop up daily. The best way to avoid being distracted is to write your objectives down. The last thing you want to say to yourself is, "Everyone is using such and such, so we should use it." Place your objectives in a prominent place, and refer to them often. If they change, revise the document.

✔ **Be prepared to be wrong.**

This is a tough one. In your role as marketer, you want to lead your company to successive victories. SMM is not a sure thing. You need to be prepared to experiment and change course using the feedback you get from customers. You may start with a small idea and develop it into a full-blown campaign. It is unlikely that you can start out with a very expensive big effort and not have to correct along the way. When management and staff start out with the notion that they are testing and experimenting, changes in direction won't seem as shocking. This cuts down on wear and tear of the psyche for everyone.

Understanding the role of the influencer

To understand how social influence works, you need to look at how people are influenced in the real world, face to face. Social influence isn't something new. Long before the web, people asked each other for advice as they made purchasing decisions. What one person bought often inspired another to buy the same product, especially if the original purchaser said great things about the product. That's how human beings function; we're influenced and motivated by each other to do things. We're social beings, and sharing information on our experiences is all a part of social interaction.

Is influence bad? Of course not. More often than not, people *seek* that influence. People ask each other for advice; they share decision-making processes with friends and colleagues; they discuss their own experiences.

How much a person is influenced depends on multiple factors. The product itself is the most important one. When buying *low-consideration purchases* (those with a small amount of risk), people rarely seek influence, nor are they easily influenced by others. Buying toothpaste, for example, is a low-consideration purchase because each product may not be that different from the next one, and they're all fairly inexpensive — so you won't lose much money if you choose one that doesn't fit your needs. On the other hand, buying a new car is typically a *high-consideration purchase* (a purchase that includes a large risk).

The price of the car, the maintenance costs, and its reputation for its safety all contribute to making it a high-consideration purchase, not to mention the fact that you want to identify with a certain brand versus another one. Social influence plays a much bigger role in car purchases than in toothpaste decisions. Mercedes Benz used social media marketing at the time of the Super Bowl to draw attention to its brand, as shown in Figure 1-2.

Figure 1-2:
The
Mercedes
Benz tweet
race.

Social influence matters with every purchase, but it matters more with high-consideration purchases than low-consideration ones. Most consumers realize that when they're making high-consideration purchases, they can make better and more confident purchasing decisions when they take into account the advice and experience of others who have made those decisions before them. That's how influence works.

Considering the types of influencers

When discussing social media marketing, people often ask us whether this means that they should add product review features to e-commerce websites or advertise on social networks. Yes, product reviews and advertising are important, but there's more to social influence than those two things. When you think about social influence in the context of your marketing objectives, you must separate social influencers online into three types: *referent, expert,* and *positional.* These categories come from thinking that social psychologists John French and Bertram Raven pioneered in 1959.

As a marketer seeking to deploy social media marketing techniques, the first question to answer is this: Which social influencers sway your consumers as they make purchasing decisions about your product? After you identify those social influencers, you can determine the best ways to market to them.

Any major brand affinity or purchasing decision has referent, expert, and positional social influencers all playing distinct and important roles. Which one is most important may vary slightly based on the purchase, but the fact remains that you need to account for these three distinct types of social influencers in your marketing campaigns. If you're a marketer trying to positively affect a purchasing decision, you must market not just to the consumer, but also to these influencers.

Referent influencers

A *referent influencer* is someone who participates on the social platforms. These users are typically in a consumer's social graph and influence brand affinity and purchasing decisions through consumer reviews, by updating their own status and Twitter feeds, and by commenting on blogs and forums. In some cases, the social influencers know the consumers personally.

Because the consumers know and trust their referent influencers, they feel confident that their advisers are also careful and punctilious. Because they're people they trust, they value their advice and guidance over most other people. Referent influencers influence purchasing decision more than anyone else at the consideration phase of the marketing funnel, according to *Fluent,* the social influence marketing report from Razorfish.

For example, if Shiv decides to make a high-consideration purchase such as a car, he might start by going online and discussing different cars with a few friends in a discussion forum or on a social network. And then that weekend, he might meet those friends over coffee and carry on that discussion in person. They tell him about the cars they like, their own purchasing experiences, and which dealerships they've had experience with. This influence is considered *referent influence* because these friends sway him by the strength of their charisma and interpersonal skills, and they have this sway because he respects them. What's worth pointing out, though, is that the friends whom he knows to be most informed about cars will probably influence him more than the others.

Expert influencers

A consumer who's mulling over a high-consideration purchase might also consult an expert influencer. An *expert influencer* is an authority on the product that the consumer is considering purchasing. Also called *key influencers,* they typically have their own blogs and huge Twitter followings, and rarely know their audiences personally.

When considering buying a car, suppose Shiv doesn't turn just to friends for advice, but also visits some car review websites like Edmunds (www. edmunds.com, shown in Figure 1-3). On these review websites, experts rate, rank, and pass judgment on cars. Because they put the cars through various tests and know the cars inside and out, their opinions matter. They're the expert social influencers — people whom Shiv may not know personally but are recognized as authorities in a certain field. Their influence is derived from the skills or expertise that they — or broadly speaking, their organization — possess based on training.

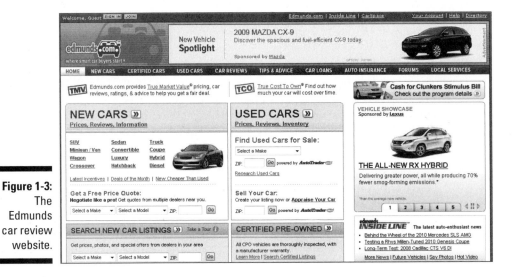

Figure 1-3:
The Edmunds car review website.

Positional influencers

A *positional influencer* is closest to both the purchasing decision and to the consumer. Called *peer influencers* sometimes, they are typically family members or part of the consumer's inner circle. They influence purchasing decisions most directly at the point of purchase and have to live with the results of their family member's or friend's decision as well.

As Shiv says, "I know that I can't make a high-consideration purchase like a car purchase without discussing it with my wife. Invariably, she'll drive the car, too, and sit in it as much as I will. It is as much her purchase as it is mine. Her opinion matters more than anyone else's in this case. After all, I need to discuss with her the relative pricing of the cars available and whether one is more suitable for our family versus another." This person derives her influence from her relative position and duties in relation to the actual consumer. She's closest to the purchasing decision and to the consumer and therefore has the most social influence.

Influencing on digital platforms

As we discuss earlier in the chapter, social influence impacts every purchasing decision and always has in some form or other. Each time people make purchasing decisions, they ask each other for advice. Sometimes, they depend upon an expert's guidance, and in other cases, that advice comes from people they know.

So why is influence such a big deal today? This is because Internet and social media consumption specifically have hit the mainstream. For example, as of October 2011, the social networking phenomenon Facebook had 800 million users worldwide, giving it a population larger than most countries. That's a lot of people talking about a lot of things (including products) to a lot of people!

People are making more and more purchasing decisions online every day. It's as natural to buy a product online as it is to go into a physical store. People buy clothes and shoes online, not to mention high-consideration items such as computers, cars (yes, cars), and jewelry. But that's not all. Not only are consumers buying online, but thanks to social media, they're also conversing, socializing, and influencing each other online on a scale never seen before.

Call it a shift in web behavior, but the way people make decisions in the real world is finally moving to the Internet in a big way. The social media platforms such as Facebook (shown in Figure 1-4), LinkedIn, Twitter, and YouTube are just a few of the places where people are asking each other for advice and guidance as they make purchasing decisions. Smart companies are realizing that they should no longer design their e-commerce websites to convince buyers to make purchasing decisions in isolation. Rather, they need to design the websites to allow consumers to bring their social influencers into the decision-making process. As consumers, people expect and want that because that's how they're used to making their purchasing decisions. That's why social media marketing matters today. People are influencing and are being influenced by each other every day on the social network platforms, community websites, and destination sites.

You may need to put a lot of effort into convincing your managers how important the social media platforms are. The best way to communicate these ideas and techniques to your staff is by organizing lunch-and-learn sessions and bringing in external speakers who can walk your managers through the major social platforms and how best to market on them. Sharing case studies from other brands always resonates well and goes a long way to establishing credibility.

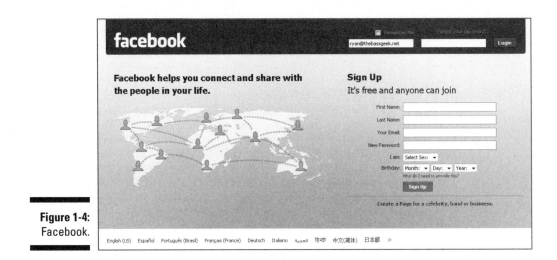

Figure 1-4:
Facebook.

Comparing Social Media Marketing with Other Marketing Efforts

It isn't enough to deploy social media marketing (SMM) in isolation of every other marketing effort. If you do, you're sure to fail. Your customers will notice that you have a disjointed, conflicted story — depending on where and how you're interacting with them. Therefore, it's important to understand how you can integrate your social media marketing within your other, more traditional marketing — direct mail, public relations, display advertising, and promotions.

Some of the social media marketing philosophies are in conflict with traditional public relations, media buying, direct mail, and promotions tactics. It's no use damning those forms of marketing and alienating your peers who focus on those areas. Put extra effort in partnering with your fellow employees as you practice these marketing techniques. Explain what you're doing, why you're doing it, and how it complements their efforts. If you discredit the other forms of marketing and the people behind them, it only hurts you in the long run.

Direct mail

Direct mail is about managing an active customer database and marketing to members of that database via circulars, catalogs, credit card applications, and other merchandising materials delivered to homes and businesses.

You've probably gotten a lot of direct mail over the years — perhaps mountains of it — and at some point, you've probably wished that these companies would stop mailing you. That's all direct mail, and whether you like it or not, direct mail has been a very successful form of marketing. The catalog industry has logged billions of dollars in sales because of it.

However, that has been impacted by social media marketing. Of all the areas of marketing, direct mail is one that will be most affected in the long run. Before you start worrying that your mail carrier will stuff your mailbox (or your e-mail inbox through e-mail marketing) even more than usual, consider this: Direct mail is most successful when the mail is targeted and personalized. That means it's reaching the people who really care about the offers (or are most likely to take advantage of them), and it's personalized toward the recipients' needs in a voice and style that's appealing to them. Pretty straightforward, isn't it?

Direct mail is as successful as the marketer's customer database. The database should contain names and addresses of people who are open to receiving direct mail. But when people stop trusting the marketing efforts of large corporations and instead switch to each other for advice, that's when direct mail loses its power. Statistically, we know that consumers are now more likely to depend on each other for advice and information than they are on the corporations that are marketing to them.

With consumers who are even more connected to each other through social media than before, it has gotten easier for them to reach out to one another for that advice. That means that when they see a piece of direct mail, they're less likely to depend on it. They'd rather go online and ask a friend for advice or search for a product online than look at that flyer in the mail. And as marketers harness social media marketing tactics more, it could see further drops.

There's another side to the story, though. The more data that you can capture about your customers through social media marketing tactics, the more opportunities you have to feed your direct mail database. That's just a factor of consumers doing more online, sharing more of themselves, and opting into direct mail efforts in exchange for information or acceptance into an online community. Your database may get richer with social media marketing in the mix, but the value of it may decrease — although that doesn't mean that you can't use direct mail as a starting point to jump-start an online community, sustain interest in it, or reward participation through mailing coupons. The solution? Think about how you collect information about your consumers differently and, more important, how you share information back to them. It doesn't have to only be via mail or only via social media; knowing when to use what form of communication is key. More on this in later chapters.

Public relations

Among the earliest proponents of social media were digital-savvy public relations experts. Many of them entered this space by treating social media just as they have treated the mainstream media. These professionals equated *buzz* (how much people talk about a specific product or brand) in the social media realm with press mentions in the mainstream media. These PR experts identified the influential (*influence* defined as those having the most reach) bloggers and tweeters and started showering them with the same kind of attention that they had been bestowing on the mainstream media. They sent them press releases in advance, offered exclusive interviews, invited them to dinners, commented on their blogs, and carefully tracked how much their brands were mentioned and how positively.

For PR professionals, this approach made perfect sense. Arguably, they recognized early on how powerful social media could be and were among the first to track brand mentions and participate in conversations. In fact, many of the social media experts today are former public relations professionals who've taken the time to understand how social media works and how they can leverage it to support a company's or a brand's objectives. Many PR professionals also understand how bad press and traditional PR disasters can be amplified by social media if not addressed immediately.

But life isn't that simple, and the relationship between public relations and social media is a complex one — which is something that the savviest of PR professionals understand and have always understood. Public relations is fundamentally about managing the press (mainstream or alternative) and pushing a company's agenda out to the press as much as possible. Whether it's the mainstream or alternative media, it doesn't matter. From a public relations professional's perspective, the press is the press, and they're only as good as their ability to amplify a company's message. That's where the problem lies.

When we look at social media marketing and how it harnesses social media, some of its core tenets are in conflict with public relations. For example, social media marketing is about social influencers influencing each other through social media. The focus is on the social influencers influencing each other and not on the PR professionals influencing people in the social media realm. The difference is that as consumers, we're trusting and depending upon each other more for advice than on large corporations. The PR professionals, for all their sincerity and skill, will still push a company's message as forcefully as they can — and in that, it conflicts with social media marketing. But still, here's something extremely important to consider: The more forward-looking public relations experts approach PR from a broader communications perspective and have taken the time and energy to understand the space deeply. Those who do that are much better equipped to understand and market through social media than other professionals.

Is there a remedy for conflicts between departments? Not necessarily, but as you deploy social media marketing campaigns, be sensitive to the fact that your goals and aspirations may be in conflict with your PR organization if it hasn't embraced social media or social media marketing. Have a conversation with them early on, find ways to collaborate and delineate boundaries, too — who does what, who reaches out to whom, and how much space is given to authentic social influencers to do the influencing versus the PR professionals. And as you do this, keep in mind that for many PR professionals, social media marketing is an evolution of PR. That's a good thing, providing for even more opportunities to collaborate.

Online advertising

When it comes to buying online advertising (also referred to as digital *media planning and buying)* on websites where your customers spend time, social media marketing plays an important role. *Online advertising* is about identifying websites your target customers visit, buying ad space on those websites, and then measuring how much those ads are viewed and clicked. It's as much an art as it's a science because knowing which sites your customers visit, where they're most likely to engage with an advertisement (where on the site as well), whether the site charges the appropriate amount for the advertisement, and how much that advertising affects purchasing is not always easy. We work with media buyers all the time, and their jobs are harder than you think, especially in the world of digital ad exchanges, data management platforms, and remnant inventory (books could be written on each of those terms alone).

But the online advertising space is important even in an economic downturn. The reason is simple: It's one of the most measurable forms of advertising, especially in relation to print and television, along with search engine advertising. You can track who views the advertisement, what they do with it, and in some cases, whether they eventually buy the product based on that advertisement. It's no surprise that the relationship to social media marketing is an important one as a result.

This relationship with social media marketing takes various forms. Here are some of those connection points:

- ✔ **Market to the social influencers who surround the customer, as well as the customer.**

    One of the ways in which you market to those influencers is using display advertising. So rather than just placing advertisements on websites that your customers visit, you place some advertisements (doesn't have to be a large percentage of your budget) on websites that their social influencers frequent, too. Is this as measurable as those advertisements targeting your customers directly? Maybe not, because these influencers are less likely to click the ads and make a purchase. But nevertheless, they remember the brand, and they influence your customers.

✔ **Place display advertising on the social platforms — like Facebook and YouTube — that your customers frequent.**

Most social platforms accept display advertising in some form, and this serves as an important part of their revenue model. Figure 1-5 shows an eBay display advertisement on YouTube. See Chapters 9 and 16 for more on this.

Granted, display advertising on social platforms used to produce bad results (users didn't notice the advertisements, and they don't click them), but the ad formats for social platforms are evolving, and today Facebook is the largest advertising platform on the Internet. One example of the evolution is *appvertising,* where advertisements are placed within applications that reside on social networks. These produce better results. Another innovation is where consumers are asked to like the ads that they're viewing on Facebook, resulting in their action appearing in the News Feeds of their friends. This helps the platform target ads more appropriately to them in the future.

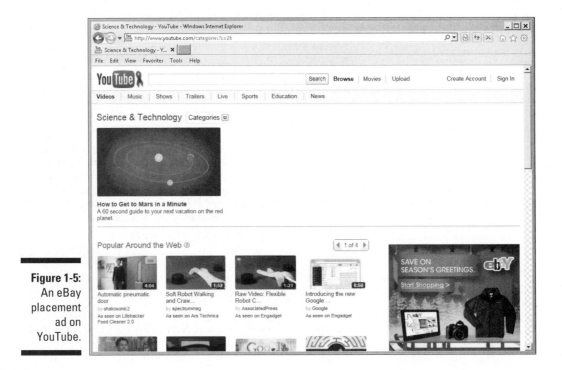

Figure 1-5:
An eBay placement ad on YouTube.

✔ **Use interactive social advertising.**

Think about this scenario for moment: You visit a major website like www.cnn.com and see a large advertisement on the right side. The advertisement asks you to sign up for suggestions about local deals in your neighborhood. That's an example of the ad unit becoming a platform for social interaction. There aren't too many examples of social ads online, but we're seeing more companies experiment in this space. Figure 1-6 shows how a Google Offers ad appears on CNN's website. See Chapter 16 for more on this.

Promotions

Promotions is another important type of marketing activity that's affected by social influence marketing, due to the fact that as people communicate with each other more, they have less time to participate in product promotions. But it also presents unique opportunities for marketers to put the potential of social influence marketing to good use.

Figure 1-6: Advertising on CNN.

Consider this: Promotions are primarily about incentives that are designed to stimulate the purchase or sale of a product in a given period. Promotions usually take the form of coupons, sweepstakes, contests, product samples, rebates, and tie-ins. Most of these promotions are designed as one-off activities linking the marketer to specific customers. However, by deploying social media marketing concepts, you can design promotions that require customers to draw in their social influencers, whether it's to participate in the contest or sweepstakes with them or to play an advisory role. By designing the promotion to require social influencer participation (it needs to be positioned as friends participating), the specific promotion may get a lot more attention than it normally would have. We discuss promotions in Chapter 4.

Taking Social Influence Beyond Marketing

As we hint in the earlier sections, the benefits of social media marketing extend beyond the core domain of marketing. If you harness the power of social influence marketing to change other parts of your business, you stand to gain the most. You can use SMM to mobilize groups of people to take specific actions, make marketers better corporate citizens, and further social change — and through those efforts, enhance a brand, too.

Using social influencers to mobilize

Social influencers, obviously, play an important role in getting people to do things. And this extends beyond the world of marketing. What makes it different on the web is that it's a lot easier to do now. Author Howard Rheingold was one of the first thinkers to identify this phenomenon in a book titled, *Smart Mobs: The Next Social Revolution* (Basic Books). He discussed how the street protestors of the 1999 Seattle World Trade Organization (WTO) conference used websites, cellphones, and other "swarming" tactics to organize, motivate each other, and plan protests. The smart mobs (an intentionally contradictory term) could behave intelligently because of their exponentially increasing links to each other. Through those links, they influenced and motivated each other to perform tasks, form shared opinions, and act together. They used social influence marketing tactics on themselves to accomplish specific objectives.

More recently, in *Here Comes Everybody: The Power of Organizing without Organizations* (Penguin Press), Clay Shirky also focuses on the power of organizing and influencing using social technologies. As he explains, every web page can be considered a latent community waiting for people to interact, influence, and mobilize one another. People with shared interests visit the web page at various times and often seek out their peers' opinions —

not just opinions from the web page's author. Shirky also discusses how Wikipedia, a user-contributed encyclopedia, can grow exponentially, publish efficiently, and self-correct using nontraditional corporate hierarchies.

We use the Seattle WTO protests and Wikipedia as examples to demonstrate how much social influence extends beyond the traditional realms of marketing into dramatically different domains. Driving the success of the Seattle WTO protests and the Wikipedia publishing model were two factors: social technologies that allowed people to contribute, participate, and converse easily and technologies that allowed people to see what others were doing. The social influencers were at the heart of these efforts and many of the other "smart mob" initiatives over the years.

Recently, Twitter directly enabled protesters in Iran to organize in the wake of their recent elections, to such an extent that the U.S. State Department asked Twitter to delay a scheduled maintenance so that it wouldn't disrupt communications among the Iranian citizens as they protested the reelection of President Mahmoud Ahmadinejad. And arguably, one of the key factors that drove the Arab Spring and the fall of the Egyptian government in March of 2011 was the ability to use social media to organize on a mass scale quickly as well as share media about the protests around the world at a time when the official government channels of communication were blocking everything. In fact, many people believe that the simple Facebook status update "Advice to the youth of Egypt: Put vinegar or onion under your scarf for tear gas" significantly helped the protestors.

But bringing this back to your company, it also demonstrates that you can harness those very same social media marketing philosophies to achieve other corporate objectives as well. We discuss them further in Chapters 3 and 18.

Social media marketing isn't just about how people influence each other by what they say on the social media platforms and on sites across the web. It also happens when people observe what others are doing online. As a result, if you'd love others to mimic a certain type of customer behavior, make that behavior visible to everyone visiting the website. We don't just listen to people we admire; we also copy what they're doing.

Marketers as better corporate citizens

As has been the case in the last few years, marketers are increasingly supporting and furthering specific social causes that are in alignment with their brands. This win-win situation results in the marketers getting more favorable press for their brands and the specific causes getting much needed sponsorship, too. One area where marketers are increasingly harnessing social media marketing tactics is in amplifying their efforts in the cause realm.

Why causes? The causes have all the ingredients to make a successful social media marketing effort. They are usually time-bound, have broad appeal, and are subjects that people like to discuss with each other. Marketers who tap into causes see their brands benefiting from halo effects by being associated with important social concerns and by gaining visibility with much larger audiences than they normally would have. If you're a marketer, it bodes well to directly support a cause, encourage its supporters to harness social media marketing tactics, or sponsor it indirectly. And then even more so, it makes sense to market your own cause efforts using social media marketing tactics in a measurable fashion.

Early in 2009, Procter & Gamble (one of the largest consumer-goods companies in the world) organized a social media education session for all its marketers. But instead of having a series of presentations by employees, P&G invited social media experts to visit their headquarters. The company divided the social media experts into teams and paired them with their own marketers. The teams were tasked with raising money for Tide's Loads of Hope disaster relief campaign using social media platforms to sell T-shirts. (The Loads of Hope website is shown in Figure 1-7.) The winning team raised $50,000, and Tide matched their contribution. Through this effort, P&G positioned itself as a better corporate citizen, raised money for a good cause, and was able to educate its marketers about the potential of social media by actually practicing social media marketing. Some detractors argued that this was just a one-day effort that got more attention than it deserved, but the fact that so much money was raised in so little time is admirable.

As you consider tapping into social media marketing to amplify your brand's efforts in the cause realm, keep in mind that consumers are increasingly skeptical of these efforts. Make sure that you're donating enough to make the effort genuine and meaningful for everyone involved.

Social graphs for social change

There's more to social causes than your ability to amplify your efforts around causes using social media marketing tactics. A larger change is afoot that demands attention, even if doesn't directly relate to your objectives. The web allows individuals to financially support a cause at the very moment that they're inspired and then encourage their friends who reside in their social graphs to do the same.

Figure 1-7:
Tide's Loads
of Hope.

When an individual provides monetary support for a cause, he can — in that very moment, using the social platforms and his own social media — broadcast his effort to his network of friends and associates. By doing so, he becomes a social media marketer, spreading the word about the cause and socially influencing his friends to contribute as well. This instant *viral effect* (the phrase comes from diseases and how they can spread rapidly from person to person) is collectively (and strongly) influencing how causes are promoted and funded — more so than the traditional big corporation backing strategies. This means that you, as a marketer, benefit from the halo effect of supporting a cause, but you can't just support it — you must be willing to participate in this viral affect the same way. Here are a few examples in this realm:

✔ **The Pepsi Refresh Project:** In 2010, Pepsi chose to give away $20 million to people across America who had ideas for refreshing their communities in positive ways. But instead of this being a traditional charity program, the Pepsi Refresh Project enabled people across the country to submit ideas that deserved funding. Ideas were chosen by other consumers. Ideas with the most votes were then funded. This award-winning social media program was social at the core (with over 80 million votes and millions of conversations about the ideas) and moved the brand's brand health metrics forward.

✔ **Causes:** This Facebook and MySpace application (which is available at www.causes.com) is a perfect example of nonprofit organizations using social media as marketing and fundraising tools. (You can see the Causes application's home page in Figure 1-8.) It allows you to choose a nonprofit, contribute funds to it, and track how many of your friends go on to support that cause after seeing your contributions or receiving your invitation to contribute. Within a year of its launch, the application had 12 million users supporting approximately 80,000 nonprofit causes worldwide. Users raised $2.5 million for 19,445 different charitable organizations. Facebook reported 60,000 daily uses of the application, whereas MySpace tracked 25,000 daily uses.

✔ **Oxfam:** The English charity Oxfam uses technology to help donors understand a problem more deeply and help them appreciate the difference that they're making. If you'd like to give the gift of giving, you can go to www.oxfamunwrapped.com (shown in Figure 1-9) and buy books, bags of seeds, clean water, and even goats in your friend's name. Oxfam delivers the gift to someone in need and also sends your friend a gift card. The site is a core component of Oxfam's fund-raising efforts.

Figure 1-8:
Causes.
com.

When Oxfam launched this program, the fact that you could buy a goat for someone in Darfur was more buzzworthy than any other marketing effort. Needless to say, it got people talking about Darfur, Oxfam, and goats, with people forming online communities based on these topics and the other charities that they support. In this case, the donors become social influencers.

Figure 1-9:
Oxfam.

✔ **charity: water:** This U.S.-based nonprofit provides clean water to developing communities using a Twitter festival (www.twestival. com) to promote the charity and encourage others to donate money as well. (See Figure 1-10.) The Twitter festival was held in 202 cities around the world, bringing together people from Twitter to support a cause. On February 12, 2009, the participating cities raised $250,000, with counting still going on. This was done with micropayments by participants related to the cause. Participants spread the word about it and socially influenced each other to contribute as well. The event was organized 100 percent by volunteers, and 100 percent of the money raised went directly to the charity. You can find out more about this charity's efforts at this website: www.charitywater.org/whywater/.

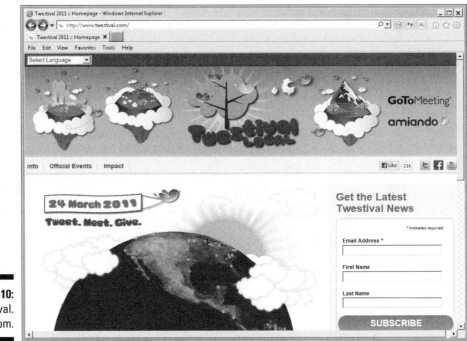

Figure 1-10:
Twestival.
com.

Chapter 2

Discovering Your SMM Competitors

*W*hich consumers are using the social web is a subject of much debate. Some see social networks as a passing fad and try to ignore it. They are just as wrong as the evangelists who believe that everyone is using the social web all the time.

The truth is that it's difficult to say who is using the social web. This is because the term *social web* is most commonly used to describe how people socialize and interact with each other across the web. With every passing day, many websites are becoming social platforms where visitors can interact and learn from one another. So then how can you find out which consumers use the social web? The best way is to understand how your company fits into the big picture and how your competitors are using social media.

In this chapter, we explain how to do that. Having a firm grip on the lay of the land in the social web makes it easier to craft a marketing plan that works with it. Understanding what your competitors are doing helps you understand your customers' expectations.

Classifying Consumer Activities

Before you launch a social media marketing campaign, you need a feel for what activities consumers undertake on the social web. After all, your marketing campaign is far more likely to succeed if it is in harmony with what consumers are trying to accomplish on the social web. Consumer activity on the social web is classified into these eight categories:

✔ **Information:** The Internet, with its academic roots, was conceived as a virtual library and an information-sharing tool. And to this day, consumers use the Internet for finding information more than anything else. In fact, it's no surprise that Google and Yahoo! are two of the top four web destinations. (Facebook is the second; YouTube is third.) It's because they're primary search engines, helping consumers find the information they're looking for. That hasn't changed, and even with the Internet going increasingly social, searching and finding information remains the number one consumer activity online. If you're running a marketing campaign for a product or service that consumers seek, you're most likely to get strong results. When people are in "information seeker" mode, they're most apt to participate in campaigns.

✔ **News:** One primary use for the Internet is news. More people read the news online than watch it on cable television. The instant, real-time nature of news makes it particularly suited for the Internet. Many cable television channels promote their websites to their TV audiences. But what's even more interesting is that practically all the major news websites integrate social media functionality into their user experience. When you go to www.cnn.com, www.nytimes.com, or www.washington post.com, you notice that journalists have blogs and the articles allow for commenting and ratings. Figure 2-1 shows the blogs offered by *The New York Times.* News sites often integrate video clips as well.

With news, your marketing opportunity differs slightly. Consumers are more receptive to the campaigns if your product or service is either contextualized in some form to what they're reading or is directly targeted toward them.

✔ **Communication:** The Internet continues to be a core communication medium for most people. With the advent of social media, this communication takes place within social networks versus personal websites or via e-mail and instant messenger programs. *Microcommunication* technologies such as Twitter, which let you communicate in short bursts of information, are very popular. The medium allows consumers to communicate with one another in new, dynamic ways, whether it be microblogging, leaving notes on friends' Facebook Walls, commenting on personal blogs, or instant messaging from within websites. When consumers are communicating with each other, they're less receptive to marketing campaigns unless the campaigns incorporate their communications with their peers in a permissible fashion. This is why social media marketing campaigns that incorporate groups of people are so important.

✔ **Community:** Online communities and social networks have seen explosive growth in the last few years. The amount of time that people spend on community websites is significantly higher than anywhere else on the web. Online communities include social platforms, such as Facebook and Twitter, and the more private online communities and forums that are often tied to company websites.

For example, The Well (shown in Figure 2-2) is one of the most famous online communities, just as Facebook is the most popular social network in the United States as we write this. The reasons people participate in online communities are myriad. (See Chapter 13 for more information on online communities.) Suffice it to say, community participation is a key type of activity online. However, when people are engaging with each other, they participate less in marketing campaigns because engaging with one another captures all their attention. They have no time for advertising because they're just hearing each other's opinions. When consumers are searching for information or looking to buy a product, they are more open to advertising. This is exactly why social media marketing, with its unique approach, is important.

✔ **E-commerce:** Consumers across the country continue to choose to buy more goods online. The fact that the products have to be shipped has done little to hinder many consumers from using the Internet to make retail purchases. The largest online retailer continues to be Amazon (www.amazon.com), with approximately $34 billion in sales each year. E-commerce represents a growing portion of total retail sales. There are some very obvious marketing opportunities in this, especially when peers are asked to recommend products. Great social media marketing opportunities abound here.

THE WₑLL™

Home   Learn About   Conferences   Member Pages   Mail   Store   Services & Help   Join Us

Username
Password   log in
☐ Remember me on this computer
Need help logging in?
SHARE

What is The WELL?

Welcome to a gathering that's like none other —
remarkably uninhibited, intelligent and
iconoclastic.

The regulars in this place include noted authors,
programmers, journalists, activists and other
creative people who swap info, test their
convictions and banter with one another in wide-
ranging conversations, using their real names.

The WELL, launched in 1985 as the *Whole Earth
'Lectronic Link*, provides a literate watering hole
for some articulate and unpretentious thinkers.
[more about The WELL...]

Where in The WELL are you?

Ed Ward, writer, broadcaster:
Living overseas, my information needs
are different: without access to U.S.
media, I find it's essential to read the
Media conference to stay aware of
what keeps Americans buzzing. Naturally, I also
check in to the europe.ind conference daily, and
Cooking has been a source of great tips and has
certainly expanded my, um, horizons. [more
recommendations...]

Fresh conversations

The picnic aquatic
Come to The WELL's annual picnic -- now
with more tugboat. (Members only)

Keeping the heart unwrinkled
How can we best help our parents as they
age?(Guests welcome) 💬🔲

Stranger than fiction
Do recent headlines sound like fictional
events? (Members only)

More discussions...

Photo festival 2009

Getting into The WELL

Membership is not for everyone, partly
because we are non-anonymous here. Here's
how to decide whether The WELL is for you,
and whether you're for The WELL. [more on
joining...]

Search our front porch

Figure 2-2:
The Well.

✔ **Entertainment:** There's no doubt that consumers look to the Internet
for entertainment. The explosive growth of YouTube and the most
recent adoption of high-end video sites like Hulu (shown in Figure 2-3)
are testament to this trend. Social games like Scramble and Pet Society
on social networking platforms and the major portals are just another
example of this trend. Arguably, entertainment is becoming a driving
reason for people to spend more time online, and this is in part thanks
to the proliferation of high-bandwidth access across the country. As
long as the marketing campaign is entertaining, consumers will respond
to it. They don't care as much whether it's an advertisement in these
instances.

✔ **Services:** Another popular consumer activity online is the use of services
to allow a person to lead a more efficient and productive life. Whether
they're paying bills, checking bank balances, looking up phone numbers,
finding jobs, or searching for apartments, consumers use the Internet
as a tool to lead more productive lives. Many of today's businesses,
such as banks and airlines, provide services on the Internet. Consumers
are typically very task-oriented when they're interacting with online
services; as a result, they don't expect to participate in advertising
campaigns, and especially not social media marketing campaigns, when
they're in this mode.

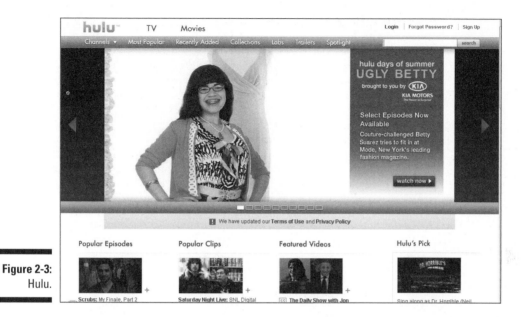

Figure 2-3:
Hulu.

✔ **Business:** And of course, the Internet is used to conduct business. This may take the form of companies talking to each other and exchanging information, establishing online marketplaces, and initiating brand launches. Businesses engage with their customers online by marketing and selling products and services and providing customer service via the Internet. Consumers expect these online conveniences from brands that they interact with, and they increasingly engage with businesses on the Internet. They also use the Internet to start their own businesses. Depending on the business, social media marketing campaigns can certainly help here.

Researching Your Customers' Online Activities

When developing a social media marketing campaign, it's important to determine what your target customers are doing on the Internet. You can use several tools to find out where your target customers are going online. Without this information, you can't formulate a smart social marketing strategy. You're simply shooting in the dark.

Tools that help you research online activity fall into two basic categories: free and paid. The free tools you can simply register for and use. Tools and services for which you must pay can get expensive very quickly. In Chapter 4, we discuss the pay tools and services, which are more appropriate when you're planning a specific SMM campaign.vln this section, we discuss some of the free tools:

✔ **Blog search engines:** These search engines *crawl* (sort through) just the blogosphere for the terms that you input. They search for those terms in the blog posts and the comments, and the searches generally include all publicly viewable blogs on the Internet. If you just want to get a sense of the conversations in the blogosphere about a specific topic or brand, these search engines can help you do that. The most popular ones include Technorati's blog search engine (`http://s.technorati.com`), Google's Blog Search (`http://blogsearch.google.com`), BlogPulse from Nielsen (`www.blogpulse.com`), and BlogScope (`www.blogscope.net`), which is shown in Figure 2-4.

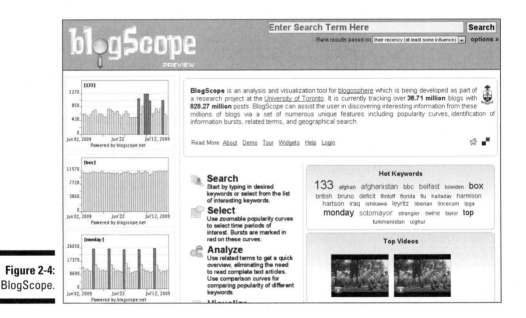

Figure 2-4: BlogScope.

A discussion on blog search engines wouldn't be complete without mentioning the official Twitter search tool (`http://search.twitter.com`). Twitter is the most popular microblogging platform. *Microblogging* is similar to blogging except that you're restricted to a certain number of characters per post. Another microblogging search engine to consider is Tweet Scan (`http://tweetscan.com`). Tweet Scan is shown in Figure 2-5, where you can search Twitter and its closest competitor, Identi.ca.

Figure 2-5:
Tweet Scan.

🖛 **Buzz charting:** Similar to the blog search engines, there are a few buzz
charting tools. These tools focus on giving you a comparative perspective
on how many different keywords, phrases, or links are discussed in
the blogosphere. They search for the terms and then organize the
responses into a chart, with the x-axis being time and the y-axis the
number of posts. Typically, you can choose the duration of time for the
x-axis. Nielsen has probably the most popular blog buzz charting tool, at
BlogPulse (`http://blogpulse.com/trend`). Omgili does similar buzz
charting for discussion forums (`http://buzz.omgili.com/graphs.
html`), as shown in Figure 2-6.

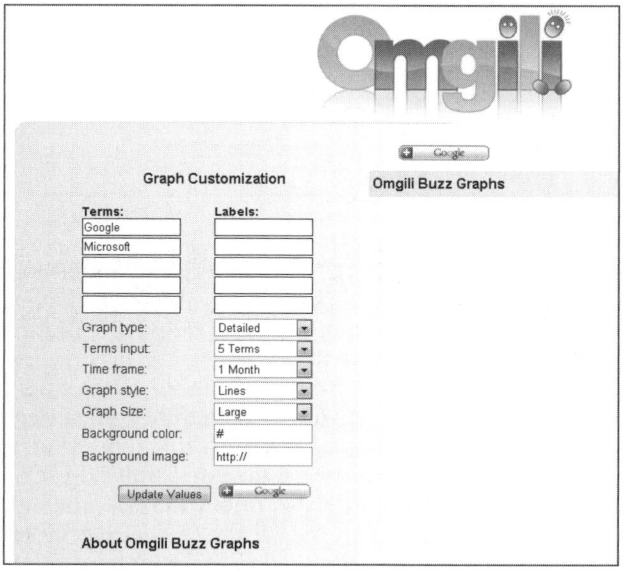

Figure 2-6:
Omgili.

✔ **Forums and message boards:** To understand online behavior in the social web, you must be able to scan the conversations happening in forums and message boards as well. Boardreader (`http://board reader.com`) allows you to search multiple boards at once. You can use it to find answers to questions that you may not find on a single board. Also, back to a marketer's point of view, you can find research people's opinions of brands or products. Boardreader is so popular that it powers a lot of the forum searches that the fee-based brand-monitoring tools conduct. Another player worth mentioning in this space is Omgili (`www.omgili.com`), which similarly focuses on forums and message boards. BoardTracker, (`www.boardtracker.com`), shown in Figure 2-7, is another popular way to search forums and message boards.

Figure 2-7:
Board
Tracker.

✔ **Video and image search:** Earlier in this chapter, we mention entertainment and the increasing number of people going online to watch videos — professionally created videos and personal ones, too. But how can you find the videos that are of interest to you or your brand? For video search, you have to depend on a couple of tools, as no single one truly captures all the videos created. All video searches must begin with YouTube (`www.youtube.com`), as it's the largest, but then you should also look at Metacafe (`www.metacafe.com`); Viral Video Chart (`www.viralvideochart.com`), which also tells you how much the clip is being discussed; and AOL Video (`http://video.aol.com/`), another notable player, shown in Figure 2-8.

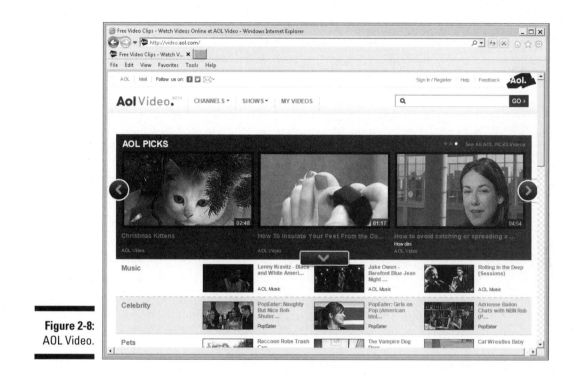

Figure 2-8:
AOL Video.

On the image side, you'd want to use the Flickr search (www.flickr.com) and, to a lesser extent, Google Images (www.google.com/images).

Google Images also searches professionally produced and published images, not just user-generated ones, so you might not get an accurate picture of what people are talking about.

Identifying Personas

After you understand what your customers do online, you can begin to define them more clearly. To do this, you can create what are known as *personas.* Personas are customer profiles that represent your actual buyers. Alan Cooper first wrote about personas in his book *The Inmates Are Running the Asylum.* He wrote, "We don't so much make up our personas as discover them as a byproduct of the investigation process." That is exactly what you need to do.

Some marketers swear by personas; others find it difficult to wrap their heads around it. We recommend the creation of personas because they help you stay focused on the buying strategies that matter. For example, suppose you identify your customer as a 45-year-old male who has an annual income of more than $90,000 and a family with two children less than 12 years old.

When you are developing your SMM campaign, you can stop your team from developing copy for a young woman of college age. This may sound obvious, but it's easy to get off track when the ideas are flying fast and furious. When a fun notion pops into someone's head, it can be helpful to look at your persona and think it through. You can remain focused and course-correct when you find you are getting away from the heart of the profile.

So what information goes into creating a good customer persona? Consider the following:

- ✔ **Demographics:** Obviously, you want to know if your customer is male or female, where they live, what their estimated income is, and so on.

- ✔ **Photo and name**: If you give your persona a name and choose a stock photo (or real customer photo), you bring life to it. When someone asks, "What would Alice want?" it makes a greater impact than visualizing a faceless and nameless customer.

- ✔ **Online places where they hang out:** This is important for your SMM efforts. Does he spend time on Facebook or a niche sports site?

- ✔ **Online places where they look for product information:** You need to know where they read product reviews and what online bloggers influence them.

- ✔ **Job level:** Is your customer a supervisor with staff to whom she can delegate? It's helpful to know the amount of responsibility she has at work.

- ✔ **Children and pets:** Clearly, childcare responsibility, family pets, and other home care chores play a factor in his product choices.

- ✔ **Hobbies and interests:** Learning about hobbies and special interests helps you speak to their desire for specific products.

Make sure your team understands the value of personas. Start with one or two until they get used to using them. Also, task someone with keeping them updated. If something changes, you want your customer profiles to be current.

You may not have all the information you want to include when you start out, but you can fill in the blanks as you go along. Don't wait until you have everything to create one. The value comes from the ongoing "investigation process," as Alan Cooper once wrote.

Analyzing Competitor Efforts

Just as it's important to understand where your consumers participate in the social web, it's necessary to understand how your competitors engage in the social web. But where should you start? The following are some types of information to consider when you are planning your SMM investigation:

✔ **Keywords being used by competitors.**

This is something you have probably heard again and again, but its importance can't be overemphasized. If you don't use the right keywords, you won't be found. Make sure to note which ones your competitors are using. They may not all be "home runs" for you, but it's important to evaluate them.

✔ **Where their traffic is coming from.**

Using Google Analytics and a host of other tools (detailed in the three sections that follow: "Setting up Google Alerts," "Setting up Twitter alerts," and "Monitoring blogosphere conversations"), you can determine how they get traffic to their website and other channels.

✔ **Rankings by important engines.**

You can do a quick look at major ranking engines like Alexa (`www.alexa.com`) to see how their sites compare with yours.

✔ **Which social media platforms they are on and which distribution channels they use.**

As we have discussed throughout this book, if you don't know where your customers spend their time, you won't be able to market to them where they are most comfortable. You can't count on them going to your website. Most businesses are now using several channels besides their websites (like a blog, Twitter, and so on), so be aware of their choices and see what could work for you.

✔ **Who they partner with.**

This is an often-overlooked source of competitive information. Businesses find synergy and partner with those who have similar audiences. Who they partner with tells you a lot about how they view their audience.

✔ **Loyalty and other programs they employ.**

Find out what programs are keeping their customers loyal to them, and see how you can tap into the same vein with your own unique program.

✔ **Their online customer service efforts.**

This one can be a secret weapon for you. If you see that your competitors aren't offering support through social media channels, you can distinguish your company with a solid effort here. According to the Word of Mouth Marketing Association (WOMMA), in 2011, 55 percent of customers recommended a company because of its customer service. And surprisingly, 27 percent of customers would pay 15 percent or more for a superior customer experience. Customers notice!

✔ **What they do offline to connect with customers.**

Check out whether your competitors have special training programs or other educational sessions available locally. This might be a way they are increasing their customer base consistently.

If your competitors are already running marketing campaigns similar to what you plan to do, yours won't attract much attention. To prevent this from happening, a combination of sleuthing and the following third-party tools can help you.

Setting up Google Alerts

You can set up these free alerts for keywords related to your competitors. These keywords can include company names, brands, senior manager names, and partner names. Every day, you receive a Google Alert in your e-mail inbox with summaries of news stories and blog posts that include those keywords. It's a good starting point and completely free.

To set up a Google Alert, follow these simple steps:

1. **Go to** www.google.com/alerts.

   The Google Alerts page opens, as shown in Figure 2-9.

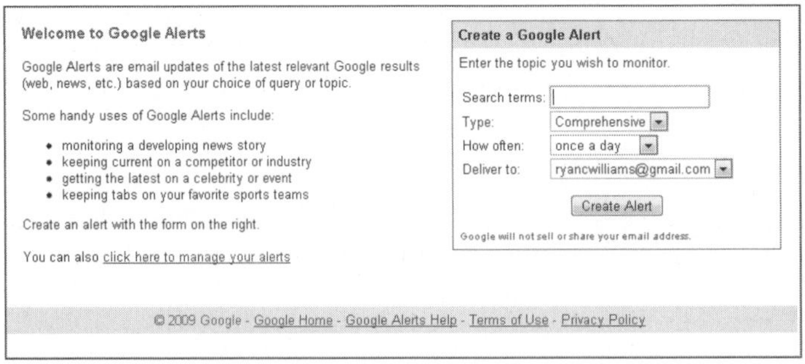

Welcome to Google Alerts

Google Alerts are email updates of the latest relevant Google results (web, news, etc.) based on your choice of query or topic.

Some handy uses of Google Alerts include:

- monitoring a developing news story
- keeping current on a competitor or industry
- getting the latest on a celebrity or event
- keeping tabs on your favorite sports teams

Create an alert with the form on the right.

You can also click here to manage your alerts

Create a Google Alert

Enter the topic you wish to monitor.

Search terms: |
Type: Comprehensive ▾
How often: once a day ▾
Deliver to: ryancwilliams@gmail.com ▾

Create Alert

Google will not sell or share your email address.

© 2009 Google - Google Home - Google Alerts Help - Terms of Use - Privacy Policy

Figure 2-9: Google Alerts.

2. **Enter the search terms for which you want alerts.**

   Try to keep these to one word or a commonly used phrase.

3. **From the Type drop-down list, choose what type of content you want Google to search.**

   We generally choose Everything so that we don't miss news items.

4. **From the How Often drop-down list, choose the frequency you want the alerts delivered to you.**

   We find Once a Day to be the best frequency.

5. **Enter the e-mail address where you want the alerts to be sent.**

   Remember that you can edit these alert settings at any time.

6. **Click the Create Alert button.**

Setting up Twitter alerts

Similarly, create Twitter alerts that track those same keywords in the Twitter world. Services like Twilert (www.twilert.com) let you follow keywords and observe all the microblogging posts in which those words appear.

A service like TweetMeme (tweetmeme.com) allows you to scan not just Twitter, but also all the other microblogging platforms at once and in real time. An example of a niche engine is InstantPulp, www.instantpulp.com/, which allows you to search celebrity topics in real time.

To set up a Twitter alert, follow these simple steps:

1. **Go to www.twilert.com.**

   The Twilert home page opens, as shown in Figure 2-10.

   In order to set a Twitter alert, you have to be signed in to your Twitter account. If you don't have one, you can sign up at www.twitter.com.

2. **Type the keyword that you want the alert set up for.**

3. **Click the Create a Twilert button.**

Figure 2-10:
Twilert.

Monitoring blogosphere conversations

Although Google Alerts can include blogs, they don't encompass the
conversations that surround a blog post. For that, you need to depend on
Technorati. Visit Technorati (www.technorati.com), and type a blog
address. You can see all the posts for that blog and all the links to it (and
their related conversations) elsewhere on the Internet. The buzz charting
tools discussed in the earlier section are helpful, too. Another tool to
consider using is BlogPulse (www.blogpulse.com), which is a blog search
engine similar to Technorati.

Monitoring social networks

You probably want to observe what your competitors are doing on the
various social networks. That's a little harder to do, as most social networks
are closed gardens, meaning that except for the public profile pages (a very
small percentage of all the pages on the network), you can't search them with
external tools, and typically, once you log in, you can't search the universe of
activity on them. However, what you can do is search and follow the pages,
profiles, groups, and applications created by your competitors. Keep in mind
that some users hide their profiles, so you won't be able to track them.

Tracking competitor websites

Look at the social media efforts that may reside on your competitors' websites. Often, those efforts are promoted or anchored in the company website or company-sponsored microsite through links. In fact, many of your competitors probably have (as they should) corporate blogs and Twitter accounts. (Start tracking those directly, too.)

Researching Your Competitors' Campaign Support

Practically every marketing campaign today has a social media component to it. As you see a competitor launch a major marketing campaign, scan the web and the competitor's website for that campaign's digital and social components. The social activity surrounding the campaign (elsewhere on the web) gives you a sense of how successful it is and how much it helps the brand. Also, watch prominent bloggers in that product category: They may be part of an outreach program and could be promoting the campaign.

Conducting qualitative research

Using the free tools and observing competitor activity is all well and good. But more often than not, you need to conduct qualitative research that doesn't just tell you what your consumers are doing, but also the goals, needs, and aspirations that drive their behavior. Here, there's good news and bad news.

First, the good news. Qualitative research, as you probably know it in the traditional marketing world, hasn't changed. You can still use interviews, focus groups, shadowing, and other ethnographic research techniques to understand your consumers. There are dozens of authoritative books on the subject — including a few excellent ones from the *For Dummies* series, such as *Marketing For Dummies,* by Alexander Hiam (John Wiley & Sons, Inc.) — on qualitative research, so I won't go into those research formats. All the same best practices of recruiting effectively, knowing your objectives, and having good interview guides and moderators apply.

And now for the bad news: The questions have changed, and you won't get all your answers from the qualitative research. Unlike qualitative research in the past, which focused on understanding a specific consumer's goals and needs, you must pay attention to the consumer's surrounding community and influencers within that community. For example, you need to ask who influences your consumers when they make specific purchasing decisions.

Running surveys and quantitative research

Similarly, quantitative research in the form of statistically significant surveys can be most helpful. Keep in mind that you must run surveys at regular intervals to get valuable, statistically significant results. The reason is that influence changes more rapidly in an online environment, and the social media platforms on which people participate change, too. Don't run extensive surveys irregularly. Run short, quick surveys about your audiences on a frequent basis to glean important insights.

Pay attention to where you run the surveys, too, as that can affect the results. A good strategy is to run the survey on your corporate website but simultaneously use a third-party survey vendor to run the same survey on the social media platforms. This way, you're gauging how people participate and socialize in their own contexts. Very often, the quantitative research can give statistically significant results about influence, with the qualitative research being used to explain the hows and whys of the responses. The two kinds of research go hand in hand.

Some of the survey vendors that you can use include

- ✔ SurveyMonkey (www.surveymonkey.com); see Figure 2-11
- ✔ Zoomerang (www.zoomerang.com)
- ✔ SurveyGizmo (www.surveygizmo.com)
- ✔ WorldAPP Key Survey (www.keysurvey.com)

As you may know, there are other important forms of research, such as content, discourse, and network analysis, which take on additional importance in the sphere of social media, but those can be relatively laborious. Generally, they're appropriate only when much deeper behavioral insights are required.

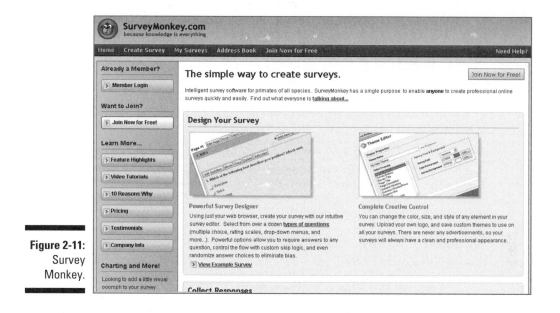

Figure 2-11:
Survey
Monkey.

The psychology behind social influence

Consumers have always been heavily influenced by each other when they make purchasing decisions. They ask each other for advice; they observe and mimic each other's decision-making; and frankly, they let peer pressure inform their decisions, whether they like to admit it or not. What's changed is that digital behavior has caught up with offline behavior, and that's why social media marketing matters to anyone who has a future in marketing.

Communication technologies such as social networks, prediction markets, microblogging solutions, location-based networked mobile phone applications, and even virtual worlds make it possible for consumers to influence each other more directly and dramatically than ever before. According to Harvard psychologist Herbert Kelman, this influence occurs in three ways:

- ✔ **Compliance:** Public conformity while keeping one's own private beliefs

- ✔ **Identification:** Conforming to someone who is liked and respected, such as a celebrity or a favorite uncle

- ✔ **Internalization:** Acceptance of the belief or behavior and conforming both publically and privately

Aside from making for good copy in behavioral psychology textbooks, these concepts do translate into tactics for social media marketing.

Seeing Why All Consumers Are Not Created Equal

A chapter on competition wouldn't be complete without addressing the fact that in discussions about social influence and social media marketing, all consumers aren't created equal. Social influence doesn't simply mean recognizing that every consumer may influence every other consumer; rather, in specific marketing contexts, specific consumers have an outsized influence on their peers around them. For example, on a social network, one of my friends posts more comments than anyone else. Just by virtue of his volume of postings, we take his opinion into account more than that of our other friends who aren't commenting as much.

In this regard, three steps help you gain a marketing advantage from influential consumers:

1. **Discover the influential consumers.**

   As you launch a social media marketing campaign and identify your consumers, pay extra attention to who is influencing your potential customers. Who are the consumers that are influencing your customers, and where is this influence taking place? (You can find out more about influencers in Chapter 14.)

2. **Activate the influential consumers.**

   After you identify the influential consumers, whether they're bloggers, forum leaders, or just conversationalists with lots of friends on the social networks, develop relationships with them, and find ways to activate them to do the marketing on your behalf. In later chapters, we discuss exactly how you can do this.

3. **Turn customers into brand advocates.**

   And finally, after a consumer becomes a customer, deepen your relationship with her so that the customer becomes a brand advocate. That's not a new strategy except that now you can ask her to take specific actions within her social networks as a brand advocate. Rather than just asking her to talk about your product, you can have her actually reach out to her peers and then reward her for her participation.

Dipping into Hot SMM Concepts

One way to stay ahead of the competition is to keep abreast of the marketing trends that directly affect your customers. Several major trends have recently impacted the social media realm. You should determine if they have application for you. Even if you do not immediately see a way to apply them, you'll want to monitor them closely. We mention them here and cover them more in depth in the chapters cited below.

Discovering gamification

There are basically two camps of people online — those who believe that online games are a complete waste of time and those who find them irresistible. But are social games actually games? They are, and again, they aren't. Social games incorporate game techniques in a social setting with the aim of encouraging you to interact with a business, a charity, or perhaps an educational entity, to name a few.

You're playing a social game if you are on one of the social media platforms and the game encourages you to take action that surrounds a brand. Where do these social gamers like to play? According to a study by the Information Services Group in 2010, Facebook is the destination of choice. Eighty-three percent of study participants play there.

Typically when you think of a "gamer," you might think of an adolescent with lots of time and energy to master ever higher levels of game play. But actually, according to the same study, the average social gamer is a 43-year-old woman. Businesses of all types are creating games that integrate the use of their products with the daily play. One example of this is Clarins, a French cosmetics company. Their game Spa Life on Facebook is about the challenges of running a spa. Their products are used at the spa and become part of the game solution.

But lest you think it's all for fun, gamification takes several different cuts at the online game experience. In September of 2011, a group of gamers who play at a site called Foldit were asked to help solve a complex protein folding puzzle that had stumped AIDS researchers for years. Surprisingly, they were able to solve it within 10 days. It is reported that the competitive nature of the game drove the teams forward. CBS News reported that one researcher called it the value of "citizen science."

If your company is thinking about creating a social game, you'll want to make sure you take a broad approach and see what's being done online. These games can be short or long term. You don't have to commit yourself to something untried.

Choosing localized marketing

Many Internet marketers are excited about the opportunities they have to reach around the globe for new consumers. What many have overlooked is the opportunity to reach into their local communities to get more customers. As Adam Metz says in his book *The Social Customer,* these customers "didn't exist at the turn of the twenty-first century."

Tools are now available to help small businesses and local sites of large businesses engage their fans. For example, Facebook has developed several types of advertising deals that help owners reward their customers for visiting the store. (We cover this in Chapter 7.)

Companies like BlitzLocal, shown in Figure 2-12, at (`www.blitzlocal.com/`), have sprung up to assist business owners in finding their local Facebook fans. Dennis Yu, co-founder and CEO of BlitzLocal, said, "It's quality, not quantity that counts" when it comes to fan numbers.

Figure 2-12:
BlitzLocal.

Creating an app for that

According to comScore, the social networking app audience grew 126 percent to 43 million users in 2011. Apps are big business and getting bigger every year. Social media marketers have an enormous opportunity to brand an app that is seen every day by their customers. Talk about product placement! Marketers can help their customers and proudly display their logo while they do it. But not all apps are a hit. It takes careful planning and research to create an app that resonates with customers. Apps can typically be categorized in one of the following eight categories:

✔ Social networking

✔ News

✔ Lifestyle

✔ Games

✔ Entertainment

✔ Education

✔ Family and kids

✔ Music

If your company sells a product or service in one of those areas, you'll likely choose to create a consumer app in that area. But what if you run a manufacturing company or do field sales? Does this mean that you can't create an app? Not at all. In fact, you can create apps that provide a solution for your employees too. For example, if you are a manufacturing company, you could create an app that searches your catalog part numbers. Areas such as transaction processing, field sales, and competitive intelligence are all possible areas to create an app for. See Chapter 17 for more detailed information on mobile marketing and creating apps.

Chapter 3

Getting in the Social Media Marketing Frame of Mind

*T*he true power of social media marketing comes from applying its principles to all parts of your business in a rigorous fashion. This begins with examining social media marketing in relation to your marketing funnel. You then need to understand how it relates to brand marketing and direct response — the two traditional pillars of marketing that support the marketing funnel. Understanding the differences helps you to better know when to deploy social media marketing tactics versus when to depend upon brand or direct-response ones.

In this chapter, we also discuss how big and little ideas relate to social media marketing. The marketing world has historically been driven by the big ideas. Whether it's been the glamorous advertising campaigns (Apple's iconic *1984* commercial comes to mind) or the clever in-store promotions that you see when you walk down the aisle at your local Whole Foods store, ideas drive marketing. That changes with social media marketing. We explain how you need to think about the big idea a little differently as you deploy social media marketing to meet your marketing and business objectives.

Putting SMM in the Context of the Marketing Funnel

The marketing funnel is one of the most important metaphors in marketing today. It differentiates between prospects and customers, and maps out the journey from the point where a prospect learns about a product to when he becomes a loyal and repeat customer. Because practically every marketer uses some form of the marketing funnel, it serves an important framework through which to understand social media marketing.

The traditional marketing funnel typically has five stages, as defined by Forrester. These five stages are awareness, consideration, preference, action, and loyalty (as shown in Figure 3-1). The last stage (loyalty) has the fewest people. Those customers are the most loyal and, therefore, among the most valuable. For many marketers, marketing is fundamentally the act of moving people from having an awareness of a product, considering it along with other products, establishing a preference for the product over the others, to eventually taking action such as purchasing it and developing loyalty toward it.

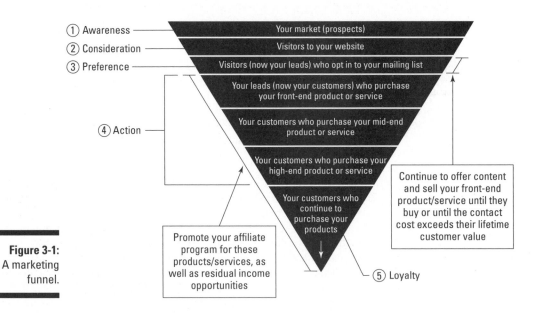

Figure 3-1:
A marketing
funnel.

You employ different marketing strategies and tactics at every stage of the marketing funnel to move the prospects along. The movement of prospects and customers is measured precisely (especially when you do this online), and if there isn't enough movement, you need to devote more marketing dollars to pushing people through the funnel. How you spend these dollars and which investments do the most to move people through the marketing funnel is always a subject of much debate and varies by product category. Regardless, social media marketing and tapping into the social influencers with differing tactics can help with this journey.

The stages of the marketing funnel may vary from company to company. Some link online funnel tracking with offline efforts, whereas others don't. You don't have to use the stages as we define them rigorously. It's more important that you look at SMM in the context of how your company tracks leads and sales. In some cases, you need to consider how you can apply SMM at the different points in an advertising campaign. Regardless, the same principles apply whether you're looking at SMM in the context of the funnel for your entire marketing efforts or for just an online advertising campaign.

SMM at the awareness stage

The awareness stage of the marketing funnel is where you introduce potential customers to your brand. You build awareness and encourage prospective customers to remember your brand name so that when they do make a purchase in the future, they include your brand in their consideration mix.

Typically, marketers use television, radio, print, and direct mail to build awareness. They also sponsor events, conduct promotions, and invest in product placements to get further exposure. Marketers also use public relations professionals to influence editorial content in magazines and newspapers.

In the digital realm, you typically create awareness using display advertising on major websites, paid searches for category-related keywords, and sponsorships across the web. E-mail marketing historically has been extremely successful at building awareness. Arguably, creating awareness online is a lot cheaper but without the same mass scale effect of a 30-second television spot.

You can use social media marketing to build awareness of your brand, too. The reason is simple. As a marketer with a loyal customer base, you can encourage your customers to build your brand by talking about your product with their friends. Many a marketer has incentivized existing customers to tell their friends and families about their purchasing decisions. You aren't the first. In fact, you can also reach out to expert influencers to help you here. One important consideration with using social media marketing at the awareness stage is whether your SMM efforts can give you the type of scale of awareness that you can get with television, radio, or print. For a long time, marketers believed that social media marketing couldn't give that scale. That's changing fast, thanks to the likes of Facebook and Twitter.

Expert influencers are the people who are experts in a field and have large audiences.

Here are some SMM tactics to consider for building awareness:

- **Publish advertisements to YouTube, and tag them with category terms.**

    For example, if you're publishing advertisements for orange juice on YouTube, use the tags *orange, orangejuice, beverage, vitamin,* and *drink* in addition to the brand name. Highlight these YouTube video clips on the corporate website, too. Figure 3-2 shows your orange juice video would be in good company on YouTube.

Figure 3-2: Does your orange juice video belong here?

- **Nurture relationships with expert influencers, such as bloggers who publish content related to the specific product category you're marketing.**

    Take the time to share product samples with this group, answer their questions, and invite them to special events. If required, sponsor a post on an influential blog. These expert influencers build awareness for your brand.

- **Set up a Facebook fan page, a Twitter account, and a LinkedIn profile.**

    Run polls, offer special discounts, publish games, promote coupons, and give members of these pages or accounts product sneak peeks. Share entertaining and educational information through them.

✔ **Provide RSS feeds for content on the corporate website.**

An RSS feed is a content format that easily allows anyone to pluck the content from your site and place it on their blog or in an RSS reader. Google Reader is probably the most popular RSS reader today. Just visit `www.google.com/reader` for instructions on how to set it up. Then each time you see the RSS icon on a website, you can click it and have that content fed into your RSS reader on an ongoing basis. Figure 3-3 shows how Apple has set up its RSS feeds.

Also allow for the easy sharing of information from your corporate website onto the social networks. Services from companies like AddThis (`www.addthis.com`) and ShareThis (`www.sharethis.com`) allow you to make your content sharable. See Chapter 15 for more information on this.

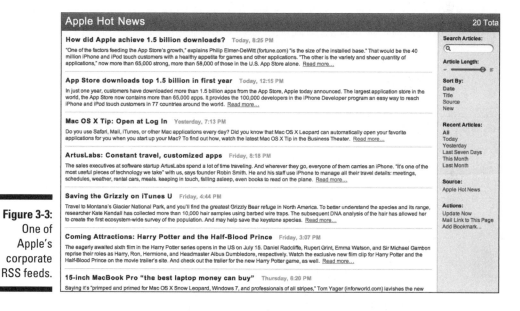

Figure 3-3:
One of
Apple's
corporate
RSS feeds.

✔ **Allow new customers to broadcast their purchases to their social networks.**

Each time a customer makes a purchase, you can ask them whether they would like to announce the purchase on their favorite social network. Services like StrongMail and ShareThis, along with Facebook Connect, allow you to set this up on your website for your customers.

If you're planning to broadcast their purchases, be sure to ask the customers for permission to do this before broadcasting the purchase.

✔ **Leverage social ads.**

Because social ads are highly engaging — by virtue of the fact that they tell the customer what his friends are doing — they're useful for building awareness and establishing consideration. For example, if a customer sees an endorsement from his friend in an ad unit for a movie, he is more likely to go for the movie. See Chapter 16 for more on social ads. Also review the new social ad options from Facebook at (www. Facebook.com/advertising), which give you awareness-building opportunities on scale.

✔ **Support a cause via a social network.**

Promise to match the contributions of participants who encourage friends to participate in the cause as well. The Causes application on Facebook allows you to do this very nicely. Go to https://apps. facebook.com/causes/ to see the app.

SMM at the consideration stage

The consideration stage of the marketing funnel is where you make sure that as the prospective customer goes about making a purchasing decision, she considers your product.

To be included in the consideration stage, use tactics like product comparisons, special promotions, sales discounts, decision tools, and calculators to convince prospects.

The consideration stage is arguably the most important one because it's at this point that you can snag a loyal customer or forever lose one to a competitor.

Social media marketing plays the most important role at this stage. This is because the referent, expert, and positional influencers (which we define in Chapter 1) help a prospect determine whether he should make the purchasing decision. Increasingly, while making choices between different products, prospective customers look to each other for advice and guidance.

They ask their friends for advice, search the web for customer reviews, and read expert opinions from credible third-party sources. In fact, according to WOMMA (the Word of Mouth Marketing Association), in 2011, 59 percent of Americans surveyed believed offline word of mouth to be highly credible, and 49 percent of Americans believed online word of mouth to be credible.

Your role at this stage is primarily connecting that prospective customer with these credible third-party sources of information. Now, you may feel that connecting a prospective customer to a bad review or to another customer who may not have liked the product is a bad idea, but it isn't necessarily so. Prospective customers are looking for the best information about a product, and they respect companies that help them research the product more thoroughly.

You can't hide bad reviews on the web, and by pointing to all the reviews and not just the good ones, you establish credibility with your prospective customer. (Besides, we would hope that the positive reviews far outweigh the negative ones.) This is important because according to the same survey cited above from WOMMA, 54 percent of the people surveyed said that a driving force to purchase was word of mouth. Thirty-one percent said an online review was a driving force.

Here are some SMM tactics that you can use at the consideration stage:

✔ **Publish customer ratings and reviews on the corporate website.**

Make sure ratings and reviews appear for all products and that you do not censor them. Even if a product gets negative reviews, publish them. In all probability, customers will choose other products from your company. You won't lose the customer completely.

✔ **Point to authoritative third-party reviews.**

It's important to point to credible third-party reviews from recognized experts so that you build trust. Doing so can make the consideration stage a shorter one.

✔ **Encourage prospects to discuss the products.**

When you're designing your online catalog, encourage prospects to discuss the product with their friends and family. Make it easy for them to take the product into Facebook to solicit opinions from others using services like ShareThis (www.sharethis.com), pointing users to the brand's business page on the social networks, and including e-mail links, too.

✔ **Connect prospective customers to each other.**

By setting up discussion forums, you can create spaces where prospective customers can exchange notes on the potential purchases that they're considering. Also point them to existing satisfied customers or real-world testimonials that visitors can rate and comment upon.

✔ **Set up a Twitter account, and respond to customer queries.**

It's important to watch the chatter about your products and brands across the social web. Where appropriate, respond in a thoughtful, helpful manner to the questions raised. Correct misrepresentations of your products in a similar way.

Twitter is useful for customer service. Companies like Comcast have had great success in using it for responding to customer queries and concerns. But the tone you respond in is critical: You always run the risk of sounding defensive. You'll probably be doing more damage to your brand than good if you allow yourself to get defensive on Twitter.

✔ **Track a list of websites, blogs, and discussion forums where the product's target customers spend their time.**

Track activity on these sites, and participate in conversations about the category, competitors, and customer needs in an authentic, productive, and useful manner. Here are some you may want to consider:

Addict-o-matic (`http://addictomatic.com/`): You can type in any word or URL to see what's being said about it from a variety of social media platforms.

StepRep (`www.secure.steprep.com/`): When you sign up for StepRep, you can set up a variety of search terms, like your competitors and important people in your industry. You'll get an instant notice via e-mail or from their control panel when there is a mention. This is a good way to monitor your own reputation online.

HowSociable (`www.howsociable.com/`): Type in your brand, and you can see where you're being mentioned around the web.

SMM at the preference stage

At the preference stage, the prospective customer leans toward making a purchase. He's considered several products and established his favorites. He likes the product that you're pushing him toward. By this time, the prospective customer is more concerned with confirming that he's getting good value for his money and that his purchase will be suitable for his needs. At this stage, you may offer free trials and 30-day money-back guarantees. Generally speaking, you hope your prospective customers have developed an emotional attachment to your brand that will push them to purchase your products.

By the time a prospective customer is at the preference stage in the marketing funnel, he's probably evaluated all the competitive alternatives to the product. He's found information about them through product brochures, the product websites, and customer reviews across the web. As he enters the preference stage, he's likely to talk to his friends some more and get their opinions. This may have less to do with whether one product is better than another from a feature standpoint, but the customer can get a feel for your brand as well. The prospective customer also views user-generated content about your brand at this stage.

You must be very careful at this stage. It's important that you establish a trusted relationship with the prospective customer. The prospective customer needs to feel that he will get good customer service after he makes the purchase. He wants to believe that his decision will be a good one over the long term, too. You can build that trust and allay those concerns by talking to the prospective customer in an authentic, personal, and genuine fashion.

This is when your product blogs play an important role. It reminds your prospective customers that actual people are behind your product or brand. Make sure to spend time answering questions, resolving product issues, and discussing how the product is evolving.

Consider these SMM tactics at this stage:

- **A blog — or several — that discusses the product:** Granted, blogs are valuable at the awareness and consideration phase as well, but they matter the most at the point of preference. Customers want to hear from you at this stage more than ever.

- **Podcasts with interviews and product explanations:** As a supplement to blogs, podcasts are an appealing way to explain the product to prospective customers in an appealing fashion when you're not in the room with them. To learn all about *podcasts,* which are audio blogs that are easily distributed online, take a look at *Podcasting For Dummies,* 2nd Edition, by Tee Morris, Chuck Tomasi, and Evo Terra (John Wiley & Sons, Inc.).

- **YouTube clips of product demonstrations:** With prospective customers establishing their preference for the brand, video clips demonstrating the product and explaining its benefits are helpful. Publish your videos to a site such as YouTube so that customers can easily find them and also give others the opportunity to comment and rate them.

SMM at the action stage

The action stage is when the prospective customer makes the purchase and becomes an actual customer. He goes through the process of buying the product, whether he does this online, via the phone, or in a store. During the action stage, focus on making the process as smooth, efficient, and as hassle-free as possible. You should put a lot of effort into making the purchasing experience a positive one because it is one of the first direct interactions that the customer has with your company.

Most marketers argue that at this point in the funnel, you should not play a role. Either the customer was positively influenced to make the purchasing decision or he wasn't. If he's at the point where he's taking action, he should be allowed to take that action without any distractions whatsoever because even a positive distraction is still a distraction. However, if the purchase is a high-consideration one, you can make the purchasing process social in a way that doesn't distract from the purchasing but enhances it instead.

At the point of purchase, the customer wants to know whether he is making a suitable purchasing decision and if his social influencers approve of his decision. Providing him with data points that he can share with those influencers and a means to broadcast the purchasing decision helps him. He can broadcast his purchasing decision and influence his friends to make similar purchasing decisions. And by providing valuable tidbits of information, he'll have valuable information to share.

The point of purchase also serves as an opportunity to upsell other products and services. This is a traditional marketing tactic that's been used in both the digital world and in physical stores as well. By highlighting other products that customers just like him purchased, social influence can play a role in encouraging that customer to make additional impulse purchases at the point of sale. For example, say you're buying a pair of Gap jeans from Gap.com (as shown in Figure 3-4) and as you're about to check out, you're told about a nice shirt to buy and that most people who bought the pair of jeans bought the shirt, too. You're more likely to add the shirt to your shopping cart. That's using social data to influence a purchasing decision.

Consider these SMM tactics at this stage:

- **Highlight related popular products:** As depicted with the Gap.com example, showcasing popular products relating to the ones already in the shopping carts often leads to impulse purchases.

- **Provide tools to broadcast the purchase:** This is necessary to allow for the customer to do remarketing for you. The customer should have the tools to easily broadcast his purchase to his various social networks.

SMM at the loyalty stage

The last stage of the marketing funnel has the fewest people. These are the customers who have purchased your product and are consuming it now. At this stage, it's most important to encourage customers to spread the word about the product and encourage others to buy it. Loyal customers are often the best marketers for your company. With social media marketing, loyalty plays an even larger role.

Figure 3-4:
Gap.com recommends a shirt for me based on what's in my shopping cart.

You must first focus on making your customers loyal and repeat customers. It's no use encouraging a customer to talk about your product if she isn't loyal to or an advocate of the product. You can incentivize your loyal customers to encourage their peers to test the product and make a purchase as well. You can do this using social media marketing tactics.

The best way to encourage loyal customers to influence their peers is to start by encouraging them to talk about the product. Having them rate and review the products is the first step. You'll be surprised how many customers are happy to rate and review products. What's more, as they rate and review the products, they're also happy to broadcast the reviews to their social network. Allow them to do that. Provide the technological means for them to share their own reviews of the product with their friends and family.

Another way that social media marketing can help at the loyalty stage is by connecting prospective customers with loyal customers. In some cases, you can link prospective customers with loyal customers who they know in the real world. For example, if you're looking to buy a Ford Taurus, and you have a network of 350 people in LinkedIn, you may find that someone else in your network drives a Ford Taurus. Now, wouldn't it be valuable if Ford told you which friend drives the Ford Taurus so that you could ask him his opinion? That's increasingly possible to do in the social networks.

Regardless of whether you have any friends who own Fords, you might be interested in learning about Ford from other Ford customers. Social media marketing is about connecting customers to one another so that they can socially influence each other to make better decisions. In this instance, Ford should definitely try to connect all the prospective Ford Taurus owners with the current ones. One simple way to do this is to set up a Facebook fan page or a LinkedIn group for Ford Taurus owners in specific locations and then point prospective customers to that page, where they can ask existing owners questions. It can only help them make more purchases. Not surprisingly, Ford does exactly that, and in fact, it now goes a step further by offering Ford customers the opportunity to put a "badge" on their Facebook profiles showcasing the fact that they are Ford customers!

The loyalty stage of the marketing funnel is important because that's where the most remarketing happens by your own customers. Just because the customer has already bought the product doesn't mean you should care about him less. In fact, with his ability to spread the word (positively or negatively) about your product across his social network and the social web in an exponential fashion, you had better take good care of him. Otherwise, you may have a PR disaster on your hands.

Probably one of the most classic examples of a PR disaster at the loyalty stage has to do with Netflix. Without consulting its customers, Netflix made two different attempts to change the nature and pricing of their service by dividing and charging separately for their DVDs versus their online streaming service. As a result, customers fled en masse, including those who had previously been among the most loyal. Management had to completely reverse themselves, and they now have to hope they can gain back their previous customers.

On the bright side, when JetBlue suffered a PR disaster, the chief executive officer decided to issue an apology via YouTube — using the very same social platform that was responsible for the propagation of the runway fiasco. That made a difference, and it helped even more when he announced a passenger bill of rights. These actions showed that he was engaging with his current and prospective customers on their own terms and on their platforms of choice.

There are hundreds of examples of brands facing online firestorms, often due to something stupid that they did. Table 3-1 highlights some of the more notable firestorms. Also listed are whether these online firestorms had offline ripples in the mainstream media.

Table 3-1	Notable Online Firestorms	
Controversy	*Online Noise Levels*	*Offline*
Nivea's racially insensitive ad	High	High
American Airlines removes Alec Baldwin from plane for not turning off his phone when requested	High	High
Gilbert Gottfried's firing by AFLAC for insensitive remarks about the Japan earthquake	High	Moderate
Dunkin' Donuts/Rachael Ray wears keffiyeh	High	Moderate
Burger King employee bathes in sink	Moderate	Low
Motrin moms	High	Low
#amazonfail	High	None
SpongeBob SquareButt	Moderate	Low
Starbucks nipples on a mermaid	Negligible	Imaginary

Deepening Your SMM Relationship

After your customers are at the loyalty stage, can you do anything more to deepen the relationship? SMM gives you the opportunity to stay in contact with your customers and help them in ways they don't anticipate. Delight is a strong element in growing your bond. Following are some areas of SMM that help you extend that trust.

SMM for customer service

After customers found that they could quickly get a company's attention on social media platforms, the notion of customer service changed forever. Previously, the only option consumers had was to get on the phone and wait patiently until they could speak to a representative. Often, the outcome was less than satisfactory.

Presently, consumers make it a point to seek out companies who offer them a voice on social platforms. The 2010 Cone Consumer New Media Study conducted by Cone LLC found that

✔ Sixty-three percent of respondents say they are "more aware of a company or brand if they can interact with it in a new media environment."

✔ When deciding whether to engage with companies or brands via new media, "forty-six percent chose one that solves my problems and/or provides product or service information (for example, customer service.)"

✔ Sixty percent of respondents said, "I feel better served by companies when I can have a conversation with them in a new media environment."

If you are dissatisfied with a purchase or service, you can use social media to tweet, post, or otherwise rate your way onto the radar screen of the company in question.

Here are some post-sales SMM tactics you can use to improve customer service:

✔ **Demonstrate that you are really able to do something.**

It will be readily apparent if your employees on social media are not really empowered to actually help customers. It's great to listen, but without action, it will prove a hollow exercise.

✔ **Provide links on social platforms to information, discounts, and special promotions.**

It's all about the customer, so make sure that there is always real demonstrable value in your response. Ask your management what options you have for rewarding the customer. How about a private briefing about your next product?

✔ **Offer tips and video from customer service on FAQs.**

Don't wait for a hail of tweets to show up. If you know there's a problem, create content that speaks to it. Then go back and show the customer how your solution cut customer service calls in half. That will get management's attention and buy-in.

✔ **Use different platforms for different kinds of customer service.**

Make sure you have several levels of response available to the customer. For example, you can use Twitter for quick responses. For questions that require more investigation, you can direct them to your website or set up an outside service like Get Satisfaction, as shown in Figure 3-5, to answer questions.

Figure 3-5:
The home
page of Get
Satisfaction.

✔ **Use photos to show there are real people doing interesting things.**

With a camera in every phone, it's hard not to take snapshots of events, celebrations, and charitable activities. At every event, pick someone as the designated picture-taker. This serves to authenticate your staff.

SMM with offline marketing

When you see a heading that includes "offline marketing," your first thought might be, "Why are they including this as part of SMM?" There's a good reason. Marketing doesn't stop at the digital water's edge. Hard as it is to remember, people still spend some part of their day offline. We think that's a good time to grab their attention and funnel them back to your social media platforms.

This means that you don't miss an opportunity to pair your social media venues with your offline ones. For example, if you send a postcard, you'd make sure to have all your "connections" like Facebook page and Twitter address listed on the back of the card.

You should always be thinking about how your marketing universe ties together. When you look at each of the tactics below, think about how you can offer online tie-backs:

✔ **Offer 30-minute training at a local venue.**

Give out the URL of the training notes online.

✔ **Host an event for charity**.

Make sure to secure donations from a safe online environment.

✔ **Send out postcards.**

List your Twitter address on the back.

✔ **Go to a conference or trade show.**

Have several types of handouts available. They could be a tip sheet with your web address or even a CD with online links.

✔ **Call your customers.**

Most SM marketers encourage you to send out online surveys. How about arranging a phone call to speak to a group of customers who have purchased your last product? Afterward, make sure to send them an online discount coupon or other bonus for sharing their ideas.

✔ **Create a joint venture.**

Work with another online marketer who complements your offerings to hold a meeting or event. Then create a bundled product to buy online.

✔ **Send an article to your local newspaper or trade magazine.**

Make sure your LinkedIn URL is listed.

SMM in the world of real-time marketing

With the advent of social media platforms, the tools you need for real-time marketing campaigns are ready and waiting. For example, just search your Twitter feed or glance at Twitter trends if you want to see where the online attention is.

Earlier in this chapter, we discussed the marketing funnel. Your first goal was awareness. That's what you're aiming for with real-time marketing. If you can garner awareness with your real-time campaign, you have the chance to move customers through your funnel.

To make this information translate into traffic, leads, and revenue, you need an understanding of what goes into a real-time SMM campaign. The following are conditions that should be present to help you succeed:

✓ **Determine your goals for this type of activity.**

You could do a plethora of things with your campaign. The key is to focus it on one major outcome. Ask yourself, "What action do I want the customer to take after engaging with the content?" (via tweet, video, link, and so on). This helps you choose the right first step.

✓ **Invest in the right real-time marketing tools.**

Within the last two years, several technologies have been launched that allow you to truly understand what consumers are thinking, talking about, and doing on a real-time basis. Real-time tracking can be around your brands or around topics that matter to both them and you. Whether it be tools that help you identify real-time trends as they surface or technologies that let you observe how trends travel from one physical location to another, operating effectively in real time when your consumers most care about you requires investments in the right tools and technologies.

✓ **Designate staff to monitor real-time activity.**

Make it someone's (or several people's) task to monitor the online activity in real time. That may sound obvious, but when you have very busy people on your staff, everyone thinks the other person will do it and they can get to it later.

✓ **Have resources available to take action.**

If you agree that you are going all in on this campaign, make sure to let your creative people know that they may be required to create something in response to feedback. As we discuss in Chapter 9, Procter & Gamble had their Old Spice guy record more than 100 video responses to celebrity comments within three days. Of course, we're not suggesting that your campaign will have to be as elaborate as that one. But you can get great mileage by simply writing back to the comments made. The idea is that real people are listening and talking back.

✓ **Monitor news in your topic area.**

When you are trying to decide how to make your campaign relevant, consider riffing off of some current event. This is an old PR trick. It's why when something of note happens, you see headlines like, "What X can learn about Y from the Old Spice Guy." When people Google "Old Spice," you show up in the results.

✔ **Use the real words and phrases customers use.**

Related to the item above is the idea that SEO (search engine optimization) should not be ignored. Pay close attention to the specific words and phrases that customers are using, and seed them in your campaign.

✔ **Determine the metrics you will use.**

It's important to understand the real value of metrics when it comes to SMM. You are not going to be able to wrap up your numbers with a bow and present them to your manager. For this reason, it's good to choose a simple metric like number of retweets or Likes on Facebook to start. This is not an exact science. You want to alert people to your message.

Treating SMM Differently from Brand Marketing

Because of the power of peer influence, social media marketing is increasingly approached differently from brand and direct-response marketing. The differences stem from the fact that the philosophical approach, strategies, and execution tactics of SMM are more community and socially oriented.

Social media marketing is fundamentally about engaging with expert, referent, and positional influencers and strategically leveraging social media in all its forms to meet marketing and business objectives. As a result, you need to understand how social media marketing fits into the context of brand and direct response marketing.

SMM in the context of brand marketing

Brand marketing focuses on building equity around a brand, its personality, and attributes. Customers purchase products based on the brand promise. Through various forms of advertising and communications, the brand promise is brought alive to generate awareness, build excitement, and get specific products included in a consideration set. Mass media channels are typically used to build awareness for the brand, reposition it with more powerful attributes, or ultimately sell product. This will always be central to marketing efforts. All brands require significant effort to penetrate a market and generate desire.

SMM complements brand marketing in some key ways:

✔ **SMM places extra emphasis on peer-to-peer marketing and allows for peer-to-peer decision-making in a digital context.**

The focus is on understanding how consumers are interacting with each other on social platforms versus how they're interacting with the brand. Consumers are asked to do the marketing for the brand by layering their own voices and perspectives on top. The result is the socialization of a message or story in a way that's meaningful and relevant to their world.

✔ **SMM rarely uses mass media, whether television, print, or radio.**

Interactive channels that allow for the socialization and redistribution of a message are more important. But the brand cannot be simply pushed through the channels. Instead, invite consumers in the channels to experience the brand and make it their own.

✔ **SMM is about becoming part of all media streams, across all channels, where consumers are responding to and discussing the brand messages.**

In many cases, they're self-organizing these conversations on the fly. In other instances, they gravitate toward existing community hubs where the conversations are already taking place. These conversations can also take on your own corporate website.

Because of this, messaging, advertising campaigns, and even the products themselves don't define successful brands as much as the communities that surround them do. A brand supported by a large and influential community becomes more successful than one with a weak, disparate, and disjointed community. You have a huge opportunity to learn from their consumers as they listen in on these conversations. This is an opportunity you shouldn't miss.

SMM in the context of direct response

Direct response marketing is designed to solicit a specific, measurable response from specific individuals. Unlike brand marketing, with direct response, for every dollar invested, you see a traceable return. The measurable relationship is established between you and the consumer.

Some of the core attributes around direct response include a call to action, an offer and delivery of enough information to elicit a response, and guidance on how to respond. Television infomercials, which encourage consumers to call a number or visit a website, and direct mail offers, which invite consumers to purchase a product or send a reply, are the most common forms of direct response. Online advertising campaigns that are designed to drive clicks and purchases on brand websites are the most common online equivalent.

SMM complements direct response but lacks some of the measurability found in direct response. Social media marketing isn't typically geared toward a specific individual with the goal of soliciting a specific, measurable response. With SMM, communities of consumers are targeted with the goal of enticing them to positively influence one another and other people within their networks of online relationships. The goals are to convert consumers into potential marketers for the brand and provide them with the tools and mechanisms to further influence others. It's very different from asking an isolated consumer to perform a specific task.

SMM isn't as measurable as direct response marketing is. Tracking how social influencers work is still difficult; when a consumer shows brand affinity or makes a purchasing decision, it's hard to tell which factors or influencers impacted those choices most directly. In that sense, SMM is more akin to brand marketing, where the measurability is weak and needs to be based on feedback similar to that collected in attitudinal surveys. It's easy to track expert influencers online using social media measurement tools, but that's just part of the equation. Often, the social influencers who sway purchasing decisions aren't the most public and noticeable brand advocates.

Another factor to consider with SMM is that the call to action can't be too heavy-handed. As a result, some would argue that SMM is much more about social influence and much less about marketing. Social campaigns that blatantly push the call to action generally fail because they lack credibility and appear calculated. For this reason, you can't always easily recognize or measure your successful SMM campaigns.

Tying SMM with brand marketing and direct response

Social media marketing, which is about harnessing and categorizing the local spheres of influence, complements brand marketing and direct response with its focus on reaching social influencers across a variety of channels and platforms at every stage of the marketing funnel. This is done so that influencers socialize the message in their own communities and conduct the marketing for the brand. Not all social influencers have platforms to project strong opinions; some are more anonymous, localized, and less recognizable — that's the bad news. The good news is that influencers obviously like to influence and have a meaningful and integral role to play in marketing online or offline.

Social media marketing resembles relationship marketing in that both focus on the relationship, not just the point of sale, and are more personal in nature. The difference is that relationship marketing focuses on establishing deeper, longer-term relationships with customers over a lifetime, whereas social media marketing relies on customers marketing the brand.

Part II
Practicing SMM on the Social Web

The 5th Wave   By Rich Tennant

"Awww jeez — I was afraid of this. Some poor kid, bored with the usual chat lines, starts looking for bigger kicks. Pretty soon they're surfin' the seedy back alleys of Facebook, and before you know it they're into a profile they can't get out of. I guess that's why they call it the Web. Somebody open a window!"

In this part . . .

Part II is very much the practitioner's part, explaining the nuts and bolts of SMM campaigns, including planning for them, how to manage participation, seeding viral video clips, and tips and tricks for turning a crisis to your advantage.

In Chapter 4, we discuss the components of a successful SMM campaign and how you can make it work in harmony with other digital marketing efforts. Chapter 5 discusses why you need a SMM voice, how it differs from a brand voice or personality, where it gets manifested, and who can play that role.

Chapter 4

Launching SMM Campaigns

In This Chapter

▶ Discovering the key components of a successful SMM campaign

▶ Managing beyond the campaign

▶ Synchronizing the SMM campaign with other channels

▶ Responding to criticism

*L*aunching a social media marketing campaign is, in some ways, similar to launching any other digital campaign. But at the same time, you need to approach certain aspects of it very differently to maximize the results.

In this chapter, we discuss the components of a successful SMM campaign and how you can make it work in harmony with other digital marketing efforts. We also discuss how best to respond to criticism, how to turn a crisis to your advantage, and finally some tactics for turning the campaign into a long-term marketing asset.

Discovering the Types of SMM Campaigns

At this point, it's important to talk about the different types of campaigns. After that, we discuss the rules and guidelines that make SMM campaigns successful. In the realm of social media marketing, how you implement a campaign is nearly as important as what you implement.

Before you launch your SMM campaign, make sure you've done an inventory of all the other major SMM campaigns going on at the same time that target your customers or are within your industry. The last thing you want is to launch a campaign in which you're asking your customers to do basically the same thing that they may have just done for a competitor.

The FTC (Federal Trade Commission) plans to impose regulations on how pharmaceutical companies can market using the social web. Those regulations cover blogger liability in the realm of sponsored conversations. If you're a pharmaceutical company or are operating in another regulated industry, be sure to check with your lawyers about what you're allowed and not allowed to do before launching the SMM campaign.

Blogger outreach

Probably the most common form of a SMM campaign is the blogger outreach program. This campaign typically takes the form of identifying influencer bloggers who reach your customers. They're the expert influencers who cover a topic and have a following. The best way to think of them is as media properties. Many accept advertising but typically have day jobs that they're balancing as well.

Blogger outreach programs incentivize these bloggers to write about your brand or product. You can give them incentives by inviting them to the R&D labs of your company and treating them with the same deference that the mainstream press gets, to sending them sample products and providing them with prizes with which to run contests on their blogs. Campaigns are sometimes built around these influencers.

It's important to note that the debate continues to rage in the blogosphere about blogger compensation. Some bloggers absolutely refuse to accept compensation, whereas others are comfortable with it. Some companies like Aveda, a natural beauty products company, give bloggers gift cards or spa treatments but no outright payments. Bloggers typically accept these gifts with the knowledge that their review will not be influenced by a gift of any kind. Companies want honest evaluations, and their readers demand it. You must know where your targeted blogger stands on this debate before reaching out to him.

Knowing how to reach these bloggers without coming across as heavy-handed, commercial, and ignorant is critical. Before you reach out to them, be sure to read their blogs so that you know how they cover your brand or category, scan the comments on their blog posts so that you get a feel for the readers and how they participate, understand their policies with regard to brands engaging with them (some prefer to go through representatives, for example), and ideally try to develop a personal relationship based on the content that they publish and the topics they cover before approaching them with an idea.

These are all common-sense ideas that apply if you were attempting to do something similar in the real world. But as the saying goes, common sense is often uncommon, and many a company has done exactly the opposite.

UGC contests

Contests in all their various forms have always been a big hit in the marketing campaign arena. But now contests structured around user-generated content (UGC) are all the rage. And with good reason: They are invariably extremely popular, engaging, and fun. You structure a contest built on participants contributing something in return for rewards. This can be something as simple as crowdsourcing a TV advertisement, as General Motors did with its Tahoe campaign in 2006, to asking users to contribute video clips of their funniest moment with a product. The best clip (by the predetermined criteria) gets a prize, with all the other participants getting some sort of recognition.

As *Wired* magazine reported, in the case of the Tahoe campaign, the microsite attracted 629,000 visitors, with each user spending more than nine minutes on the site and a third of them going on to visit the main Chevy.com website. Sales took off from that point, even though environmentalists tried to sabotage the UGC campaign by creating video clips that highlighted their views about on the environmental toll the vehicle takes on the environment. HP ran a successful contest in which it asked designers around the world to help design the exterior of one its new laptops. HP got tons of press, rallied a lot of support for the contest among budding designers, and also got some great ideas in turn.

Brand utilities

The basic idea behind brand utilities is that instead of providing the consumer with some advertising, you build their trust (and get their dollars) by giving them a utility application that provides actual value. If the utility serves a purpose, users adopt the application and think more favorably of your brand. Dollars that would have normally gone toward buying media go toward building the application instead.

For example, Estee Lauder has launched a Facebook brand utility called "Shine a Light on Breast Cancer." It lets breast cancer survivors and their families post "messages of hope." It also lets you know where breast cancer events are being held around the world. This connects people from all corners of the world to support one another in the fight against breast cancer.

An application doesn't always have to take the form of an application or a widget on a social network. The famous Nike + solution, which is considered the world's largest running club, shown in Figure 4-1, is a virtual community that helps users track the distances they've run and compare themselves to their peers. The advertising industry moves between trends very quickly, and it seems that brand utilities are already out of the limelight.

Figure 4-1:
Nike+
Running
Monitor on
Facebook.

What's gaining favor now are apps that use *crowdsourcing.* For example, Best Buy used this type of application on Facebook for the 2011 holiday shopping season. After you log in, the application shows you the items your Facebook friends purchased from Best Buy so that you can ask them for their opinions. Conceivably, this could lead to a purchase at Best Buy because it was recommended by a friend.

Podcasting

A *podcast* is a digital audio file that is made available via web syndication technologies such as RSS. Although strictly speaking it's not social media, it's often classified as such because it allows anybody to easily syndicate their own audio content. You can use podcasts as a way to share information with your audiences. Often, podcasts take the shape of celebrity interviews or discussions about your product or brand. A successful example of a podcast is the Butterball Turkey Talk podcast. It's a seasonal podcast including stories from Turkey Talk hotline workers. You can subscribe to it via iTunes and other online podcast directories.

Podcasts typically don't form a whole SMM campaign in and of themselves but work well with other parts of a campaign.

Sponsored conversations

Sometimes the most effective SMM campaigns are the simplest ones. These campaigns engage with consumers in a straightforward, authentic fashion on a social platform while also aggregating other conversations, pointing to new ones, and stoking the community. Recently, Disney partnered with Savvy Auntie (www.savvyauntie.com), an online community focused on aunts without kids for one such effort, which is shown in Figure 4-2. Melanie Notkin, who runs SavvyAuntie.com, tweeted about Disney's *Pinocchio* movie in March 2008 to coincide with its Disney anniversary release. She tweeted about themes in the movie, often in question form, encouraging others to respond. Her 8,000 followers on Twitter at the time (today, she has more than 17,000) knew that she was doing this for Disney (every tweet about Pinocchio had a special tag), but because the tweets were appropriate for the audience, entertaining, and authentic, the campaign was a success.

Figure 4-2:
Savvy
Auntie.

Recognizing What Makes a Good SMM Campaign

A *social media marketing campaign* is one that specifically allows for social influence to take place digitally. A few years ago, marketing through social media was a niche activity, and the notion of targeting influencers was an obscure one. The closest comparison was word-of-mouth campaigns conducted in the offline world to build brand awareness for a product by incentivizing people to talk about it among themselves. Digital campaigns, for the most part, were about display advertising across large publisher websites, complemented with paid search campaigns and maybe e-mail campaigns. These campaigns were used to drive prospects to a *microsite* (a site devoted to that particular campaign) or a website, where they were encouraged to make purchases or engage with the brand.

With a SMM campaign, you mustn't drag people away from the social platform on which they're communicating and interacting with each other. They don't want to be distracted, and you'll probably only waste precious marketing dollars trying to lure them to your website. Instead, it's more important to execute the campaign on those very platforms where your potential customers are in conversation. You have to engage your customers where *they* want to participate, not where you want them to be. And unlike in a digital marketing campaign of yesteryear, the customers of a SMM campaign ignore you unless your SMM campaign is aligned with their objectives and behavior patterns on those social platforms. In the following sections, we outline specific guidelines you should follow when launching a SMM campaign.

A good example of a failed "build it and they will come" attempt was Bud. TV by Budweiser. They tried to create an entertainment destination bypassing YouTube. The effort failed miserably, as they had to spend valuable advertising dollars to encourage consumers to do something that they had no interest in doing — moving away from YouTube, where they had the most entertaining content (and all their friends), to a corporate-sponsored website. What's more, the fact that users couldn't embed the video clips elsewhere (including YouTube) hurt the effort. Bud.TV launched in January 2007 and was shut down early in 2009.

Creating Your SMM Roadmap

Just like in any other good marketing campaign, you need to construct a roadmap that shows you where you are going and how you'll get there. In this section, we discuss seven steps you can take to bulletproof your campaign structure. They are as follows:

✔ Define your objectives.

✔ Develop a powerful story/experience.

✔ Create an action plan.

✔ Craft the content path.

✔ Execute for influence.

✔ Create partnerships.

✔ Track the results.

Define your objectives

This may seem obvious, but it is amazing how many of us forget about articulating the objectives when it comes to a SMM campaign. Your objectives need to be tightly defined, and they must be practical and actionable too. The objectives must be specific to the stage of the marketing funnel that you're playing in as well. See Chapter 3 for more on the marketing funnel. Saying that the objective of the campaign is simply to take a TV advertisement and make it *go viral* is definitely not enough.

The objectives must also specify *where* you're planning to run the campaign, *whom* you're targeting (which customers and which influencers), the *duration* of the campaign, and *how it synchronizes* with other digital and offline marketing efforts. It is easy to forget that no SMM campaign happens in isolation. How you participate on the various social platforms is always a mirror of what you do and think in the physical world. If you ignore that fact, you'll lose your customers even before you've had a chance to meaningfully engage with them.

Develop a powerful story/experience

People's expectations about how they will learn about your business/products have changed completely. Because the Back button on the browser is ever-present, waiting to take users away from your website, you have a very short window to engage and educate. The days of posting a simple data sheet and a price are over. You have to work to communicate the intrinsic value of each offer.

Also, because people want to know who they are dealing with, you need to inject the *why* into your business story. You need to let them know why you started your business and what you care about. The social aspect must be visible. The following are stories you should consider telling during your campaign:

✔ **Why we are running this campaign:** Yes, you want to sell things, we understand that. But what is the larger picture? Are you contributing to charity, helping others be successful, providing a solution, or providing content that doesn't currently exist? You have to be specific.

✔ **What value you (as the customer) will get from participating:** Customers want social proof that others you have dealt with have had a great experience. You need to gather testimonial stories to share. If you can provide video of them speaking, you have a way to demonstrate authenticity.

✔ **People who are impacted; show visual stories:** Provide visuals that tell a story. Well-known screenwriter Robert McKee has said that stories "unite an idea with an emotion." Make sure yours does.

✔ **Who the hero is:** Have a story about the person or thing that is leading this effort. It can be a product that works, a founder who wants to do good, and so on. Show that hurdles have been overcome. The late Steve Jobs was a visionary who figured heavily in the promotion of Apple products because he was the heart and soul of the business.

✔ **How internal staff feels about what they do:** A current commercial by General Electric shows people who make medical equipment meeting the cancer survivors who have benefited from that equipment. The message comes through loud and clear that these employees care about the products they produce.

Create an action plan

Obviously, the actions you take are dictated by the length and complexity of the campaign. Every campaign has special features and highlights that need showcasing. However, following are some things that are common to most SMM campaigns you'll want to consider creating:

✔ **A clear call to action.**

Decide what action you want the user to take, and make sure everything you do supports that. If they have to sign up for something, have the sign-up process front and center at all times.

✔ **Hash tags and other tools.**

Most SMM campaigns create a hash tag for Twitter so that people can follow the conversation. A hash tag has the number sign (#) and a word or phrase related to the project. For example, a 2011 campaign to feed people on Thanksgiving was started by Pepto-Bismol with the hash tag #HelpPeptoFeedAmerica. Whenever someone retweeted the message with that hash tag, the makers of Pepto-Bismol donated money to hunger relief.

✔ **A venue for crowdsourcing.**

Are you going to create your own web page for people to share and submit their comments, or will you use the current platforms? Decide whether you want to create a Facebook page or a community on someplace like Ning, or host your own. There are pluses and minuses to each choice. If it is important to own the content, by all means create your own. Just remember that it's easier to get people to participate where they normally hang out. A new venue could be an impediment.

✔ **Content that can be shared.**

The key to every great SMM campaign is the content you create to get attention. If you are a small business and can't afford to create something splashy, you can still do a video and create PDF posters, contests, and graphics. Look at all the content you have already created, and see what you can repurpose. If it makes sense, have your customers create content, and pick a winner.

Craft the content path

When creating SMM campaigns, people often forget to map out where their actual touch points will be and how they will look. It's not enough to say, "We'll send out a tweet with a link." You need to be specific about it. You need to document that you will send out three tweets a day at 9 a.m., 5 p.m., and 9 p.m., say, with certain text and link.

As a handy way to document your campaign, you can map out each of your channels and the content that will go into it. One of the best ways to do this is to create a mind map that shows you the big picture of your campaign and all the moving parts on one sheet of paper. Mind maps start with a circle in the middle and radiate ideas that relate to it. For example, you can put your campaign name in the center circle and then radiate circles of the different platforms you are using. From each platform circle, you can note the content that will be sent.

Your preplanned content is only the first part of what you will be doing. You have to also organically create messages that respond to the ongoing campaign to make it real. When people post something about your campaign on Facebook or Twitter, make sure you respond to it in a reasonable amount of time. The preplanned items are just the starting point. Social marketing means reacting to real-time events.

Execute for influence

Traditionally, most campaigns have focused on getting a potential customer to take a specific action or to view a specific brand message. The focus has always been on that individual engaging with the brand in some form. However, with a SMM campaign, you need to design for sharing, influencing, reciprocity, and social currency.

Unlike most other campaigns, a SMM campaign needs to accomplish two objectives concurrently:

✔ **It needs to engage the individual who's being targeted via the campaign.**

This is similar to any other type of digital marketing campaign. You want to engage with your target audience in a specific fashion and solicit a specific response.

✔ You also need to design the campaign so that the target person shares or discusses it with someone else.

Sharing is the social currency element. The person should feel that by sharing the campaign with someone else, he derives greater value from it. This greater value could be something as tangible as further discounts or something as intangible as status among his peers. The point is that the more people the person shares the campaign with (or discusses it with), the more value he generates from it. In this sense, the campaign takes on a network effect, with its value growing each time someone participates.

Create partnerships

Few SMM campaigns are successful in isolation. Just as regular digital campaigns come together through a series of partnerships between the agency, the advertiser, and the publisher, so is the case with a SMM campaign. However, in this case, the participants vary slightly. Rather than having a regular publisher, you have the social platform to contend with. Your campaign must be in compliance with that platform's policies; otherwise, they won't let it run on their platform. For example, Facebook (www.face book.com) and YouTube (www.youtube.com) have strict terms of service regarding the type of advertising that can appear on their platforms.

The platform players aren't the only things you have to take into consideration. With most large brands, ad hoc user groups that have a sense of ownership over the brand or product category spring up on the social platform where you're planning to run the campaign.

For example, on Facebook, if you were to search for "Ford," you'd find not just the Ford Motor Company page (shown in Figure 4-3), but literally hundreds of groups created by and for people interested in Ford Motor Company. If you're a marketer at Ford, when you're planning a SMM campaign on Facebook, it's not enough to talk to Facebook and your own agency about the campaign. For it to be a truly successful SMM campaign, you must engage with these ad hoc groups when the campaign is starting. They can be your biggest marketers, helping the campaign succeed. On the other hand, if you upset them, they can turn into saboteurs.

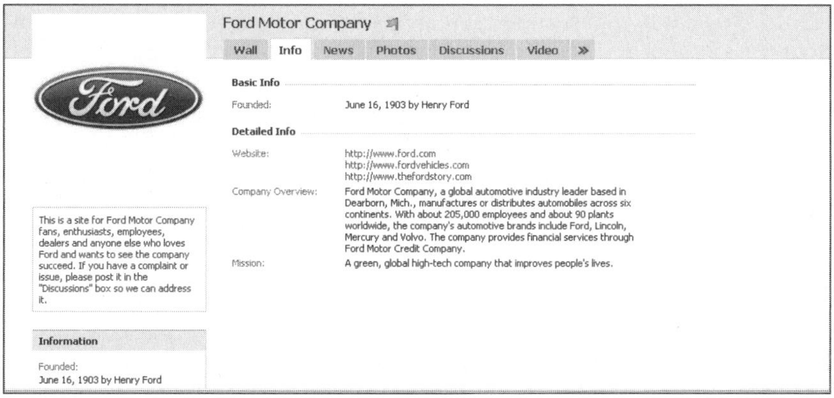

Figure 4-3:
Ford's
Facebook
page.

Irrespective of the social platform you're running a SMM campaign on, the ad hoc user groups are already there. Be sure to engage with them. A SMM campaign means new players and new partnerships that need to be forged early on for it to be a success. Finding and engaging with those communities of people becomes critical.

Track the results

There's a saying in the world of social media that only successful SMM campaigns can be measured; failures can't be. The point is that marketers often say that SMM can't measured if in their heart of hearts they know that their campaign has failed. If the campaign is a success, you bet they'll be telling you about it and explaining why exactly it was a success.

You can measure a SMM campaign in a lot of different ways. The best method depends on the objectives, the targeted audience, and the social platform on which the campaign is running. But you must determine what you're going to measure and how *before* you run the campaign. Otherwise, you're never going to know whether it's a success. SMM campaigns often spiral out of control, and the law of unintended consequences starts applying.

That's not a bad thing, but it doesn't take away from the fact that the campaign you're running is being run for a purpose, and you'll know whether you've achieved that purpose only if you're measuring the results. It's also important to measure a baseline of online activity before you begin the SMM engagement and decide what to measure. This helps you determine how successful your campaign is relative to the level of conversations and online activity before running it.

We get into measurement later in the book (see Chapter 19), but it's sufficient to say that you must measure not just how many people you reach or who is aware of your campaign, but also the influence generated; the *brand lifts* (increased awareness of the brand); and, most important, whether any of this effort led to purchases. With the measurement tools in the marketplace (many of which are free or close to free), you can easily track your SMM campaign to the point of sale on the website or potentially even in a physical store. Don't hesitate in trying to measure this.

Participating — Four Rules of the Game

Many different factors can make or break a SMM campaign, and sometimes it's even just a matter of luck. But four rules matter above all else when it comes to SMM campaigns.

These rules don't always apply to other forms of marketing. Pay attention to them, and make sure that your SMM campaign abides by these.

Be authentic

Authenticity is a tricky word. It's tricky because it's overused in the context of social media. Everybody talks about being authentic when marketing in the social media realm, but what that means is rarely explained. Authenticity is being honest and transparent: It's as simple as that.

Here are some examples:

✔ **When you set up a blog as part of your campaign, make sure that you're using your own voice.**

Don't outsource the publishing of content to a third party or to your PR team. If you have to, make sure that the writer accurately identifies himself as contributing on your behalf. George Colony's blog The Counterintuitive CEO is a great example, as shown in Figure 4-4. The blog is written in the first person by Forrester's chief executive officer, George Colony. There's no doubt that he is writing.

✔ **When you're publishing your thoughts, opinions, or simply sharing information, don't do so anonymously.**

In the world of social media, your consumers don't relate and care about brands as much as they care about the people behind them. People build relationships with each other and not with anonymous brands. Let your customers know who is behind the voice blogging, tweeting, or the contest on Facebook. You're not authentic if your customers don't know who you are.

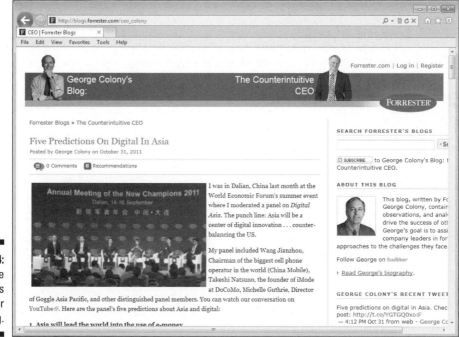

Figure 4-4:
George
Colony's
Forrester
blog.

✓ **Learn from the community, and respond to their feedback.**

A key part of being authentic is telling your customers the way it really is, hearing their feedback (both positive and negative), and being willing to respond to it. It's no use participating in the social realm if you don't respond to commentary or feedback. If you're worried about not having the time to respond, consider not participating at all.

✓ **Be humane in your approach.**

It is easy to forget that for every comment and every unique visitor, there's an actual person somewhere in the world. Make sure that you participate with consideration and with the same respect that you'd reserve for someone you're talking to face to face.

For more information on authenticity as it applies to word of mouth marketing and social media marketing, visit the Word of Mouth Marketing Association website (`http://womma.org/ethics/code`), and review its ethics code.

Operate on a quid pro quo basis

For all the altruism associated with the social web, it's easy to forget that it operates on the premise of quid pro quo. We're all good human beings, but most people expect something in return if they're giving you their time. As you develop a SMM campaign in which you'll be demanding your customers' attention (and often a lot more than that), think about the possible quid pro quo. Are you giving enough back in exchange? If you're not giving something back, your customers won't participate. They'll simply ignore you. The social web is littered with marketing campaign failures. These campaigns assumed that just by putting a banner advertisement in front of customers, they would achieve their objectives.

Here's an example of a SMM campaign that provided a strong quid pro quo for its audiences and was highlighted by *Adweek*. The All brand of laundry detergent created a promotion that aired April 5, 2009, on the TV show *Celebrity Apprentice*. Instead of focusing on the attributes of their detergent (how much can you talk about the attributes of laundry detergent, after all?), they associated All with a charitable cause through viral marketing. *Celebrity Apprentice* viewers saw a 30-second TV ad directing them to a website to watch videos that featured *Celebrity Apprentice* contestants Joan and Melissa Rivers (they could alternatively watch the video clips on YouTube).

The videos featured them using All in ridiculous settings. Each time viewers forwarded the videos, All donated 50 cents to charity. This was a SMM campaign that entertained the customer, encouraged him to share elements of it with his friends, and rewarded the customer for sharing. Success of the campaign was defined by the number of visits to the website, the number of unique visitors that registered for a coupon, the number of e-mails sent, and the amount of money raised for the charity.

Give participants equal status

Many marketing campaigns are designed to make the consumer feel special — more special than everyone else around them. That's a good thing. They feel special, and they end up having favorable feelings for your product and go out and buy it. Apple and Harley-Davidson are two brands that personify this philosophy: They make their customers feel special and different from everyone else.

That's wonderful, but it doesn't apply to the SMM realm in the same way. People across the social web like to believe that they're as special and as unique as the next person, as they should. If someone is doing something special, they want to do that as well. If a person does something interesting, others want to access to it as well. That's human nature, and the social web encourages behavior through the voyeurism it allows for.

Let go of the campaign

By virtue of starting the campaign, you probably feel that it is your responsibility to moderate and shape it. That doesn't have to be the case. Successful SMM campaigns are the ones in which the brand advocates take the campaign in new directions. As you develop the campaign, think of yourself as a participant and not just the owner of the campaign. You make better decisions regarding its evolution that way, and by letting go, you allow others to take it new and much amplified directions. And as always, remember your consumers will be in control of the campaign. That's what makes social media marketing different. However, you will always be in control of your own response to the consumer participation, and that always presents exciting opportunities.

Killing the Campaign Expiry Date

You're probably used to thinking of campaigns as having a start date and an end date. And they usually need that. You have a finite marketing budget; the campaign is geared around a series of events (like Christmas sales); new products replace old ones several times a year, and that forces you to end campaigns and launch new ones. However, SMM campaigns are unique in that after they start, they may not stop when you want them to. It's like turning off the lights midway through a dinner party. If you have a conversation going and have gotten a community of people to come together around your brand, product, or campaign, the last thing you want to do is to suddenly disown them. It is very important that you plan for migrating that community of people to a broader purpose or goal.

Here are four ways to do that successfully:

✔ **Give participants new reasons to engage with your brand.**

Your original SMM campaign has a set purpose and objectives. After they're accomplished, don't turn off the lights. Instead, think of the next campaign that you have planned and how you can customize it to this community of people.

In fact, try to weave the campaigns together into a program that benefits these people. As you do this, remember the four rules of participation we outlined previously: authenticity, quid pro quo, equal status, and disowning the campaign.

✔ **Encourage participants to coalesce into communities.**

Often, the people who participate in your SMM campaign all share something in common. This may not always be the case, but depending upon the campaign type, they may indeed be interested in forming a community. If you believe that to be the case, encourage them to coalesce into self-supporting communities. It only helps you in the long run and gives new life to the campaign. Campaigns that have generated good will transform into customer communities that you can tap into for future marketing and business efforts.

A good example of this is the Walmart ElevenMoms. Walmart tapped eleven mommy bloggers to go shopping at Walmart stores (they were given a budget) and then blog about their experiences. They did so successfully (at least from the perspective of Walmart) and are now organized into a social network. In fact, over time, they have added more moms and are now simply called Walmart Moms, as shown in Figure 4-5.

Figure 4-5:
Walmart
Moms.

✔ **Treat participants like existing customers.**

Someone who's participated in your SMM campaign may not have bought your product, but he has given you his time and probably has shared a bit of himself with you in the process. This may have taken the form of commenting on a blog post, participating in a contest, sharing your viral video clip with friends, or testing a product and writing a review about it. Because he's done more than someone who experienced a traditional marketing campaign, you owe him more.

Treat him like an existing customer, whether that means sending him special offers, inviting him to participate in focus groups, or beta testing new products. But as you do this, always remember that when you send your customers a special offer, it must be opt-in. Don't spam them if you don't have their permission to communicate with them.

✔ **Extend the campaign to the website.**

Many a SMM campaign has failed because it was kept separate from the corporate website. The campaigns are traditionally built off micro sites with display advertising promoting them. When the campaign has run its course, the micro site is shut down, and the advertising is stopped. In the case of a SMM campaign, don't shut down the micro site. Instead, promote the SMM campaign on the company website, and when the campaign winds down, find a place on the website for it. That way, your customers can always find it, and if they coalesced into communities during the course of the campaign, they always have a place to return to. (See Chapter 15 for more information.)

Often, your participants may know better than you how to create greater meaning from the SMM campaign in the form of a community. Ask them what you should be doing, if anything at all. You'll definitely get strong advice from the people who care the most.

Monitoring Brands and Conversations

It's no use running a SMM campaign if you can't measure it. You should always measure your SMM campaigns. Depending on the SMM campaign, different measurements may matter more than others. The brand and conversation monitoring tools help you measure the success of your SMM campaign and your ROI (return on investment). But they do a lot more than that. These tools help you plan and design your SMM campaigns. They give you a peek into actual user behavior on social platforms, telling you what people are discussing, whether those conversations are positive or negative, and where they're taking place.

Any time you're planning to launch a SMM campaign, you must begin by knowing what your target audiences are doing across the social web. These tools help you do that. They can be classified into three groups:

✔ **High-end tools and services** that use linguistic analysis and deep data mining to provide insights into the conversations, who is having them, and where. These tools can cost anywhere from $5,000 a month to $50,000 a month, based mostly on the number of topics mined and the frequency. Included in this category are Cymfony, Nielsen BuzzMetrics, and MotiveQuest.

✔ **Low-end tools** that primarily focus on the volume of the conversation over a period of time and cover only positive and negative sentiment. Many of these tools are free or dirt-cheap. Included here are HootSuite and Social Mention.

✔ **Middle-of-the-road tools** that do some analysis but don't always have the breadth of sources or the depth of analysis that the high-end tools have. Tools in this category are Crimson Hexagon and J.D. Power and Associates. Visible and Converseon straddle the high and low ends with different service levels and capabilities, including workflow and the ability to identify influencers.

When choosing which tool to use, keep the following factors in mind:

✔ **Your audience:** If you don't know your audience and aren't sure what their motivations are, where they are participating, and how, you want one of the high-end tools.

✔ **The length of your SMM campaign:** If you're running a short campaign targeting a small population of users, you probably don't need to use one of the high-end tools. It won't be worth the money.

✔ **The size of the campaign:** If your campaign touches lots of people, you need a higher-end tool that can help you track the activity and manage responses too.

✔ **Influencer identification:** If you're planning to focus on influencers rather than the mass population, choose a tool that's strongest at *influencer identification* (the ability to assist you in identifying influencers who influence customers about your brand). Not all tools do this equally well.

✔ **Regulatory considerations:** If you work in a highly regulated industry, you want a tool that lets you view commentary and glean insights anonymously. Higher/midlevel tools have this capability.

✔ **Dashboard functionality:** Some marketers require interactive dashboards through which they can view the conversation in real time. If you're one of them, be sure to look for a tool that allows for that.

 Lots of free tools for brand and conversation monitoring are out there. Regardless of the complexity of your SMM campaign and tracking needs, there's never any harm in beginning with the free tools. It'll cost you only the time in setting up the domain names. Also keep in mind that these tools are valuable to departments like public relations and customer research, too. They may be willing to share the costs of the tool or service with you.

Responding to Criticism

No SMM campaign is a complete success. It never is. Although you may reach many more people than you could have ever imagined, more likely than not, you're still bound to upset some people and even potentially spark an inflammatory response among a few others. From the outset, before you launch your SMM campaign, you need to plan for the potential criticism that may come your way. There's no perfect way to respond, and the answer usually depends on the type of criticism, how widespread it is, and where it is coming from. Your PR department is usually more versed in responding to criticism (and crisis management more broadly) than anyone else, so you should be sure to bring them into the process early.

Regardless, here are some guidelines to keep at the back of your mind as you launch your campaign and prepare for the criticism that may come your way:

✔ **Respond early and often.**

There's no greater insult to people criticizing your SMM campaign than to be ignored. Ignoring criticism results in greater anger and more vitriolic responses that can snowball into a full-fledged crisis as the anger percolates across the social web. Before you know it, your CEO — or maybe the *New York Times* — is calling your desk, so respond quickly.

✔ **Respond honestly and clearly.**

Be sure to use your own name when you respond. Just as you have to be authentic with your campaign, you need to be with your response. Be clear about your rationale for why the campaign is designed the way it is, admit mistakes when the fault is yours, and be inclusive in your responses.

✔ **Be prepared to change based on the feedback.**

It's easier to be stubborn and not to change your SMM campaign. But if there's valid criticism about the campaign, whether it's of the structure, the creative aspect, or the rules regarding the type of conversation, you should incorporate the feedback and make the appropriate changes. You'll win back trust quickly.

✔ **Don't hesitate to bring humor to the situation.**

Some of the best responses have been those that included a touch of self-effacing humor. Brands aren't above people, and neither is yours. Humor goes a long way in the social web, and sometimes the response becomes the new SMM campaign.

✔ **Use the same channels for the response.**

This may seem obvious, but it really isn't. Respond to people in the way they've criticized you. Don't go on national television to respond to a YouTube outburst. You'll become the laughingstock of the social web.

Chapter 5

Developing Your SMM Voice

A social media marketing campaign, program, or strategic approach won't be successful if no observable people are behind it. Consumers want to know who the people behind the brand are. Being a trusted brand is not enough. Putting your chief executive officer's name on the About Us page of your website isn't either. When consumers engage across the social web, they want to engage with real people who have personalities and opinions. In other words, the people representing the brand need to be SMM voices that people can search on Google or Bing to find out more about. That means the consumer should be able to search the person representing the brand and see via the search results that the brand has put forth a real person to talk on its behalf. That's why you need a SMM voice.

Having voices that can be researched through the search engines is instrumental to establishing credibility and being authentic. This chapter discusses why you need a SMM voice, how it differs from a brand voice or personality, where it is manifested, and who can play that role. We then discuss using that person's relationships to help with *crowdsourcing* (asking people in a community to provide their content for a specific purpose).

Figuring Out Why You Need a SMM Voice

As we write this chapter, the United States, and indeed the entire world, is in a major economic downturn. Practically every major corporation has had to lay off employees and ask their remaining employees to take on more responsibility. In this economic environment, does it make sense to introduce a new type of role into your organization with potentially overlapping responsibilities? On the surface, it may not appear so, but it's actually more important than ever. If the economic downturn has taught us one thing, it's that consumers are tired of engaging with large, impersonal brands and often turn against them on the social web. They simply do not trust big brands anymore. In fact, half of the respondents to a survey conducted recently by *The Economist* magazine said that the economic crisis has intensified their distrust of big business. The magazine went on to say that the downturn is accelerating the use of social media because people are placing more value on the recommendations of their friends than they are in big business. According to the 2011 Edelman Trust Barometer, trust in business increased 2 percentage points from 2010 to 2011 (from 54 percent to 56 percent). This is just another point on how trust in big business has not bounced back from the downturn. The stock market gyrations in markets around the world should indicate to everyone that people are scared and confused.

If you run a business trying to reach consumers in the social web, this distrust presents a problem. Those consumers don't want to listen to you anymore. They'd much rather listen to their friends. This means that they're not paying attention to all the advertising that you're pushing at them and certainly aren't making product-purchasing decisions based on it. This means that you have to change your marketing strategy, and because you purchased this book, you've probably already realized that you need to. It also means that if your consumers trust their friends more than big brands, you have to become more like their friends to earn their trust. And at the heart of becoming more like their friends is developing a SMM voice that's associated with a single person in your company through whom you reach out to those consumers. It can't just be your brand name, your logo, or your witty copy that does it. It has to be a *real* person within your company who's reaching out to your consumers.

Sometimes, the best way to discover whether you need a SMM voice is by scanning the conversations about your brand across the social web. You'll probably find people talking about you or your product category at the very least. That'll give you a sense of how important it is, and the volume of conversations may serve as a guide to how quickly you need to establish your SMM voice.

Defining SMM Voice Characteristics

The SMM voice is fundamentally the voice through which you engage with your consumers in the social web. Every conversation touch point on any social platform from YouTube (www.youtube.com) and Facebook (www.facebook.com) to Twitter (www.twitter.com) and your own discussion forums needs to be in the SMM voice. This strategy can take the form of one voice, or it can be several who work closely together to speak as one. But all SMM voices share certain characteristics in contrast to a brand voice. In the next few sections, I look at some of the key characteristics.

Multiple and authentic

Most companies have multiple, authentic SMM voices. The reason is obvious. They are generally too large to have one person representing them in all the conversations digitally. There are multiple people who focus on different conversation areas, whether it's customer support, industry insights, product information, or awareness building. In some cases, each person represents the company on different social environments. Each person talks in her own voice and loosely follows centralized guidelines. Zappos (twitter.zappos.com) is a good example of a company with multiple SMM voices. The company is proud of its multiple SMM voices and trusts those employees to represent the brand effectively without losing their own authenticity. One of Shiv's previous companies has its SMM voices represented at razor fish.alltop.com/. They have social influence marketing guidelines that the employees adhere to, but beyond that, it's all in the hands of those SMM voices.

Transparent and easy to find

Your SMM voices can't be anonymous voices. They have to be real people who are traceable; otherwise, they won't be taken seriously. Now, this may seem to be a bad strategy because so much is invested in the one person or very small group who's playing the role of the SMM voice, but it's necessary. When making these decisions, think about celebrity endorsements. People recognize that a celebrity may not be the permanent SMM voice, but they would much rather be talking to someone with whom they can form a relationship and relate to, even if it's only for a finite period, than an anonymous brand voice. For a SMM voice to be real, it has to be someone people can find through Google: There's no question about that.

Engaging and conversational

Some people know how to have a conversation, and some *really* know how to. Your SMM voice, whoever she is, needs to be truly conversational. She needs to be a person who can start a conversation, build trust, and be responsive. The person needs to have more of a customer service mentality than an on-message marketing or PR mindset. This is not about marketing or PR but about more genuine, deeper conversations.

Social web savvy

Your SMM voice needs to be someone who knows the social web intimately: the rules, social norms, and the best practices of participating in the social web. This person ideally should have individual credibility that extends beyond the brand that he works for and must be easily accessible on all the major social platforms. Keep in mind that your SMM voices will make mistakes, and they will probably get flamed at times too. You have to allow for that to happen. It is all part of the learning process.

Unique to the person

In contrast to a brand voice, this SMM voice must be unique to him and not unique to the company. This is incredibly important for the trust to develop. Otherwise, the whole effort is a waste of time. Furthermore, this voice should be irreplaceable. When the person goes on vacation, the voice cannot continue to participate and be responsive to customer queries. Someone else has to take over and introduce herself first. Think of it like a news anchor in a major television channel who takes the night off. The replacement is a different person, and that's not hidden from the viewer.

Distinguishing Between SMM Voices and Brand Voices

At this point, you're probably thinking that your SMM voice is similar to your brand voice or personality. You're probably already thinking of people — maybe representatives from public relations or corporate marketing in your organization — who can be your SMM voice. Before you jump into this decision too quickly, check out Table 5-1, which compares brand and SMM voices. Use this table to explain to team members why the two voices are different and why this effort may not be best relegated to the public relations department.

A SMM voice is very different from a brand voice. Someone who's spent a lifetime representing your brand and keeping everyone else around on brand message is probably not the best person to be the SMM voice.

Table 5-1	Brand versus SMM Voice
Brand Voice	**SMM Voice**
Singular, anonymous company voice	Multiple, authentic individual voices
Reflects the brand personality and attributes perfectly	Transparent, easy to identify online, and only loosely on brand
Everybody follows the brand voice strictly	Engaging, conversational, and responsive
Designed to appear across all brand touch-points	Mostly relevant only where the conversations are
Usually unique to the company	Usually unique to the person
Sometimes manifested in a person but not always	Always manifested in a real person or many people
Used everywhere from signage to ad copy	Used only in real conversations by real people

As you compare the two voices, ask yourself whether you have a SMM voice and, if so, how it relates to your brand voice. It can be closely associated with your brand voice, but it doesn't have to be. In some cases, the SMM voice may be closer to the product brand than the corporate brand. That doesn't matter as long as it is driven by an individual or several individuals and is truly authentic.

Establishing a SMM voice may appear in conflict with brand and public relations objectives. The best way to avoid this conflict is to include your brand marketers and your PR team in the early conversations about your SMM voices. It'll prevent an adversarial relationship from developing because they'll truly understand why you're creating it. They'll also have a lot of valuable advice for you based on their experiences in dealing with the mainstream press and customers through other channels. It is worth noting that you can have multiple SMM voices, some of whom can be people who currently are your brand marketers and PR representatives. For them to be successful, however, may require a change in how they're used to talking to the outside world but that will only be discovered in time.

Outlining SMM Voice Objectives

When you're defining your SMM voice, it's important to consider what you'll be using the SMM voice for. Knowing the objectives it serves and how it supports your marketing and business efforts more broadly is instrumental. If you haven't defined the objectives for the SMM voice, don't take up valuable time (and potentially resources too) in identifying those voices and putting a program around it.

Some of the more common objectives served by having a SMM voice include the following:

✔ **Providing industry and company insights to all stakeholders.**

A lot of people are probably talking about your brand in the social web. Many of them are probably forming strong opinions about your industry, your company, and your brand, too. Some of these people may be very influential. They could be key influencer bloggers, shareholders, customers, competitors, or market analysts. An important objective for having a SMM voice is to share your company's own take on industry and company issues with the broader world and negate any false or unfairly biased perspectives.

✔ **Building awareness for your products and services.**

Every month there appears to be a new social platform on which your brand needs to have a presence. This may be Facebook, MySpace, CafeMom (www.cafemom.com), LiveJournal (www.livejournal.com), Twitter, or foursquare (www.playfoursquare.com). Your customers may be gravitating to that service and could be discussing your brand and forming opinions about your product there. Your SMM voice is needed to simply build awareness for your products and services, communicate accurately about the products, and dispel any myths about them on these social platforms.

✔ **Forging deeper more trusted relationships with your customers.**

Sometimes, your SMM voice is important to simply deepen your relationships with your customers. It may be focused on giving them category purchase advice, sharing tips and tricks about your product, and helping them through product purchase or upgrade decisions. In other instances, it may be about simply participating in conversations and being a helpful representative of your brand.

✔ **Responding to customer service and product complaints.**

When customers are struggling with products, they often complain about them in conversations with their peers or other people who are facing similar challenges. You have a huge opportunity to listen in on these conversations, hear those concerns, provide customer support where you can, and learn from those complaints. Some of the most dynamic examples of companies embracing the social web successfully have been from companies hearing complaints on platforms like Twitter, responding to them in real time, and providing superior customer service. The ROI (return on investment) of this is easily measurable. The shoe company Zappos (www.zappos.com), acquired by Amazon in 2009, does this successfully, as shown in Figure 5-1.

✔ **Providing discounts and promotional information.**

Most brands offer discounts and special promotions on a regular basis. What better way than to share these than via the social platforms as well? Increasingly, brands are forming micro-communities with passionate brand advocates for the purpose of offering them special discounts and promotions before extending them to the wider public. This strategy builds buzz for the brand in the social web and deepens the connection between the most loyal customers and the brand.

If you do offer discounts and special promotions, you must be prepared to redeem them. Account for the promo to be successful; when it is, your company won't have trouble redeeming it.

Figure 5-1:
Zappos'
customer
service
Twitter feed.

Choosing the Owner of Your Organization's SMM Voice

There's no question that you need a SMM voice for the social web. It is instrumental to forging relationships with prospects, customers, and expert, positional, and referential influencers in addition to the industry at large. But setting your objectives up front is as important as knowing the difference between your SMM voice and your brand voice. It's no use participating if you do so in a manner that's in conflict with the fundamental ethos of the social web. You invariably do more damage to your brand and credibility than you may realize. Remember that whatever mistake you make in the social web gets quickly amplified, so set your objectives carefully, recognize how different your SMM voice is from your brand, and choose the right people to play the roles.

If you're a small company, either the CEO (chief executive officer) or the CMO (chief marketing officer) should always be your SMM voice or at least one of your SMM voices. Even Zappos, a mammoth shoe company, uses its CEO, Tony Hsieh, as its key SMM voice even after its acquisition by Amazon. The strategy works well, and given that it's building and establishing the brand primarily through social media marketing, the question of how the SMM voice conflicts with its brand voice doesn't really arise. The brand and SMM voices are perfectly aligned. That may not be the case for you, so as you wade into the social web, think carefully about your SMM voice and whether you're even comfortable having one before participating.

Richard Branson, chairman of the Virgin Group, has his own presence on Twitter (with over 1.3 million followers) and represents himself and his company (www.twitter.com/richardbranson). The airline Virgin America (which is part of the Virgin Group) also has its own Twitter presence (twitter.com/virginamerica) that is used to interact with passengers, share special offers, and announce travel advisories. With over 250,000 followers, arguably the Twitter activity makes a difference.

Now that you know what a SMM voice is, how it differs from your brand voice, and have a sense of what business objectives may drive the need for this voice, the only remaining question to answer is "Who exactly in your organization should serve in this role?"

In the next few sections, I look at the most common types of people who serve as the SMM voice and what they're typically best at doing.

CEO

A CEO can be a SMM voice. In many cases, he is already close to being a SMM voice anyway. He's representative of the brand but is recognized and noticed as an individual personality with independent opinions that happen to drive the business's direction. This person is best used as a SMM voice providing industry and company insights. After all, he has the credibility and the experience to do so. In many cases, you can use the CEO SMM voice to forge deeper relationships with customers as well. The CEO of Forrester, George Colony, is actively blogging, and you can tell that it's really him. The CEO participating in the social web and sharing his insights (and responding to blog comments) has done an immeasurable amount for the Forrester brand. If your CEO does not have time to truly commit to the online community, do not ask him to. It is better that he have no presence, whether it be a Twitter or a blog presence, than to have an abandoned one.

Never let your CEO, or for that matter any employee, comment about your company on discussion forums anonymously. Although this may seem obvious, the CEO of Whole Foods Market, John Mackey, was caught commenting on an investor forum about his competitors. He got into trouble for trying to influence the stock price of his competitors.

When choosing SMM voices, be mindful of the PR disaster experienced by Domino's Pizza when two young employees at a franchise put up what they thought was a funny YouTube video about sanitation behind the scenes. The video went viral, and the CEO had to issue a major apology. The fallout was definitely not funny. Although more junior staff may know the social platforms the best, they probably also require greater supervision and education. This is because they may not know the culture of the company that they represent or be familiar with what's good practice versus bad practice when representing a company to its customers. This is why the SMM guidelines are so important. Those are discussed later in the chapter.

CMO

Along with the CEO, another good person to play the SMM voice for the company is the CMO (chief marketing officer). Often, she is closest to customers along with the actual retail outlet employees, talking to them most often, hearing their complaints, and feeding insights from them into new product development. The CMO, as a result, is also a natural choice to be the SMM voice. CMOs are typically useful for providing industry and company insights, building awareness for products and services, forging deeper relationships with customers, and in some cases (but rarely) sharing special discount and promotional information. At Best Buy, Barry Judge, the CMO, has his own blog and Twitter account; see Figure 5-2. He's very much a SMM voice and a very vocal one, too. Mr. Judge's blog also illustrates that committing to a full-time blog can prove to be burdensome as roles change. He decided to travel much more than before and couldn't keep posting on a regular basis. This was a result of the Internet's role in enhancing the company's worldwide reach. He decided to begin blogging again when he realized that he had formed a relationship with his audience and was missed.

Figure 5-2:
Barry
Judge's
blog.

Social media lead

The social media lead is becoming a more common role within many large organizations. This person coordinates all social media activities across the company between all the different departments and out to customers as well. She is of course the most natural choice to be a SMM voice or one of the key SMM voices. This person knows the social web well, often has independent credibility within it, and understands how to strike the right balance between representing the brand and speaking authentically as an individual. This person can accomplish practically any of the objectives with the exception of company and industry insights, which may need to come from the CEO or CMO to carry credibility. In some organizations, this person has the title of community manager, social media manager, community evangelist, or outreach coordinator. Ford Motor Company (with Scott Monty as its social media lead) best exemplifies this approach. Figure 5-3 shows Scott Monty's Twitter feed.

Figure 5-3:
Scott
Monty's
Twitter feed.

PR manager

The PR manager typically manages relationships with the mainstream press. Arguably, managing mainstream press relationships and being a brand voice can and does conflict with the SMM voice, but that doesn't mean that an enterprising PR manager can't play the role of the SMM voice. He may need to choose to take on the responsibility at the cost of being the brand voice to do this authentically, however. After he does, he, like a social media lead, can accomplish all the major SMM objectives with the exception of the industry and company insights.

Agency

A social media, digital, or advertising agency can also represent you in the social web as your SMM voice. At the outset, having a SMM voice outside your company may seem inauthentic, but as long as the agency representative is transparent about it and is only building awareness for your product and sharing discount information, it's not a problem. Sometimes, the agency can monitor conversations and provide recommendations on how and where to participate. But the actual participation with the objectives of deepening customer relationships, addressing customer complaints, and providing industry and customer insights must be conducted by someone within your business. The agency can also be used to help with training the internal representatives, monitoring conversations, creating reports for senior management, and providing strategy and insight.

Other external voices

Outside your agency, spokespeople for your company can serve as SMM voices. For example, if your company uses a celebrity or a series of celebrities to promote products and services, they too can serve as SMM voices. These celebrities can engage with your customers and build enthusiasm for your products and services. But each time you use an external SMM voice, keep in mind that they may not be as loyal to your brand as you may like them to be. They could be representing other brands as well as your own. If you have an independent expert serving as a SMM voice, keep in mind that she may not always be available to participate on your behalf when you need her to. Often when external SMM voices are used, they're used in conjunction with internal ones and not in isolation.

Crowdsourcing SMM Voices with Guidelines

For all the strategies that you may put into place to support your SMM voice, you need to do still more. If you're a large company with hundreds or thousands of employees, you can't stop your employees from participating in the social web. Just as you cannot stop an employee from talking about your company at a dinner party, you can't prevent him from talking about you online. That's not necessarily bad: The more people who know your brand and talk about it favorably, the more it can help you. But it is important to establish some guidelines so that your employees know how to talk about your company online.

Employees care about their companies, and they'll welcome the guidelines. They'll see it as a way for them to better represent the company in the public domain — that is, of course, as long as you don't make the guidelines too restrictive and do incorporate feedback. If you develop the guidelines in isolation from your employees, ignoring how they typically participate online and want to represent your company, you're sure to face backlash. It is also important to design the guidelines to be adaptable based on how the social web is evolving and how behavior is changing on the different social platforms.

Before you write the guidelines, be sure to check whether your organization has any existing guidelines and policies that can serve as a starting point.

Here are elements that you can incorporate into your SMM policy:

- **Purpose:** Start with the objectives. You need to explain why the guidelines are being established, what they hope to accomplish, and how they help the employees.

- **Declaration of trust:** Just as important, you must establish that the goal of the guidelines isn't to restrict employees or to sensor them, but to encourage them to be better ambassadors of the company. Similarly, it's important to establish that no one will monitor employees, nor will you ask them to edit or delete posts.

- **Statement of responsibility:** Make clear that employees are personally responsible for all the content that they publish online, whether it is on a blog, a wiki, on YouTube, or any other form of social media. They should do so in a manner befitting their identity as an employee of the company, recognizing that whatever they publish may be attributed to the company.

- **An identification of themselves as employees:** Employees must know that although they do not have to always identify themselves as employees of a company, they must do so when discussing company or industry matters. In those instances, they should either speak as a representative of the company or include a disclaimer emphasizing that they are sharing their own personal opinions. Similarly, employees should declare any conflicts of interest when discussing professional matters.

- **A SMM voice:** Employees should speak as a SMM voice by being engaging, conversational, and authentic but recognizing that they aren't the official brand voice of the company. And furthermore, it is important to do so in one's own name and not anonymously. The CEO of Whole Foods Market commented on discussion forums about his competitors anonymously. When he was caught, it hurt him and his company.

✔ **Engagement principles:** Being a good SMM voice also means following certain engagement principles. These include responding to comments immediately, providing meaningful and respectful comments, being transparent in all social interactions online, and always looking to add value.

✔ **No unauthorized sharing of business information:** Employees should not share client, company, partner, or supplier information without express approval from the appropriate owners. When referencing somebody, link back to the source.

✔ **Respect for the audience:** As with any other form of communication, by virtue of being associated with the company, the employee is an ambassador and a SMM voice. He can easily tarnish the brand without meaning to do so and without even realizing it. It is therefore important to avoid personal insults, obscenity, or inappropriate behavior that is outside the company's formal policies. This is especially important because when something is expressed in the social domain, it's easily amplified by others. Just ask Domino's about the crisis it faced when two employees published obscene videos online.

✔ **Respect for copyright, fair use, and financial disclosure laws:** Regardless of the media being published, employees should still respect all local, state, and federal laws, especially in the realms of copyright, fair use, and financial disclosure.

✔ **What to do when they make a mistake:** Regardless of what an employee publishes, at some point, he is going to screw up. We're all human, after all. The guidelines must address what employees should do if they make a mistake. That means being up front about the mistakes, correcting the errors immediately, and accepting responsibility.

These guidelines are culled from an analysis of several social media guidelines, with the IBM guidelines, shown in Figure 5-4, serving as the primary source of inspiration, as they represent the most complete set. If you'd like to see the complete set, go to www.ibm.com/blogs/zz/en/guidelines.html.

SMM guidelines can get long and unwieldy. You may not need every element mentioned in the preceding list. If you're a small company, these guidelines may fold into broader employee guidelines and may not need to be a stand-alone document. But you definitely need them in some form. They provide direction to your employees without hampering their enthusiasm for social influence marketing. And with the right excitement around SMM, you may find yourself turning every employee into a marketer who is representing the company in her own SMM voice, authentically and convincingly. You can't ask for more than that from your employees. Invariably, these spontaneous, natural grass-roots efforts complement your more formal brand and SMM voices. They don't contradict but strengthen each other.

Figure 5-4:
IBM's social
media stan-
dards.

Be sure to invite employees across your company to provide feedback on the guidelines. It is no use creating and publishing guidelines in isolation. Your employees provide you with valuable feedback. By being included in the creation process, they're more likely to follow the guidelines.

Some SMM guideline resources and examples

Here are some of the most helpful online resources for creating SMM guidelines:

✓ **IBM Social Computing Guidelines:** www.ibm.com/blogs/zz/en/guidelines.html

✓ **HP Blogging Code of Conduct:** www.hp.com/hpinfo/blogs/codeofconduct.html

✓ **Intel Social Media Guidelines:** www.intel.com/sites/sitewide/en_US/social-media.htm

✓ **U.S. Navy Web 2.0: Utilizing New Web Tools:** www.doncio.navy.mil/PolicyView.aspx?ID=789

✓ **U.S. Air Force New Media Guide:** www.af.mil/shared/media/document/AFD-090406-036.pdf

Part III
Reaching Your Audience via Mainstream Social Platforms

The 5th Wave   By Rich Tennant

It was on the WhaleNet site one night that Capt. Ahab caught up with his obsession.

WHALE CHAT

White? Really? Where can we meet?

In this part . . .

*W*hen you're ready to start your campaign, Chapter 6 helps you choose which of the major social platforms on which to launch, sustain, and promote your brand. In Chapter 7, we look at why Facebook is one of the "must-haves" for social media campaigns.

Chapter 8 focuses on Twitter. You see the variety of tweet types that exist and how you can exploit them in your advertising. Chapter 9 covers how to create a winning YouTube strategy that can stand out among your competitors. In Chapter 10, we discuss how the relatively new social platform foursquare can help you bring local customers into your store and grow your business.

In Chapter 11, we discuss how using LinkedIn can benefit your SMM campaigns as well as your own personal brand. Chapter 12 looks at how Google+ is gaining traction at a fantastic rate and how it can work for you.

Chapter 13 moves away from the major platforms to discuss the niche social networks. In Chapter 14, we discuss why social influencers matter, how you can reach them, and what best practices to deploy in the process of doing so.

Chapter 6

Finding the Right Platforms

*I*f you have been an Internet user since the mid-1990s, you probably know that the popular social platforms today are not the first to have been launched. Many came before Facebook and MySpace. In some cases, those early social networks and online communities were extremely successful too. For example, back in the mid-1990s, The Well was considered the most influential online community. It wasn't the largest, but it was the most influential.

GeoCities, which rose to fame in the late 1990s and was bought by Yahoo! for a whopping $3.57 billion at its peak, boasted millions of active accounts. Friendster, which was the darling of the social networking world in 2003 and 2004, fizzled when its technical infrastructure and lack of new features pushed people in America away from it. (Approximately 80 percent of its traffic comes from Asia today.) And even in the last two years, users have moved away from MySpace, which was the largest social network in the country, to Facebook, in what appears to be an unstoppable and extremely worrying trend for MySpace.

The point is that customarily, social platforms such as online communities, social networks, and loosely connected personal spaces online have periods of immense growth, plateaus, and then slow, painful declines. It appears hard for a social platform to avoid this evolution. We've seen this happen time and again. This poses a difficult challenge for marketers.

Where do you invest your marketing dollars if you don't know whether a specific social platform is going to be around in a year or two? Similarly, how do you know which up-and-coming social platform your users are going to gravitate toward after a major social platform starts fizzling? Knowing which social platform is going to have explosive growth next and where your customers will spend their time is not always easy. Nevertheless, you must try to answer those questions.

This chapter helps you identify which combination of social platforms on which to launch, sustain, and promote your brand.

Before marketing on these social platforms, you need to figure out your social voice. See Chapter 5 for more information on how to do that.

Choosing Social Media Platforms

The first step is to recognize that no *single* social platform is going to be enough for your SMM activities. It's extremely unlikely that your potential customers use only one of the social platforms exclusively. In fact, research shows that a user is rarely only on one platform. It is far more likely that your customers have profiles on two or three social platforms and use some of them more than others.

You've probably also noticed that marketing on several social platforms isn't that much more expensive than marketing on one, as long as most of your energies are focused on a few. It makes sense to choose several platforms versus just one to do your marketing.

Still, that doesn't answer the question of where to market. You can't be marketing on MySpace, Facebook, Friendster, LinkedIn, YouTube, hi5, Bebo, orkut, Flickr, Twitter, and Classmates all at once with the same amount of effort. Although SMM is considered cheap, it still takes time, money, and effort when you're doing so on many social platforms at once. (You're probably going to confuse customers who have presences on several of the social platforms to boot.)

The answer is to put a lot of effort into marketing on a few social platforms where your customers participate the most and to have lighter presences on the other platforms.

To pick the right platforms, you can start by looking at the audiences with which you interact. For purposes of this discussion, they can be broken down into the following three groups:

✔ **Customers:** Obviously, this is your main target. You want to connect, interact, and prompt them to buy from you. You need to understand why they buy and where they buy.

✔ **Industry:** These are the people who may be competitors, vendors, governing bodies, and so on. In the social media world, this group helps to support your visibility and influence.

✔ **Employees:** They can be either your greatest strength or weakness, depending on how you prepare them to participate in social media. If you don't have staff to dedicate to a project, you have a different kind of problem to solve.

Following is a look at how to work through the issues of picking platforms that support each group.

Learning about your customers

Choose where to practice SMM by researching and understanding where your customers are spending most of their time. This doesn't mean identifying where most of your customers have registered profiles, but instead researching where the customers have the highest levels of engagement. This means

✔ **Finding out what amount of time they spend on the social platform, what they specifically do, and how they use it to interact with each other.**

Tools like Quantcast (www.quantcast.com) can you help you understand engagement, but you may need to reach out to the social platforms themselves to understand the details of the engagement. Keep in mind that with Quantcast, only if the site has been Quantified (which means that the site owner has added Quantcast code to his site) are the statistics the most accurate. comScore (www.comscore.com) is a paid solution that can provide more accurate numbers for non-Quantified sites. Figure 6-1 shows the Quantcast home page.

✔ **Understanding the user behaviors on the social platform.**

For example, if you're a business-to-business (B2B) solutions provider, and your customers use LinkedIn to ask each other for advice when making business-related purchasing decisions but spend a lot more time on Facebook, LinkedIn may still be a better place to practice SMM. That's where they're making the purchasing decisions that matter to you. It doesn't matter if they're spending more cumulative minutes on Facebook.

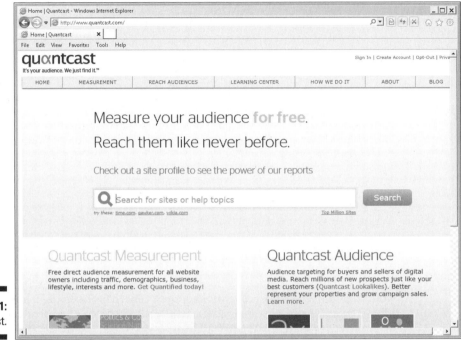

Figure 6-1:
Quantcast.

Invariably, you discover that three to four social platforms match your customers' demographics, have high engagement levels for them, and are what we loosely call *locations of influence* as far as your product category is concerned. That's where your customers make their decisions, get influenced by others, and observe how their peers are purchasing or discussing their own purchases. These three factors together tell you where to practice SMM. And as you do so, recognize that you must also consider two broader aspects:

✔ **The macro trends of the social platform.**

   For example, does the platform look like it's emerging, has it settled into a plateau, or is it fizzling? Accordingly, you may want to devote more or fewer dollars and effort to it.

✔ **Whether the social platform is a place where your brand will have permission to participate and one in which you will want to participate.**

   Participating in some social platforms may hurt your brand. For example, if you are a high-end exclusive brand like Chanel, it may not be appropriate to engage in conversations in a casual, music-oriented social environment like MySpace.

Your customers move between platforms as time passes. As a result, be prepared to adjust your social media marketing campaign significantly. Your customers may not always stay on the platforms that you're targeting them on currently. This matters especially with small business marketers.

Each social network has a reputation. Make sure that your brand is in alignment with that reputation. For example, MySpace is known to be more music-oriented and has a reputation for attracting a young, less affluent audience. Keep that in mind as you choose where and how to market.

Addressing your industry influence

A look at your industry yields a very long list of potential competitors, partners, vendors, and associations for you to connect with. The SMM goal is to make this group aware of your influence in the marketplace. We address the importance of influence and the role of influencers in Chapter 1.

Here, we take a brief look at four free tools you can use right away to make a quick assessment of your overall business influence. Obviously, you want to take a much more thorough look, but the following can give you some feeling for your current state of influence:

- ✔ **Klout** (`www.klout.com`): Klout measures what they call "true reach, amplification, and network impact." It has become a very popular measure because you can evaluate your organization across such platforms as Twitter, Facebook, and LinkedIn (also includes seven others and growing) at the same time. If you have an employee who has her own influence on these platforms, you can also check her out separately.

- ✔ **Website Grader** (`Websitegrader.com`): Evaluate your website using HubSpot's tool for grading websites. It looks at a variety of measures, including your traffic rank, indexed pages, and linking domains.

- ✔ **Technorati Authority** (`Technorati.com`): Technorati is the granddaddy of online tools. To get a quick assessment of your blog's influence, you can go to Technorati to see your "authority" rank against all the other blogs online. It's a macro look but interesting nonetheless. It gives you a perspective on how many blogs are actually out there.

- ✔ **TweetLevel** (`Tweetlevel.edelman.com`): You can evaluate your Twitter account with global PR firm Edelman's tool for measuring influence, as shown in Figure 6-2. This one measures just your Twitter feed according to influence, popularity, engagement, and trust.

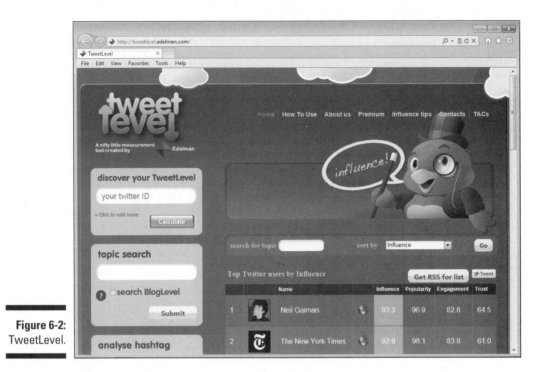

Figure 6-2:
TweetLevel.

Preparing Your Employees for Social Media Networking

A great social media campaign can be damaged if your employees are not given the information they need to support it. How often have you had a store employee say to you, "I don't know anything about that promotion. They never tell us anything"? It seems like it would be obvious, but in the whirl of planning and executing, managers often leave out the staff completely. If you are planning a social media campaign, you must make sure that everyone on staff supports the effort. Following are some important issues you must equip your employees to understand:

✔ **Your employees must know the real value consumers place on your products.**

Reality can sometimes be in limited supply when managers plan their SMM promotions. It's important to know the real value customers place on your products, not the value you hope for. Social media tools allow you to get direct feedback and reviews from your customers. In order to plan effectively, your staff needs to know what they will encounter when customers talk back. Make sure that someone who has been on the front lines (like customer service) is part of the team.

✔ **Employees need to mine the intellectual property hidden inside your business to create products and services.**

Some managers wonder why their employees are not more innovative. The answer may be simple. Innovation is not prized or rewarded in their company. Sometimes it's intentional. Most often it's not. Your staff has the opportunity to determine which website content your customers respond to. For example, if they find that customers are remarking about a multimedia video on a particular topic, they need to bring that up at meetings where creative solutions are welcomed. It could effect changes in your products and help build your social media influence.

✔ **Employees need to understand who your real competitors are.**

It's easy to wear blinders when you're working on SMM campaigns. You are so focused on your own product that you can forget that the competition is everyone that your customers can turn to for advice, training, education, and entertainment about the topic. When customers are not limited by geography or time zone, their choices open up. Develop a full list of competitors that everyone can monitor.

Evaluating Your Resources

It's often said that SMM takes a lot more time than money. This isn't true when you begin to factor in the amount of resources it takes to implement a full-blown strategy. You can't overlook the fact that either you or your staff will have a variety of tasks to complete even before you start tweeting, blogging, and so on. With this in mind, consider the following resource issues before you begin:

✔ **Time:** Determine how much time your resources permit you or your staff to spend on SMM each day. How much employee time can be devoted to actually communicating with customers? This is the goal. You want to make authentic contact. This takes time.

✔ **Technical skills:** Examine the breadth of technical skills you have in-house. Who will do the technical work involved? Some of the platforms are plug-and-play, but more often than not, integrating them into your own sites can present problems. For example, if your website uses proprietary software, you might need to have technical staff write new code to connect the two applications without causing problems. This might be a quick fix or a long, involved project. You'll want to know that before you move forward.

✔ **Design skills:** Understand the design skills needed to create visuals, charts, and so on. The quality of graphics and multimedia online continues to increase. You either need a designer on hand or have to hire someone to create the graphics to match your own branding on one or several of the SMM platforms.

✔ **Computing power:** Look at whether you are prepared to handle more traffic and sales. You've heard the warning, "Be careful what you wish for." What if you get more leads than you can presently handle — or if your site can't handle the traffic surge? It sounds like a great problem to have, and it is, unless you wind up disappointing potential customers who can't reach your site or get support.

In September of 2011 during Fashion Week, Target stores found themselves in this spot when they promoted their new limited line of Missoni for Target. They underestimated the amount of traffic that the sale of the luxury brand at affordable prices would generate. They suffered repeated website crashes and had to calm a lot of unhappy customers in their stores after items sold out in a flash.

Target spokesman Joshua Thomas called it "Missoni mayhem." Contrary to what you might think, this publicity was not the kind Target was looking for. You want to have sellouts but not angry customers who can't buy (see Figure 6-3).

Be realistic about the quality of your hosting and customer support. Prepare by evaluating how much traffic you can actually handle, and plan for a bit more than you estimate. That way, you won't look amateurish if your promotions succeed beyond your wildest dreams.

Figure 6-3:
Missoni for Target goods created a frenzy.

Assessing What Each Social Network Offers You

Now that you've looked at the factors that influence your choice of a platform, it's time to look at the platforms themselves to determine which ones are a good fit. In Chapters 7 through 13, we cover each of the major social media platforms in depth.

In this chapter, we look specifically at the user profile for the top three social media platforms and add a fourth, YouTube, which is not usually covered as a social media platform, but is in fact the fourth-most-visited platform online. As reported in *Social Media Today* by Paul Kiser (http://socialmedia today.com/paulkiser/285851/who-uses-facebook-twitter-linkedin-myspace-4thq-1stq-stats-and-analysis) in April of 2011, the statistics are as follows:

- ✔ **Facebook:** Facebook users are 61 percent women; 72 percent of users are between 25 and 54. Users focus primarily on social interaction.

- ✔ **Twitter:** Fifty-seven percent of Twitter users are women; 54 percent are between 25 and 44. They focus primarily on world events and business-related topics.

- ✔ **LinkedIn:** Fifty-five percent of users are men; 61 percent of the users are between 35 and 54. Users focus on jobs, marketing themselves, and selling services.

- ✔ **YouTube:** Fifty-two percent of users are women; approximately 22 percent are 25 to 34, and another 22 percent are 35 to 44. Roughly 50 percent have "some college." (Stats for YouTube are from the *2011 Social Network Analysis Report* from IgniteSocialMedia.com at www.ignitesocialmedia.com/social-media-stats/2011-social-network-analysis-report/#YouTube.)

This gives you the broad strokes of the user demographics on these platforms. Next, you'll want to dig deeper.

Using platforms as audience research tools

You can use several tools to analyze demographics. See Chapters 19 and 25 for more information about tools that delve deeply into this area. In this section, we discuss the use of two platforms not usually used to do market research — YouTube and Flickr. Mining these platforms can bring you unexpected findings:

✔ **Check out YouTube.**

If you have uploaded videos to YouTube, you can use YouTube Insight to get a variety of analytics. But what about looking at YouTube as a large research lab? By using the home page search function, you can drill down on an almost unlimited number of topics. By using the Sort By drop-down list as shown in Figure 6-4, you can determine the following:

- **Relevance:** This is the default search. It brings you the videos most closely associated with the topic you requested.

- **Upload Date:** With this, you can see what's most viewed right now as opposed to something older. You can find out what's hot here.

- **View Count:** This shows you the general interest in a topic. With the millions of people on YouTube, you can see what's of interest to a big chunk of them.

- **Rating:** This is an interesting measure. YouTube used to use five-star ratings but found them to be ineffective. Most people would rate everything either a 1 or a 5. This didn't really give the viewer enough feedback. YouTube now relies on likes and dislikes, which gives you a quantitative measure.

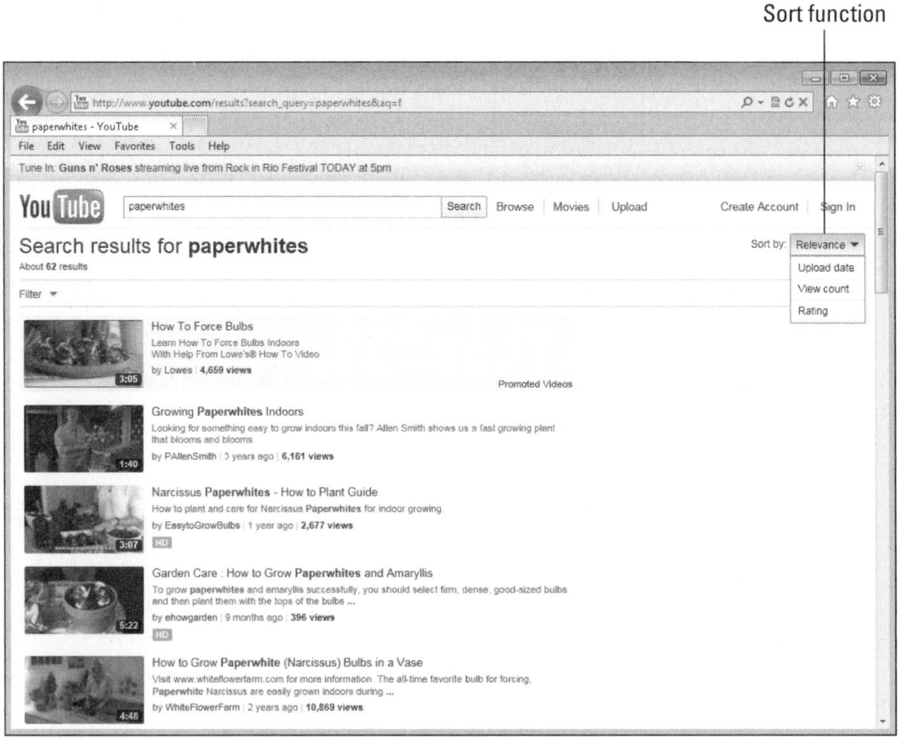

Sort function

Figure 6-4: YouTube's sort function.

✔ **Peruse Flickr.**

When marketers look at Flickr, shown in Figure 6-5, their first instinct is to think about how they can display something — their products, conference photos, or staff pictures. Next, they think about how many people have viewed the photos they've posted. Those are both useful but are by no means the only way to use Flickr.

You can also use it a research tool. For example, if you sell wedding invitations, you can use Flickr's search capability to find wedding photos that may include invitations. The idea is to use it as your doorway into customer's lives. Before the Internet, friends and neighbors would regale each other with stories, using slide carousels in their living rooms. Think of Flickr as a grand view into everyone's living room. If you want to see what kind of shoes people are wearing when they travel or millions of other things, you'll find that here. If you think creatively, you can get an enormous amount of information on Flickr.

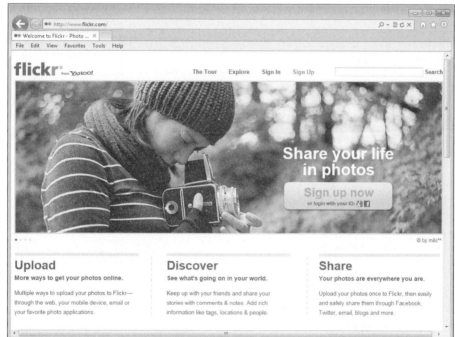

Figure 6-5:
Flickr's
home page.

Getting niche-savvy

In addition to picking the right major social networking platforms for your business, you should investigate niche platforms your customers may frequent. The Top 100 Directory has a list of the top 350 niche social media sites. It can be found at `http://dir100.com/resource/top-350-social-networking-sites.html`, as shown in Figure 6-6. You'll be amazed at the variety of sites you find there. For more information on niche platforms, see Chapter 13.

See if you can find something directly related to your audience. The sites are categorized in the following way:

✔ Books

✔ Business Networking Professionals

✔ Family

✔ Friends

Figure 6-6:
The Top 100
Directory.

✔ Hobbies and Interests

✔ Media

✔ Music

✔ Mobile

✔ Shopping

✔ Students

✔ Travel and Locals

For example, if you sell eco-friendly baby toys, you may want to check out CafeMom, shown in Figure 6-7. It is listed in the Family category and can be found at `www.cafemom.com/`. Here, you can read about what types of toys moms are looking for and what they are currently buying. If you engage in a low-key, respectful way, you learn a lot without offending anyone. Any kind of "hype-y" sales pitch would not be appropriate here.

Figure 6-7:
CafeMom.

Chapter 7

Exploring SMM Strategies for Facebook

As you do your analysis of which social platform is best for your SMM campaign, you'll likely discover that Facebook (www.facebook.com) is one of the platforms on which you have to engage. It has had explosive growth in the last several years (Facebook now has more than 800 million users) and is the largest social network in the United States. More than 50 percent of users log in to Facebook every day.

Approximately 145 million North Americans are on Facebook in some capacity or another, so it is fair to assume that at least some of your customers are going to be on Facebook.

According to Facebook Chief Operating Officer Sheryl Sandberg, speaking at the Association of National Advertisers convention in 2011, you should be "social by design." By that, she means that SMM should be a part of everything you do. As such, we want to spend a few minutes explaining what SMM on Facebook is like today and provide a few pointers too.

Looking at Facebook Basics

Deciding how to practice SMM on Facebook can seem intimidating because so much is going on at once. The profile page for each entity has a host of links, ads, posts, and so on. In addition, changes to the platform itself are being made continuously. You may feel that as soon as you understand how something works, it changes. One way to overcome this sense of feeling overwhelmed is to remember the following:

✔ **The key to SMM on Facebook is to understand that your network is the key.**

Together, you and your friends do things online that may affect each other's behavior. Marketers try to harness this activity to their own advantage. That's what you need to focus on. For example, if several customers Like your product, their friends will see that recommendation and perhaps buy it too. By understanding the interconnectedness of SMM, you can build your business.

✔ **The heart of Facebook is a user's timeline.**

It is easy to forget that the heart of Facebook is not your Facebook page or a user's profile page; rather, it is the timeline. This is the page that a user sees when she logs into Facebook. It shows her friends' activities (including potentially your brand's activity). As a result, it is extremely important to focus your Facebook marketing efforts on the timeline. A lot more users may learn about your company or your product through the timeline than by visiting your particular company page.

✔ **Using Facebook requires constant experimentation.**

There is no one right way to market on Facebook. Your audience and products are unique. There are some best practices, but for the most part, you have to determine what works for your specific audience. If you understand this going in, you will not feel you are failing because things are moving slowly at first. Try something, and see how it works. Then use feedback and results to point you in the right direction.

✔ **You have powerful tools at your disposal to enhance all your other channels.**

Facebook gives you tools to link to other channels on which you promote. For example, you can link to your blog, your Twitter account, and so on. Provide a link anywhere you have an opportunity. Don't forget to link all your e-mail addresses and newsletters to your Facebook account. For example, when people are on your website, make sure they see a widget for your Twitter account. Go to `https://twitter.com/about/resources/widgets` to get the widget to link your Twitter account to your website and social media platforms.

✔ **Facebook gives you an SEO (search engine optimization) advantage.**

The search engines regard Facebook Connect as very important content. By publishing to your Facebook page, you can see a potential boost in your rankings.

✔ **You can easily reach local customers.**

Facebook makes it easy to let customers know where you are, and you can choose to include a map. When customers are there, they can also choose to let their friends know. Furthermore, you can target specific posts in Facebook to certain customers only.

✔ **Pay attention to the Wall.**

Your Wall is the place where everyone goes to get your updates. Keep things lively. If you publish only once in a while, people lose interest. Make it a point to put a process in place, and use content calendars to manage the frequency and types of postings to the Wall.

✔ **The number of Likes you have should not be your only measure of success.**

The number of Likes you have are only one indicator of interest at a particular point in time. You may have lots of Likes and few engaged customers or buyers. Use several measures, including looking at Facebook's own Insights, to see how you are doing. Pay particular attention to Facebook's new People Talking About metric, which represents how many people are doing such things as Liking your page, posting to a wall, and commenting or sharing your content. This is found in Facebook Insights.

Facebook is still in the process of evolving its social platform. In September of 2011, it launched two new functions that received a great deal of attention — the Facebook timeline and Media Sharing.

Besides the guidance we give in the sections that follow, we recommend visiting Inside Facebook (`www.insidefacebook.com`) and All Facebook (`www.allfacebook.com`) to keep pace with the evolving marketing opportunities and advertisement formats on the platform.

Starting with search

"In the beginning, there was search." Okay, we're paraphrasing, but just as you do with any good investigation into a subject, you may want to start with a search. When you are determining what's already on Facebook and how that relates to your own SMM plan, you want to use Facebook search, which can be found at `www.facebook.com/search.php`.

You can narrow your search by using the drop-down menu to select the following:

✔ All Results
✔ People
✔ Pages
✔ Groups
✔ Apps

✔ Events

✔ Web Results

✔ Posts by Friends

✔ Public Posts

✔ Posts in Groups

By starting with search, you can get a good understanding of what exists in your product or service category. For example, if your category is productivity, you could type in that search term and get the results. Then you could narrow it down by one of the terms such as Apps, as shown in Figure 7-1.

The idea is to get an understanding of your customers, competition, and Facebook users' way of doing things. We recommend that whenever you want to investigate a question about the Facebook universe, start here.

Note that the previous list of search options includes Web Results. This is a result of the partnership that Facebook has with Microsoft to use Bing as its search engine.

Figure 7-1:
Search in
Facebook
for
productivity
apps.

Facebook pages

Think of Facebook pages as company profiles on Facebook. Everything starts here. You can set up a page for your brand and encourage others to Like it. It doesn't cost anything to create a business page, but it does take time and effort to make it relevant and worthwhile.

Don't confuse a Facebook page with a personal profile. A personal profile has your name on it, and is about you and your friends. A page is devoted to an entity such as a business, charity, or public figure.

The first thing you need to do is decide what type of page it will be. The choices, as shown in Figure 7-2, are as follows:

- ✔ Local Business or Place
- ✔ Company, Organization, or Institution
- ✔ Brand or Product
- ✔ Artist, Band, or Public Figure
- ✔ Entertainment
- ✔ Cause or Community

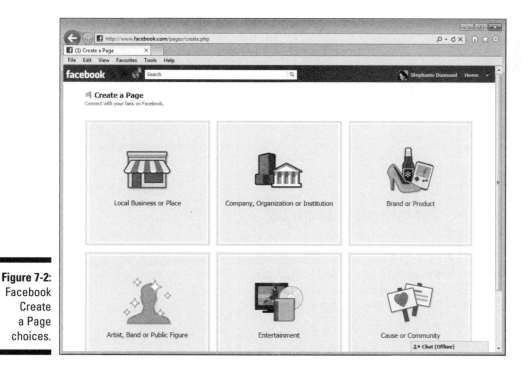

Figure 7-2:
Facebook
Create
a Page
choices.

As you can see, you are provided with a variety of options for your business. It should be easy to get started.

After you've selected your type, you need to decide what you will add to your page to make it garner attention. If you begin to think like a social media marketer, you want to consider publishing media including the following:

- ✔ **Posts and location-based posts:** Ongoing posts that keep your community informed are necessities. Post as often as you can, but keep it relevant.

- ✔ **Photo albums**: It's very easy to add a set of photos to Facebook in the form of an album. You can add up to 200 photos per album and an unlimited number of albums. Make sure to add any pertinent photos of your products, services, staff members, and anything else that will inspire your customers.

- ✔ **Multimedia content:** To ensure that you provide a variety of formats, you can link to slides, video, and podcasts. Remember that your audience likes to be surprised.

- ✔ **Twitter feeds and blog posts:** You can easily link your Twitter feed or blog to show up in your status updates using a plug-in. For example, to link your Twitter feed to Facebook, go to this URL: `www.facebook.com/twitter/`.

- ✔ **Event information:** The opportunity to alert your community to your events is priceless. You can also show the location with a map. (See the section "Facebook Events" later in this chapter for more information.)

- ✔ **Coupons and other promotional items:** You can provide printable coupons to customers who Like your page. Two things to remember here: First, make sure you take down expired coupons. Second, some people may un-Like your page after they print the coupons. Hopefully, they'll still buy the product.

PBS Kids, shown in Figure 7-3, has a popular Facebook page that sometimes offers coupons.

Facebook groups

In addition to pages, your brand and product category could well be a part of one of the hundreds and thousands of conversations in the Facebook groups. These groups are set up by users and are for them to use to discuss topics of interest and express their points of view. In order to join a group, you have to be invited by another member.

Figure 7-3:
PBS Kids
offers a
coupon on
Facebook.

Coupon

You can't market directly in the Facebook groups, but you can certainly identify the ones in which your brand is being discussed extensively. In some cases, groups may be dedicated solely to the discussion of your brand. In those cases, you may want to observe the conversation, learn from it, and maybe participate as a SMM voice when and where appropriate.

You may want to also contact the group administrator to see whether they'd be open to doing a joint promotion with you. If your brand has an official group, Facebook will help you move it to a page. As a brand, it's better for you to have a page than manage a group, which is really designed for user-to-user interaction only.

Facebook Events

If you're holding an event for your customers, employees, or business partners, you can promote it on Facebook by listing it as an event. This can be a virtual or a physical event supporting your company, its products, special promotions, or milestones.

People can be invited to attend the event (you invite them from within Facebook), and the event page can include content about the event, your brand, and your products and services. (See Figure 7-4.) Conferences, product previews, and special promotions are popularly highlighted through Facebook events. After the event is complete, you can share photos and write-ups of the event on the event page.

If the event is a virtual one in real time, you can do a lot to encourage visitors by creating posts that tease the event beforehand. You can have different types of events, such as a Q&A session with a guest, or questions about your latest product. People who use Facebook often appreciate the opportunity to stay there to get answers to their questions. They don't have to make a phone call or log into another online chat service.

To stream video events in real time, you need to use a plug-in like Ustream or another outside app. You can find the Ustream plug-in at `http://www.ustream.tv/`.

Facebook applications

Creating pages and events that are supported by advertisements and sponsored stories may not be enough. Some companies choose to build applications that can be installed in a user's profile or on a Facebook page. For a branded application to be a success, it must engage users in a meaningful fashion, whether that is utility- or entertainment-driven. The most successful applications can take weeks to build and promote within Facebook, so don't expect this to be a simple endeavor.

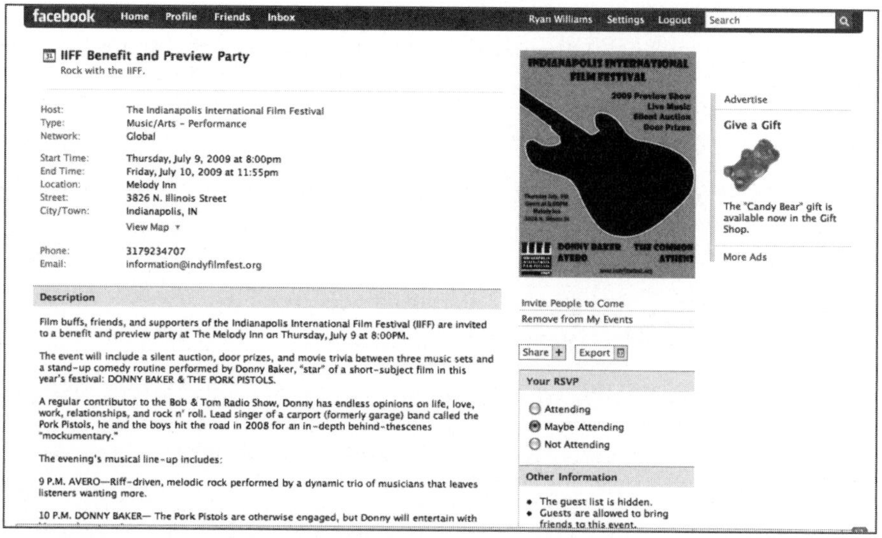

Figure 7-4:
A Facebook
event.

Popular applications include games, quizzes, badges, calculators, and tools that analyze a person's social graph. For example, TripAdvisor's Cities I've Visited application lets you show your friends which cities around the world you've visited. It has been an extremely popular application. For more information on building Facebook applications, visit the Facebook Developers page (`http://developers.facebook.com/`).

For a list of the top Facebook applications, visit `http://statistics.all facebook.com/applications/leaderboard` or `www.insidefacebook.com/2011/09/30/the-guardian-photos-page-tabs-cards-and-more-on-this-week%E2%80%99s-top-20-emerging-facebook-apps/`.

Facebook Connect

Facebook Connect has continued to evolve since its introduction in 2008 and is now commonly referred to as Login with Facebook. In a nutshell, when you use an application that allows you to use Login with Facebook, you have the ability to bring your Facebook social graph to a third-party website. (A *social graph* is a global mapping of people and how they relate to each other — in this case, your Facebook network.) More and more websites are supporting it.

This means that when users log into those sites with their Facebook credentials, they can see which of their friends have participated on that website in some fashion, whether by commenting, rating, or writing a product review. Whatever the users do is also sent to Facebook and appears in the News Feeds of all their friends. But the News Feed has a lag. They can instantly see what their friends are up to by looking at the ticker on the right side of the page.

This allows users to share their activity on third-party websites with their friends in Facebook, which inadvertently gives the site more exposure and greater power from a recommendation perspective. Facebook Connect is discussed in more detail in Chapter 15. Figure 7-5 shows the home page.

For more information about Facebook Connect, visit the Facebook Connect Developers page (`http://developers.facebook.com/`) or view this SlideShare presentation that Shiv put together with a friend about Facebook Connect's potential (`www.slideshare.net/shivsingh/portable-social-graphs-imagining-their-potential-presentation`).

Figure 7-5:
Facebook
Connect.

Using Ads on Facebook

To increase revenue using Facebook, you can do something as simple as a Facebook Ad. Facebook has done a great deal to enhance their advertising in the last year. They have provided very robust statistics by the name of Insights and continue to improve the value of their ads. They have a unique ad format in which demographics, user interests, and other keywords that are listed in profiles target the advertisements.

When you set up an advertisement, Facebook tells you how much you're narrowing your audience with each additional criterion you specify. You can also add social actions to those advertisements that include asking the viewer to rate the advertisement and become a fan of the brand directly through the advertisement.

When you create the advertisement, you can also have friends of the viewer who have endorsed a brand appear in the advertisement itself as an endorsement. It's a clever way to capture your attention and tell you that a friend likes the brand, so maybe you should give it serious thought too.

These can be bought on a cost per click (CPC) or a cost per impression (CPM) basis and have been very popular with small businesses because of their low cost and the ability to pick a daily budget for how much to spend.

The following are ad formats you should consider using.

Sponsored stories

As the name implies, sponsored stories appear with a title, body copy, and images, and they look and feel like stories. They appear on the right side of the page and may link to a Facebook page or even to an external site. (It is usually recommended that you link to a Facebook page and keep the user within Facebook itself.) The sponsored stories are targeted through profile data like the social advertisements and are popular because they're highly visible.

The News Feed is what a user first sees when he logs into Facebook. The ads appear on the right side (not in the news stream) but are easily noticed.

 A variation on the sponsored story is the sponsored video, which functions in a similar fashion. The sponsored videos are popular because they don't require the user to leave the News Feed to view them. You can learn more about these at www.facebook.com/ads/stories.

Check-in deals

If you have a physical location, consider trying a check-in deal. It allows you to reward customers who show up at your store and use the check-in on their mobile phone. People love to be rewarded for something that requires very little effort. If they are near your store and can get 25 percent off (or whatever the offer is) by showing up, they will. It's a great way to help your customers establish the habit of dropping into your store. The potential is also there for customers to tell their friends and find you new customers.

The following are the four kinds of deals you can create:

- ✔ **Individual deals:** This is a one-time deal. Create it when you want to launch something new or bring old customers back.

- ✔ **Loyalty deals:** This mimics the loyalty deals with which people are familiar. They can be rewarded after as few as 2 check-ins or as many as 20 check-ins.

- ✔ **Friend deals:** You can offer a deal to up to eight friends who check in together.

- ✔ **Charity deals:** Help your customers donate to a worthy cause of your choice. *Note:* You need to have a way of handling the contributions outside Facebook.

Chapter 8

Marketing on Twitter

● ●

In This Chapter

▶ Discovering Twitter basics

▶ Understanding organic engagement

▶ Using paid advertising

▶ Discovering new tips and tricks

● ●

*N*o social platform has had more explosive growth in the last few years than Twitter, the microblogging service. Twitter (www.twitter.com) is similar to a blogging service, except that you're limited to 140 characters per message, or *tweet.* Also, only people who follow you on Twitter see your tweets in their Twitter stream. You reply to other people's tweets, forward their tweets, or send them direct messages. All of your followers see anything that you tweet.

Today, Twitter has 100 million active users around the world, half of whom log in daily, posting on average 250 million tweets a day. Every day, more people create accounts on Twitter than they do on any other social platform. Unlike on the other fast-growing social platform, Facebook, Twitter users are typically older. Although the total number of Twitter users is still relatively small compared to Facebook, it is growing so rapidly and has such an influential user base that marketing on Twitter requires a specific discussion.

You can market on Twitter using paid and unpaid methods. You can buy specific Twitter ad products that allow you to draw attention to your Twitter account, attach yourself to specific trends, and align with certain keyword searches. Third-party services let you also buy attention by associating with celebrities.

But in a similar fashion to Facebook, marketing on Twitter must start with the basic unpaid tactics. And as you do that, remember that Twitter is most powerful for building and nurturing relationships between people, even more so than Facebook. It's because you're limited to 140 characters. When marketing through Twitter, focus tightly on building the relationships, and everything else will follow. Don't worry too much about pushing messages to the community. But when you have to, there are smart ways to do that via the Twitter ad products that don't hurt your reputation in the community.

If you do not take ownership of your company or brand name on Twitter, someone else may do so on your behalf. This could be a competitor, another business with a similar name, a customer, or a fan. If that happens, you'll probably have to spend a lot of time (and maybe money, too) to get back the username. Most Twitter users automatically associate your brand name on Twitter with your company. Many may not realize that the person behind the Twitter account is not from your company.

Figuring Out the Basics of Twitter

Twitter is fundamentally an asynchronous communication platform that drew inspiration from SMS (short message service, or texting) and Facebook when it was first designed. It allows you to publish 140-character tweets (not one character more than that) and view tweets from other users of Twitter. To view someone else's tweets in your feed, you simply have to follow them. In a direct contrast to Facebook friending, when you follow someone on Twitter, they're not automatically made to reciprocate in return.

A second important contrast to Facebook is that on Twitter, your account is automatically set to public viewing by default. This means that anybody can view a tweet that you publish. This differs from Facebook, where posts by most people are private and viewable only by their friends. On Twitter, you can choose to make your account private, but most people don't. As a result, tweets by the 100 million Twitter users around the world serve as a treasure trove for academics and marketers who want to learn how people talk online and what they talk about.

Following are some of the activities you can engage in on Twitter:

- **Mentions:** As a user on Twitter, you can publish tweets as soon as you've signed up. Just enter your tweet in the message box, and you're on your way. To draw attention to another user, you can mention their account in your tweet by preceding their account name with the @ symbol. For example, to use the Pepsi Twitter account in a tweet, you would need to type **@pepsi**. Then when a user clicks the Pepsi handle (@pepsi), he would automatically be taken to the Pepsi Twitter page.

- **Retweet:** Another uniquely Twitter feature is the ability to resend (or retweet) someone else's tweet. Think about this as a forward button. You can retweet by clicking the Retweet link that's below every tweet in your Twitter feed. If someone has tweeted something interesting, and you want to share it with your own followers, the Retweet link is the one to use.

- **Message:** Through Twitter, you can also send direct messages to specific users. These messages are seen only by that Twitter user and not by anyone else. To send a direct message to someone who is already following you, begin your tweet by typing **DM**, and follow that with the

@ sign and the person's account name. For example, to send a direct message to John, you'd type **DM @john** followed by the actual message. Direct messaging is useful when you want to communicate directly with a customer in response to something they may have tweeted. You cannot direct-message people who do not follow you.

✔ **Hash tags:** Preceded by a hash mark, these are used as spontaneous categories for people who want to participate in a conversation around a specific topic. For example, during the Super Bowl, people who want to tweet about the game end their tweets with #superbowl. Then, whenever a person would search for #superbowl, they see all the tweets related to the game. Clicking a hash tag allows a user to see all the other tweets related to that category too.

A Twitter handle

It is very important to take ownership of your brand on Twitter. Sign up for Twitter with your brand or company's name as the Twitter handle. If you're lucky, no one has already taken it. Use this account to communicate company or brand news, special promotions, and product offers; respond to questions; and resolve customer service issues.

Should you follow every person who follows you? It's good Twitter protocol to do so if you're looking to build relationships with lots of people. But if your goal is just customer service, don't feel the need to follow everyone. However, when you do so, watch out for spam and viruses. Both spam and viruses have made their way onto the Twitter platform, and probably the easiest way to put your account at risk is to follow another account that is then used to send you links to viruses. So when you choose to follow other people, make sure that they're legitimate people and not spambots or virus malware.

Searches

For anyone looking to market via Twitter, the first step is to monitor the conversations for your company, brand, and product mentions. You want to know how people are talking about you. You can set up these searches easily within Twitter itself or by using a separate application like TweetDeck (`www.tweetdeck.com`), which is shown in Figure 8-1. Make sure you track not just your company brand, but also your competitors. You'll probably learn more from people talking about your competitors than from their conversations about you. You can use the Twitter search engine (`http://search.twitter.com`) or one of the real-time engines like TweetMeme (`www.tweetmeme.com`) or Twazzup (`www.twazzup.com`). You could also try TweetBeep (`www.tweetbeep.com`), which gives you Twitter alerts via e-mail on an hourly basis.

The reason for using a platform like TweetMeme or Twazzup is that you can find sorted information in real time. When you use Twitter search, you get a deluge of tweets that you have to sort through. The tweets may be current or a bit older. When you use the real-time search engines, you get up-to-the-minute tweets that can be sorted by category. These are the best tweets to use for real-time marketing campaigns.

Responses

It's not enough to just listen in on the conversations. You have to participate in the conversations too. This means responding to questions directly addressed to your Twitter username, whether the questions are customer service–related or more general. It also means watching your brand mentions and correcting misinformation (although don't appear too defensive when you do this because it can backfire), providing helpful advice when and where appropriate, and broadening relationships with the people who are talking about your company.

Part of being a good social voice is allowing your own personality to shine through, which means opening up and being willing to talk about your own life and not just the brand you represent.

Figure 8-1:
The
TweetDeck
website.

But there can be challenges in doing this too. For example, if you're a mass brand with lots of followers on Twitter and lots of people talking about you, you may have a hard time responding to everyone. It can become cumbersome and resource-intensive, and worse still, it may make your Twitter account look like a series of individual responses versus being one that balances responses with fresh, original content.

Managing this can be difficult. If you are a company has lots of customer service queries, you may want to set up a separate Twitter handle to manage those. Similarly, if you are a brand that has lots of consumers asking questions, you may want to create FAQ pages on your website to which you direct your consumers. Answering everything completely via Twitter may not be always possible, especially when you're restricted to 140 characters per tweet!

Keep in mind that when your customers talk about your brand, they may not always expect or demand a response from you. Knowing when to join Twitter conversations about your brand and, more important, how to do so is very much an art. Don't try to join every conversation, and at the same time, don't ignore all conversations. Apply common sense, try to understand the people behind the conversations, think about whether you can add value to it, and then choose to join or not.

Following and followers

The core of activity on Twitter is following other people and getting followed yourself. First and foremost, make sure you follow anyone who follows you. Second, consider following all the employees at your company who have Twitter accounts. You'll build good will with them, and they'll generate followers for you.

Next, identify influential tweeters who have large followings to follow and establish relationships with. These people are similar to influential bloggers. They're the experts in a specific domain, with large audiences who can encourage people to follow you and who can influence others. In some cases, they may not be experts but celebrities of one kind or another. Twitaholic (www.twitaholic.com) has a list of the most popular people on Twitter by follower count. Not surprisingly, many of them are celebrities, starting with Lady Gaga, Justin Bieber, and Katy Perry. Next on the list are President Obama, Kim Kardashian, Britney Spears, Shakira, and Taylor Swift.

Different applications can help you identify these users, but one we like that measures a user's influence is called Twitalyzer (www.twitalyzer.com). You may want to also try WeFollow (www.wefollow.com), which is a popular Twitter directory that helps you find interesting and influential people and brands to follow. When deciding who to follow and who not to follow, think about it like a cocktail party. First, start with the people you know and the people that they know, and then people talking about subjects important to you, and finally random (or influential!) people and those that approach you.

Marketing via Twitter

Twitter can be used in any number of ways to market. But there are a few critical ways in which you can leverage the Twitter platform to reach your customers. Here they are listed in order of priority:

1. **Listening:** There's no doubt that Twitter is a powerful listening platform for you to learn how your customers think about your products, your company, and the category that your product sit in. Don't miss that opportunity to listen to your customers talk about you in real time. Comcast changed the way customers thought about it by starting to listen seriously to customer concerns expressed via Twitter and responding through the platform itself.

2. **Promoting product launches and events:** The real-time news element of Twitter has been fundamental in catapulting the platform into the mainstream. There are few faster ways for news to spread more quickly than via Twitter. In a similar fashion, marketers can use Twitter effectively to announce products and market events capitalizing on the newsworthiness of the announcements. In fact, marketing efforts can be announced this way. For example, Pepsi asked Snoop Dogg to announce its Pepsi Max commercial via his Twitter account to his followers first. It helped that he was in the ad itself.

3. **Making special offers, deals, and discounts:** Timely special offers, deals, and discounts are often communicated through Twitter. Customers respond quickly to these Twitter deals and often spread the word to their own followers. Some companies have set up special deal handles through which they tweet about deals. One example of a company setting up a special deals handle for tweeting about deals on a regular basis is @delloutlet. The Dell Outlet twitter handle has 1.5 million Twitter followers.

4. **Customer service:** Companies use Twitter as an alternative customer service option. They listen for customer complaints and respond to those customers via Twitter itself, or at the very least, they begin the response on Twitter before moving to a phone call or an email exchange. Comcast, JetBlue, and Home Depot are all examples of companies that have successfully used Twitter for customer service.

5. **Engaging meaningfully with customers:** Different companies take different approaches to engage meaningfully with their customers via Twitter. The award-winning Best Buy Twelpforce was set up to enable customers to ask any Best Buy associate a question about what product to buy. Whole Foods asks their customers what they like to read and watch, and then recommends new food podcasts and invites the customers to upcoming company or in-store events.

Using Promoted Accounts

In the last year, Twitter has launched several advertising products that enable marketers to reach their customers more effectively via Twitter. The first of these available to advertisers is Promoted Accounts, as shown in Figure 8-2, which draws attention to your Twitter account. When you buy the Promoted Account offering, your Twitter account name appears in the Who to Follow area in the right side of the Twitter screen, with Promoted captioned below it. Be aware that as of this writing, you need a budget of at least $5,000 to get started using Promoted Accounts.

Promoted Accounts encourage other users to follow your Twitter account. You can target who should see your Promoted Account via factors such as geography, interests, and profile descriptions. Promoted Accounts are priced on either an impression basis, which means you pay for the number of people who see the Promoted Account listing, or by the number of people who choose to follow you. The latter can vary dramatically based on consumer interest levels.

Although having the most followers on Twitter isn't a true measure of success, it is valuable to build up a base of followers who in turn can then help you get others as they interact with you on the platform. Promoted Accounts helps you build this base and is especially valuable for when you're about to launch a new product or marketing program and want to have a large number of people to whom you can get the word out about the announcement.

Promoted Accounts help build that base with the additional benefit that after people become your followers, they typically stay your followers. This differs from display advertising, where a dollar spent on an impression is lost after the ad campaign has run. You get no real long-term benefit from that investment.

Promoted account

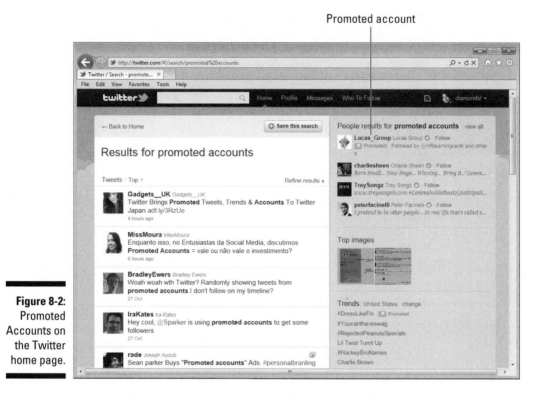

Figure 8-2:
Promoted
Accounts on
the Twitter
home page.

Making Use of Promoted Tweets

Promoted Tweets let you draw extra-special attention to a single tweet.
Promoted tweets are primarily sold attached to a specific search term, although
Twitter is currently testing it in a user's feed too or for their followers.

When you buy a promoted tweet, you are choosing to have a specific tweet of
yours appear at the top of the search results page for certain Twitter terms.
This could be any number of terms. As with Promoted Accounts, you can add
a layer of targeting to this so that the tweets reach the people who you really
want it to.

Following are the types of Promoted Tweets, also shown in Figure 8-3, and
what they're best for:

✔ **Promoted Tweets in search:** This product is best used to target users
who do not follow your brand on Twitter. When using this product, you
can reach users against a specific search term in a similar fashion to the
way Google allows you to advertise against searches on its website.

Bear in mind that only one advertiser can buy a search term at any given time. As a result, if you're looking to buy popular search terms like those related to pop culture events or TV shows, you may need to spend a lot of money. Promoted Tweets are bought via an auction model. Whoever is willing to pay the most get the rights to advertise. Often during the course of an evening, you can see different brands run Promoted Tweets against the same search term as they try to outbid each other for the attention.

Promoted Tweets is popular because it allows brands to attach themselves most directly to consumer intent. For example, if you search tweets about holidays, airlines know that you'll probably be thinking about flights too and that it is valuable for them to advertise against the term.

✔ **Targeting followers:** Promoted tweets can be used to target followers of your brand on Twitter as well. You may wonder why you should use advertising dollars to target followers when they're already following you. But the reality is that when you tweet to your followers, your tweet quickly drops below the fold and can be missed by your followers. When you use Promoted Tweets to target followers, the promoted tweet stays at the top of the feed. As a result, it becomes practically impossible for the follower to miss the tweet.

Promoted tweets are valuable when you want to promote something to your followers — the people who are typically your biggest brand advocates. This strategy works well when you have something to share that you believe will spread organically after it's seeded to a small group of brand loyalists.

✔ **Geotargeting:** Promoted tweets get even more powerful when you geotarget them at the country or even the DMA level (Nielsen-designated market areas). When you target a Promoted Tweet to just the people in specific locations that matter to you, your Promoted Tweet costs get much lower. This matters most for local businesses who care to advertise only in the actual locations where their businesses exist. Geotargeting can be applied as a layer over any kind of Promoted Tweets.

Promoted Tweets are bought on a cost per engagement (CPE) basis versus a cost per thousand impressions (CPM). Cost per engagement means that you pay only when a user retweets, replies, clicks, or favorites your tweet. You are not paying for the number of people who see the tweet, but those who take an action with it. (Paying for everyone who sees your tweet would be paying on a cost per thousand impressions basis.) This makes Promoted Tweets an extremely cost-effective performance-based form of social media marketing and a nice complement to other forms of digital marketing.

Figure 8-3:
Promoted
Tweets
in Twitter
search
results.

Promoted tweet

Using Promoted Trends

Twitter is an exciting social media platform for many reasons, but our favorite Twitter feature is how trending topics work. (This feature is in beta as of this writing.) Every minute of every day, Twitter analyzes all the millions of conversations on its platform to determine what's trending in a particular moment.

The trending topics get featured next to the user's feed on the right side. They can be filtered by geography as well, so for example, you can choose to see only the United States trending topics or even trending topics that are pertinent to certain cities. What's trending on Twitter serves as a barometer of how much something may be topical in the physical world in any given moment. Trending topics are definitely not to be missed.

Promoted Trends complement the organic trends and help brands build mass awareness, announce product launches, highlight events, and build the brand by association with other cultural events. They work in a similar fashion to trending topics except that Promoted Trends are defined by the advertiser. A user sees the Promoted Trend on the right side of the screen with the other trending topics but with the word *Promoted* below it.

Like Promoted Tweets, Promoted Trends can be clicked to view all the tweets containing the hashtag or trend terms associated with that Promoted Trend. Clicking the Promoted Trend takes a user to a search results page that has a Promoted Tweet from the advertiser at the top of it. Other tweets on the search results page will be unfiltered and open.

Promoted Trends, shown in Figure 8-4, are typically most valuable to buy on days when major pop culture events are happening and then best when aligned in some meaningful form around those pop culture events. For example, when the VMAs (Video Music Awards) air on TV, you might want to buy a Promoted Trend about music or, more specifically, about an award-winning artist from the VMAs because a lot of people will be on Twitter talking about the VMAs.

Promoted Trends are extremely popular with marketers, and it is worth buying the Promoted Trend in advance of the actual day that you want it to run. Because only one Promoted Trend can run on Twitter on a given day, marketers buy those terms well in advance of the actual day that they want the ad to run.

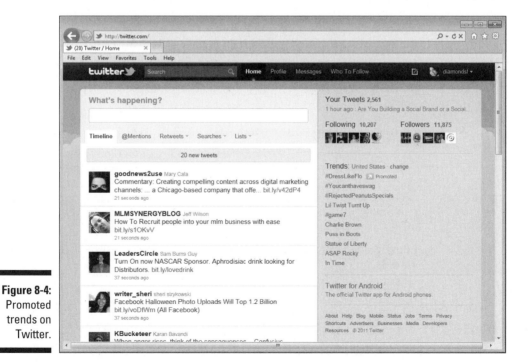

Figure 8-4:
Promoted trends on Twitter.

Working with Sponsored Tweets

One other current advertising opportunity that blends into the paid-tactics domain is sponsored tweets. In a similar fashion to sponsored posts on blogs, some Twitter users with very large followings are open to publishing sponsored tweets. This is done independently of Twitter. This means that you would discuss the marketing campaign with those users and they would tweet about it in their language and style to their audiences.

Typically, Twitter users do this only if they can declare that these are sponsored tweets and if the marketing messages are in sync with their own personal brand and the type of information that they like to share with their followers. This is an emergent marketing tactic. An example of a company that provides this service is Sponsored Tweets. You'll find them at `http://sponsoredtweets.com/`.

Discovering Twitter Tips and Tricks

Twitter is a versatile platform, and marketers use it in many different ways to achieve their marketing and business objectives. In fact, the versatility of Twitter is what has made it such a valuable platform for marketers. Some use it primarily for customer research, some to promote specific marketing programs, some for outreach to influencers, and others for customer service.

Regardless of how you use it, you should keep in mind some key tips and tricks when using Twitter. They help you build a loyal, committed base of followers and drive up your digital engagement with them:

✔ **Provide value to your customers.**

It is easy to forget that Twitter wasn't built as an engagement platform for marketers to use to connect with their customers. Rather, it was built for people to connect with each other, learn what their friends are doing, and broadcast their own activities. For brands to participate meaningfully, they must add value to the experience; otherwise, they will be ignored.

✔ **Recognize that different strategies make sense for different marketing needs.**

It is important to remember that your Twitter strategy needs to align with your overall marketing strategy. If your business is all about customer service, use Twitter for customer service. If it is for providing exclusive access, use Twitter as a distribution engine for promoting how you provide exclusive access. Match the Twitter tactics to the marketing strategy.

✔ **Prepare to adjust your Twitter approach.**

There's no better way to evolve your Twitter approach than by paying attention to how your customers respond to your participation in their social conversations. Learn from them, and adjust your Twitter approach based on what you see working effectively in real time. Are your customers responding to questions posed by you? Do they shy away from talking about your product? Are they more interested in learning about future marketing activities? Use their participation as a guide for how to market on Twitter.

✔ **Use Twitter advertising to jump-start conversations.**

Nothing beats organic engagement on Twitter. To be able to hear from your customers in real time, participate in conversations with them, and watch them go about their lives through the conversations that they have on the platform is extremely powerful. However, there are times when you need to use the mass reach of paid advertising to jump-start those engagements or draw special attention to what you're doing. The Twitter advertising products help that process.

✔ **Remember that knowing your customers is as important as ever.**

Some marketers make the mistake of believing that simply because this is a 140-character communication format, you don't need to know your customers as well. That's not true. Before you respond to a tweet from a customer, take a minute to understand who they are, what else they tweet about, and what matters to them.

✔ **Listen, listen, and listen.**

It may have become a cliché, but it's still very true. Listening to how your customers talk to each other, talk about culture, about your product category, your products, and your company is critical to succeeding on Twitter. Listening is the first step in participating in conversations and mustn't be skipped.

Chapter 9

Creating a YouTube Strategy

. . . .

In This Chapter

▶ Exploring the benefits of SMM on YouTube

▶ Creating custom content for your channel

▶ Harnessing the value of comments on videos

▶ Discovering advertising on YouTube

. . . .

YouTube (www.youtube.com) is another social platform that has had explosive growth in the last few years. Launched in 2005, it is now the number one website for online videos. Whenever marketers think of viral marketing, they think in terms of YouTube. You can't afford to overlook it as a marketing vehicle. In fact, today some marketers liken it to a TV network both in terms of its importance to consumers and its potential reach. (Not surprisingly, YouTube itself has noticed this and in early 2012 will be launching "premium channels" that will function just like TV channels.)

What some marketers seem to forget is that developing a SMM strategy for YouTube is no less important than it is on Facebook or Twitter. You have to look at it strategically. Although YouTube started out as a fun site, its marketing value has risen dramatically. In this chapter, we look at how YouTube fits into your SMM plan.

Looking at YouTube Basics

If you think that YouTube isn't a marketing goliath, consider the following facts, as of February 2011:

- ✔ It has approximately 800 million unique users per month

- ✔ More than 3 billion videos are viewed each day.

- ✔ Approximately 70 percent of the traffic on YouTube is from outside the United States.

- ✔ More than 500 tweets per minute contain a YouTube link!

Clearly, YouTube has all the muscle you need to drive your video SMM efforts.

Benefitting from SMM marketing on YouTube

The first thing you need to decide is the extent to which you will market on YouTube. You know that you want to participate, yet you're not sure how much time and effort to devote to it. To help you decide, here are some benefits you can derive from marketing on YouTube:

- **Visibility:** First and foremost, being on YouTube puts you where the action is. People come to YouTube to search for videos, and you want your video nuggets to be found.

- **Branding:** Extending your branding to your videos is pretty straightforward. Your logo and other design elements should be present; this assists in brand recognition. If you don't have these elements, you need to get them for all your SMM efforts!

- **No cost to set up:** Unlike setting up a website, putting a video on YouTube is free. If you already have videos you've created, all you need to do is sign up. See the section later in this chapter called "Always create a customized channel."

  The cost to create videos and all the work that goes into maintaining them should also be factored in. It's free to set up the YouTube channel, but everything else has a time or money cost associated with it.

- **Fixed placement options:** You don't need to worry about how your video will be placed and viewed on the site. Yours will be displayed along with all the other videos. Your goal should be how to stand out, not how to fit in. If you have a developer who can use the YouTube API to help you stand out, that's an advantage.

- **SEO done for you:** Thanks to the built-in SEO (search engine optimization) format of YouTube, Google displays your videos in their search results, along with everyone else. However, you should pay extra attention to the keywords you use to describe the videos so that they get the extra attention they deserve.

Attracting subscribers

People on YouTube who choose to subscribe to your videos are known as YouTube subscribers. Every time you upload a new clip, they're notified, and their names and icons are visible on your YouTube channel page.

Think of the subscribers as similar to followers on Twitter or fans on Facebook pages. Just as you'd nurture relationships on those other social platforms, you should do so here, too. So what's the best way to build a following of subscribers? Consider doing the following:

✔ **Publish quality video clips**.

You've probably heard many times that online, "content is king." Think about your YouTube channel as you would a TV channel. If the content is weak, you won't build a community of subscribers who clamor for more. You don't have to have Spielberg-like quality, but you do need to project a certain professionalism.

✔ **Encourage commenting on your clips.**

Comments on YouTube are not unlike the comments you find on blogs or other social media sites. Some have value; some are just silly or worse. Your goal is to develop a community of people who appreciate and look forward to your new videos. If they post comments that indicate that you are meeting their needs, you've met your goal.

✔ **Subscribe to other people's videos.**

There is twofold value in subscribing to other people's videos. The first is that you see what the experience is like. You want to understand how it feels to subscribe and how other channel owners engage with their subscribers. Second, it gives you an opportunity to meet and share with others on their turf. They are interested in getting subscribers as much as you are. Remember, this is a social platform.

✔ **Share the clips on the other social platforms.**

You build good will, increase views, and get more subscribers by doing this. It also burnishes your image on those other platforms. Show generosity.

Promoting on YouTube

Knowing how to publish and promote your marketing video clips is essential to getting them the attention they deserve. The following are some recommendations for promoting your video clips on YouTube.

Always create a customized channel

Having a YouTube channel dedicated to your company or brand is important because it allows you to showcase all the related video clips in one place. A YouTube channel is your brand's account home, where clips that you have published can appear. Setting up a channel is very easy, so don't hesitate to do so.

A channel also allows you to create a profile for yourself and have a place to link your website. Make sure that you customize the channel to match your company's or your brand's visual identity. You do not need to manually create a YouTube channel. As soon as you sign up for an account (using the Create Account link in the top-right corner of the home page) and upload a video clip, a channel is created for you. To reach your YouTube channel, just click your username after you log in. Figure 9-1 shows one such channel.

Don't forget to provide a link to/from your website to your custom channel. Also, make sure that your other channels like your Facebook page and blogs also have links to your YouTube channel. Reciprocal links are very important to a cohesive SMM campaign.

Create custom content for YouTube

It is not good enough to simply add your TV advertising spots to YouTube. Create custom content that matches the style and format of YouTube. Keep the running time to five minutes or less, and stay within the 100MB limit on file sizes. Group the video clips into themed playlists for increased viewing.

Often, a clip that lasts a minute or two can have great impact. You are trying to get your audience to share your video with others. Don't expect viewers to devote a lot of time to one video. As you know, the site has millions of users and tons of clips to watch. The worst thing you can do is bore your audience.

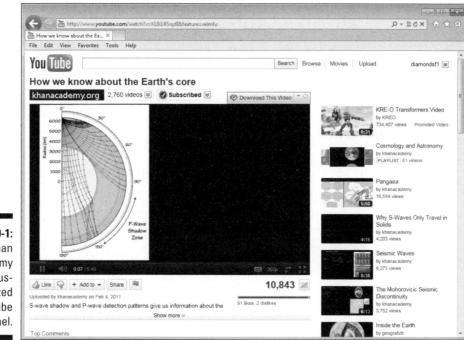

Figure 9-1:
Khan
Academy
is a cus-
tomized
YouTube
channel.

Tag and categorize all your clips

Choose the category for your video clip carefully. Start by looking at how popular video clips in your category have been tagged (see Figure 9-2), and consider using some of the same tags. Those tags have probably worked for the popular clips, and they'll work for you too.

Your content may not fit into a category neatly. Choose your category based on the number of similar video clips that reside in it.

Use tags to make up for the limits of categorization. YouTube does not limit the number of tags that you can add. These tags also make unsearchable data (like photos and video) searchable by adding metadata to them. Video titles and descriptions can also help with this.

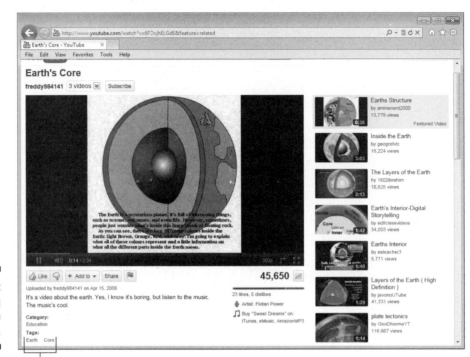

Figure 9-2:
Tagging
displayed on
a video clip.

YouTube tags

Promote your video with YouTube E-mail and Bulletins

YouTube helps you with the promotion of your clips through the E-mail and Bulletin features. Reach out to other users through YouTube E-mail and tell them about your content and why it is of interest to them. On a similar note, leverage bulletins, which let you post short messages to your channel or on other user pages. You can manage YouTube e-mails, bulletins, subscribers, and friends all through your channel page on YouTube.

Be careful not to spam other users. If someone hasn't asked for e-mail from you, don't send it.

Leave video responses

Don't forget that you can build good will with other users by leaving video responses to their clips. This matters, especially with the extremely popular clips in your category. Don't hesitate to create YouTube video responses. When you do, make sure that your responses are civil and relevant.

Procter & Gamble used this technique to great effect with their very popular Old Spice guy campaign with Isaiah Mustafa, as shown in Figure 9-3. First, they created a funny video promoting the product. Then they followed up by creating video responses by Mustafa to the comments made online. This captured even more attention and doubled their sales. The great news about this technique is that although it's inexpensive, it can pack a punch. Imagine the surprise of your viewers when you respond back to their comments with their own personalized video.

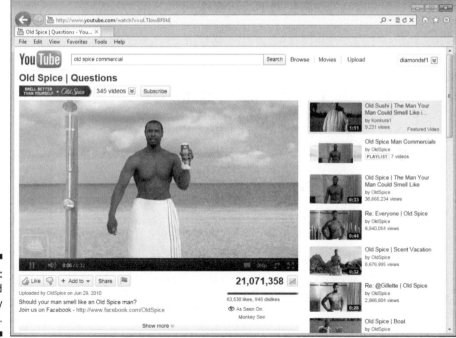

Figure 9-3:
The Old
Spice guy
video.

Include a call to action

In every good commercial you've ever seen on TV, you are asked to buy or do something after watching. That's called a *call to action*. Promotional videos are no different. Just lose the hard-sell. If you create a how-to video, it should include a link back to your site for more how-tos. If you discuss a customer problem, give an e-mail address they can contact for the solution. Make these videos pay off by engaging your customers. When they're gone, they're gone. Don't miss an opportunity to generate a lead or a sale.

Have some fun, too

Your customers are typically looking to be entertained when they're on YouTube. Have some fun with the clips that you post. Even if they're educational in nature (which can be very valuable and popular on YouTube), don't shy away from injecting a bit of humor into them (like Old Spice did). Keep in mind that the clips should be engaging enough that they encourage the user to share the clip with others.

Seeding a Viral Campaign

Viral videos are of two types, and it is important to know both:

- ✔ **Organic:** This is a video that creates a national frenzy, and people rush to see it and share it with their friends (like singer Susan Boyle). Usually, it just happens organically without planning. It captures the imagination of viewers, and off it goes.

- ✔ **Seeded:** This video has a carefully planned viral seeding campaign with lots of thought and advertising dollars behind it. It may go viral, but there's no guarantee. Some companies specialize in viral seeding, or you can go through a general social media agency to get assistance. Companies like Sharethrough (www.sharethrough.com) and TubeMogul (www.tubemogul.com) can help in this regard.

Can you *make* a video go viral? Decidedly no. If you could, marketers would be launching them by the armload. However, these few tips and tricks may improve your chances of creating a viral video:

✓ **Keep the content fresh:** Nothing beats fresh content when it comes to creating viral video clips. The content needs to be so engaging and unique that people can't help but want to share it with everyone they know. Always start by focusing on the content.

✓ **Use celebrities if possible:** If you're representing a large brand and can afford to use celebrities, don't hesitate to do so. Adding celebrities to the mix typically makes the videos more viral. We're a celebrity-obsessed culture, and celebrities drive views. It is as simple as that.

✓ **Make it surreal:** A video that you want to watch many times over and share with your friends is often a video that has a surreal element to it. Someone is doing something in the video that is so out of the ordinary or so crazy that you can't help watch it several times or talk to others about it. Better still is if a celebrity is doing something surreal.

✓ **Arouse emotions:** More broadly speaking, studies by psychologists have shown that the videos that get the most attention and are shared most frequently are the ones that arouse emotions in the viewer, whether that be emotions of awe, anger, amusement, or disgust. Although surreal videos are often the ones that get shared the most, don't ignore the other ways in which you can arouse the emotions of your potential viewers.

✓ **Make it short:** People online have no time at all. You must keep the viral clip short. Sometimes clips as little as ten seconds long are long enough for a video to go viral. Focus on quality versus quantity more than anything else.

✓ **Don't make it an ad:** Sometimes marketers can't resist the temptation to turn everything into an advertisement. Don't let that happen. The content needs to be thought of as entertainment, and in fact, the more it is in a user's casual language (both in terms of words and shooting quality), the more likely it is to do well.

You can also do a viral seeding campaign on the cheap. Someone in your organization can be in charge of developing a campaign. You need to decide how high the stakes are and what your overall goal is.

Viral seeding involves sharing your video in a very targeted way to increase its shareability (if that's a word). Those elements can include the following:

✓ **Targeting influencers:** People who are influential in that category may comment to their audience about the video content, either online or off.

✓ **Placing it on social networks:** Links to the video start showing up in tweets, Facebook posts, and other venues.

✔ **E-mailing it to popular lists:** Popular newsletters may include a link to the video.

✔ **Advertising:** Video owners buy different types of advertising — Google, YouTube, Facebook, and so on — to encourage sharing.

✔ **Blogging:** Well-known bloggers include a link to the video in one of their posts.

✔ **Doing giveaways:** Links to the video mentioning free prizes start showing up online.

One example of viral seeding is the campaign Procter & Gamble created for Cheer detergent, as shown in Figure 9-4. In August of 2011, they launched a music video on YouTube that contained clickable links to prizes. When you clicked any of the prize links, you were taken to a Facebook app that allowed you to register to win. Creative campaigns like this are going to become increasingly popular because they involve the viewer and get strong word of mouth. The seeding aspect of this campaign — the sharing across social platforms, the advertising, and the contest with prizes — all worked together to help this campaign go viral.

Figure 9-4: The Cheer detergent viral music video.

Advertising on YouTube

If you're a marketer at a large brand, you may have the dollars to invest in some paid advertising tactics. YouTube provides several options based on your objectives. They categorize the objectives as Brand Awareness, Product Launch, Direct Response, and Reputation Management.

After you've determined your objective, you are offered ad formats including the following:

- ✔ **Home-page ads:** This provides the advertiser with a premiere spot on the YouTube home page, as shown in Figure 9-5. More than 50 million unique users go there every day. It's prime advertising real estate.

- ✔ **TrueView Videos ads:** YouTube is trying out this new format that allows users to click a Skip This Ad Now button after the user has viewed the ad for three seconds. Advertisers can also opt out of this and provide the regular ad that can't be skipped.

- ✔ **Brand channel:** This category offers several levels of customization for a channel dedicated to your brand. This is different from a user channel, which is free when you sign up.

- ✔ **Mobile:** Video ads are served up on your customer's mobile devices — iPhone, Android, and BlackBerry. comScore lists YouTube as the number one destination for mobile video.

With these paid tactics, YouTube provides all the standard media metrics with YouTube Insights. (See Chapter 19 for more about YouTube Insights.) These include impressions, click to play, click rate, and quartile viewed in addition to the community metrics (likes, views, and comments). A *quartile view* shows the data segmented in equal quarters so you can determine how well each is doing.

These advertisements can also be targeted to run next to select partner content, if you prefer. This matters to many marketers who worry about what their own advertisements (video or otherwise) may appear next to.

Home page ad

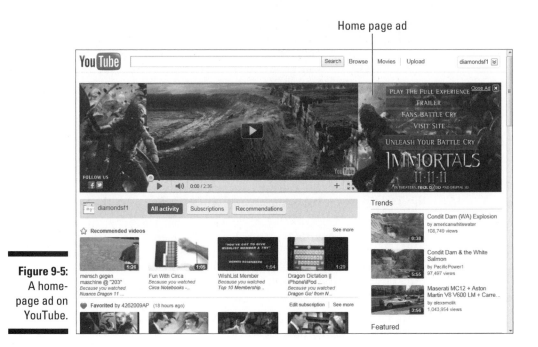

Finding Marketing Inspiration on YouTube

Nobody said that SMM using video was a snap to figure out. The folks at YouTube would be the first to say that we're all still learning. To assist in this learning process, they have put together a feature called Show & Tell, which can be found at www.youtube.com/user/YTShowandTell, as shown in Figure 9-6. Here, they collect what they call "the best creative marketing examples on YouTube."

In the spirit of Pablo Picasso, who said, "Good artists copy, great artists steal," they provide examples that help you "steal" from the best. They divide the examples into the following categories:

✔ **Interactive Video:** In this category, you see hundreds of videos that engage the viewer by asking them to click the video. This breaks you out of the passive viewing mode.

✔ **Brand Channels:** This category shows you the very best examples of brands that own channels, as shown in Figure 9-7. Lots of creative graphics and features here can give you and your team ideas about what's possible.

✔ **Home Pages:** As you'd expect, this section shows how some of the heavy hitters spend their advertising bucks to grab your attention on the YouTube home page. Disney, Warner Brothers, and Volvo show up here.

✔ **Viral Hits:** As you peruse this section, you'll see that the videos that actually go viral are incredibly diverse. You can find lots of inspiration but no blueprints here.

✔ **Creatives' Corner:** This section is for the people who do the actual creating and crafting of videos. It features interviews about how to think about the making of things.

Figure 9-6:
The Show &
Tell section
on YouTube.

Figure 9-7:
A featured
Brand
Channel ad
in Show
& Tell.

Chapter 10

Making foursquare Work for You

*W*hat is foursquare? It's a location-based social network that is accessed primarily through mobile phones. The service was started in March 2009 and in the span of just two and half years has grown to 10 million users around the world. Users can check in at locations primarily using their mobile phones. Upon checking in at a location, they see tips for that location, receive points for their check-in, are rewarded with special badges, and can also see who else has checked into that location. The service includes a leaderboard that shows users how many points they have relative to their friends. As of September 20, 2011, the service had surpassed a billion check-ins.

Over the last year, foursquare has opened itself up to the marketing world, and today, major brands from Starbucks and American Express to PepsiCo and 7-Eleven are active on foursquare. Although marketers may sometimes think that the best way to market on foursquare is by having a brand badge, foursquare actually offers other deeper and more meaningful ways to interact with consumers on the social network platform. Before we get into how brands can leverage the foursquare platform, however, we discuss how individuals use the platform on a regular basis.

Utilizing the Platform

foursquare is accessible on smartphones via foursquare downloadable applications. The devices supported include iPhone, Android, Symbian, BlackBerry, webOS, and Windows 7. Users can also access foursquare from the foursquare website, but when they do, they cannot check into specific locations.

Following are some of the activities an individual can perform on foursquare:

✔ **Check in at locations**: When an individual opens foursquare, he has the ability to scan for check-in locations in his vicinity. These locations may have been created by foursquare or by other users. Upon finding his location, he can then check in and share the fact that he's checked in with his friends. His check-in can be shared with other people on Facebook and Twitter. If he cannot find his location on the foursquare location screen, he has the option to create his own location for the check-in.

✔ **Get points and tips:** As he checks into the location, a few other things happen. He gets *points,* which are based on a variety of factors, including whether this is his first check-in, how many times he's checked in at the location, how far the location is from his previous check-in, and other similar factors. He can also view tips left by others about the location. In the case of a restaurant, the tips may be related to what to eat. In the case of an airport, the tips might tell him which security line to get in for faster service. These tips are available not just for his friends on four-square, but also for anyone checking in at that location. Furthermore, when he checks in at the location, he gets to see who else has checked in there.

✔ **Become a mayor:** After a user has checked in more times at a specific location than anyone else over a 60-day period, he is crowned mayor of that location. He remains mayor until his check-ins are exceeded by someone else, in which case the mayorship immediately passes on to the next person. When the person is recognized as a mayor of a location, he gets extra points. He is then visible as the mayor of the location each time anyone else checks in at that location via foursquare.

✔ **View the feed:** Like Facebook and Twitter, foursquare has a user activity feed. This feed tells you all the activity of friends, including their check-ins, tips that they may have left at a location, photographs shared, and mayorships attained. When you join foursquare, you're invited to bring your friend or follower list from Facebook or Twitter with you. A link asks you to Find Your Friends. Click that link, and you are taken to a page with icons for those platforms. After you click an icon to connect with one of those networks, invitations created by foursquare are sent to all of your Facebook and Twitter friends or followers who are also on foursquare, asking them if you can connect with them on foursquare too.

✔ **Discover new places via foursquare:** foursquare serves as a powerful discovery tool to find places to eat, drink, shop, and be entertained. The Explore button shows you recommended places that are in your vicinity based on their popularity among your friends and in your city. You can view those locations, their tips, and whether they have any four-square specials available (more on those in the section "Using Advanced Marketing Strategies with foursquare"). The Trending tab tells you which venues are getting more and more popular by the moment, based on the number of check-ins in a very short period of time.

✔ **Use the Lists function:** Finally, the Lists function lets you bookmark your favorite locations and compile them into a public list that can be viewable by others. You can add your favorite restaurants. After you've created a list and shared it, others can view the list and see how many of those locations they have checked in at.

Setting Up Shop on foursquare

A brand can use foursquare in a number of different ways. Just as with Twitter and Facebook, how you use foursquare should really depend on your brand, the business you're in, and what you're trying to accomplish. There's no single way to use foursquare that all brands must follow.

However, before you can get into some of the more innovative ways of using foursquare for your social media marketing efforts, here are a few things you must do:

✔ **Set up your brand page on foursquare.**

Borrowing from both Facebook and Twitter, foursquare allows brands to create their own pages on `www.foursquare.com`, as shown in Figure 10-1. After you've created a brand page, other users can follow your brand on it. Users who follow your brand can see the tips you place at specific locations.

✔ **Claim your physical location.**

If you're a merchant with a physical store location, you can claim the location (with foursquare verification) and then run specials for your customers, whether you are a restaurant, a hotel, or a shop. Specials, which are typically discounts or special offers, serve as another way to attract foursquare users into your specific venue to buy merchandise from you.

✔ **Create a location for your headquarters.**

If you aren't a merchant with a physical store location, you should at the very least create a location for your company headquarters. It is important for people visiting your company to know that you're on foursquare. It makes an important symbolic point and often results in friendly employee competitions to become the mayor of the office.

✔ **Leverage the API to add location data to all your web products.**

The foursquare places database can be used by developers in your company to add location information to your applications or websites. This can add more texture to whatever application you may have on your website. For example, if your website includes restaurant reviews, using the foursquare API, you can also highlight tips from the restaurants as well as showcase the foursquare specials.

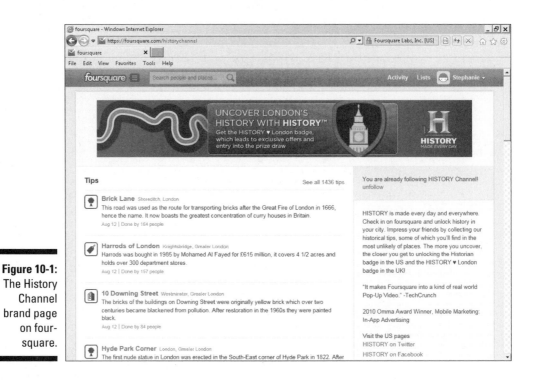

Figure 10-1:
The History Channel brand page on foursquare.

Using Advanced Marketing Strategies with foursquare

To understand the true potential of foursquare and its application programming interface (API) is to learn how brands like Pepsi, American Express, Tasti D-Lite, and Neiman Marcus have launched marketing programs that drive not only awareness for their brands, but also sales and customer loyalty. These marketing programs benefit their customers, their brands, and foursquare too — a sure sign that the program holds lots of merit.

Following are a few examples that highlight the potential of the platform for marketers:

✔ **PepsiCo Shopper Loyalty Program:** In November 2010, Shiv's digital team at PepsiCo partnered with foursquare to create a "load to card" program with participating supermarket chains. This program allowed you to register your foursquare card with the loyalty card program of a particular retailer. Then when you checked in on foursquare at that supermarket, depending on what foursquare badges you'd received in the past, you got special offers and discounts on PepsiCo products geared specifically for you. This program depended on your past foursquare behavior to target the right kind of offers to you.

For example, if you've already gotten the Gym Rat badge on foursquare for making frequent trips to the gym, upon your next check-in at the participating retailer, you'd be given a special offer on a Gatorade product. The offer is tailored to everything that you've done in foursquare in the past, which is what makes it valuable to both the consumers and the brand. After all, the company gets to learn about their consumers behaviors' (anonymously) and which offers matter to whom and in which location.

✔ **American Express:** American Express is another poster child example of a company that has partnered with foursquare to uniquely drive business value for its customers and partners. Their relationship started as a test at SXSW 2010. It was then made it into a national program for customers who use their American Express cards at select retailers.

The first step in using foursquare with AmEx is to link your American Express account with your foursquare account via the American Express website. Next, check into specific participating stores on foursquare, and tap Load to Card on the special. After that, each time you check in, you are eligible for discounts that get automatically reflected on your monthly AmEx statement. Companies like H&M and the Sports Authority offer specials to AmEx customers in this way.

✔ **Tasti D-Lite:** Who'd have thought that an ice cream company would be one of the first to dynamically tap into the power of location-based social networks? That's exactly what Tasti D-Lite did, as shown in Figure 10-2. They partnered with foursquare to integrate their loyalty program into foursquare. Now whenever you check out at a Tasti D-Lite and swipe your loyalty card, you're automatically checked in on foursquare.

In a sense, the signature behavior on foursquare — the ability to check in — has smartly been made a passive one through the loyalty card. Each time you swipe the loyalty card, you're also given special offers and points that pertain to that specific location (it now knows your location), and depending upon your past behavior, other offers maybe served up to you.

But there's still more: When you swipe your loyalty card and get checked in on foursquare, creative messaging is pushed to all your friends on foursquare. (A message pops up automatically, and you click it if you want it to be sent.) This messaging, which is typically like "I just earned five Tasti rewards points at Tasti D-Lite, Columbus Circle", goes further to build the brand. Needless to say, you get extra loyalty points if you allow these messages be shared with your friends on foursquare.

Figure 10-2:
The Tasti
TreatCard.

✔ **Nokia:** A natural partner for foursquare is Nokia, which, as a technology company, partnered with foursquare during Social Media Week to launch a vending machine that allowed for check-ins. Each time a person checked in at the vending machine, she would receive candy bars, Nokia accessories, and even in some cases Nokia phones.

The idea was built on the notion of random acts of kindness — all driven via foursquare check-ins at the vending machine. It served two purposes. One was to showcase how the location-based social network behavior can be used to drive activity in a different machine. The second was to draw attention to the power of the foursquare API. It also had the added benefit of encouraging people to share their check-in and promote Nokia in that fashion.

Tips and Tricks for Marketing on foursquare

As you can see from the previous discussion, there are numerous ways to market on foursquare. Every brand should be using some of the basic tactics. Taking advantage of some of the more advanced features really depends on your imagination, resources, and broader marketing objectives.

Regardless of which approach you take, here are some tips and tricks to consider as you approach marketing on foursquare:

- **Don't think of foursquare as location but as an activity platform.** Even in its short life, foursquare's mission has evolved considerably. It's no longer about where you are; it's about what you're doing at a given moment. Brands that recognize that subtle but important distinction have much better success in harnessing the platform and its API to market more effectively.

- **Carry your social graph into foursquare.** As a brand, you too have a social graph built by encouraging people to like you on Facebook and follow you on Twitter. One of the best ways to trigger interest on foursquare is to encourage these very same followers and fans to join you on foursquare too. It certainly doesn't hurt to encourage this behavior with a few special offers available only to foursquare users who are connected with your brand. This core base of loyalists will then bring others into the fold.

- **Make your paid media marketing efforts work for you.** The best way to harness foursquare is by treating it as a component of your broader marketing efforts. PepsiCo followed this tactic last summer when it launched its "Summertime is Pepsi Time" advertising campaign. This TV led campaign was about having fun at the beach. The TV advertisements ended with a call to action to check in at fun summer locations (beaches, amusement parks, and the like) around the country for more Pepsi fun.

  Checking in at three or more locations earned participants the Pepsi badge, which in turn opened up a series of discounts at participating retailers. The program made sense because it nicely complemented the narrative of the TV commercials but made them more real.

✔ **Use badges wisely:** Badges on foursquare are important. As users, we all like to earn badges and show our friends how many we've accumulated and why. But badges can be overused, and sometimes marketers jump to badges too quickly. It may make sense to have badges for your brand, but keep in mind that only people who follow you are eligible to get those badges. More valuable is to use other tactics like encouraging check-ins and spurring them on to "become mayor" (many of which we discuss earlier in the chapter in the section "Utilizing the Platform") to build a large following on foursquare. After you've built that following, it may make sense to award badges for specific behaviors as rewards.

✔ **Use your imagination to harness the foursquare API.** As American Express, PepsiCo, Tasti D-Lite, and Nokia showed, there are innumerable ways to make the foursquare API work for your brands and your customers. All it takes is the imagination to think of those ideas and then the resources to be able to execute and promote them. In this crowded media ecosystem, every good idea still needs some promotion.

✔ **Deepen your relationships with foursquare.** You may not always have all the answers or the best ideas on how to make foursquare work for your business. This is a new platform that evolves practically every other day. Here's one solution — talk to foursquare directly about the possibilities and bounce ideas off of them. They are a relatively young company that's eager to work with brands. You'll be surprised how much they'd love to help you achieve your own marketing objectives.

✔ **Employ the "Keep It Simple, Stupid (KISS)" philosophy.** It is easy to get carried away and craft a foursquare marketing program that is both incredibly complex and expensive. It doesn't have to be, and it certainly shouldn't start out in that fashion. Some brands have crafted extremely simple yet powerful foursquare marketing programs by just using the built-in features of the application. For example, by leaving tips at each of your company's retail locations, you may run a special foursquare treasure hunt with rewards at every step of the way. Or as many restaurants do, you can offer a special reward to whoever is the mayor of your retail location. You can then promote that, widely encouraging others to check in at the location frequently.

Chapter 11

Considering LinkedIn

· ·

· ·

The old adage "It's not what you know, but who you know" is even more true with the growth of the web. People used to be limited in their ability to stay in touch and nurture their small cadre of relationships. With the advent of new web tools, you can connect with people in ways never before possible. An outgrowth of this capability is the ability to identify people who are connected to you by virtue of their proximity to your contacts — or "degrees of separation." You now have the ability to identify and request an introduction to the connections of your connections!

LinkedIn is different from the other major social media platforms like Facebook or Twitter in that it focuses specifically on the world of work. Information about your favorite restaurant or new shopping acquisition is best shared elsewhere. The tone is serious, and the social media marketing potential is vast because people join to network. If you sell to a business audience of any kind, LinkedIn can provide you with a great focus group of interested members. According to a study done by *BtoB* magazine in April of 2011, 26 percent of B2B marketers cite LinkedIn as their single most important social channel, with 20 percent choosing Facebook, 19 percent citing blogging, and 14 percent citing customer communities.

When LinkedIn (www.linkedin.com) launched in May of 2003, many questioned whether it truly fit the mold of a social media network. With the addition of over 120 million worldwide users, that question is answered. As of August of 2011, LinkedIn was rated the third-most-popular social media networking site. (See Chapter 13 for details.) According to comScore, LinkedIn has seen a growth of 65 percent, from 48 million users in March 2010 to 79 million as of March 2011. That's growth!

Why did LinkedIn grow so robustly? Like all the other popular social networks, it met a need. It provided a way for like-minded business people from around the globe to find each other, share information, and give advice. It legitimized a way for professionals to communicate in an environment that had guidelines and accountability.

The key to success is remembering that LinkedIn is just one channel of your social media strategy. You need to pay attention to how your connections here can drive traffic to other channels. For example, you may want to provide a link to a discount on your website. By integrating selling with everything else you're doing, you won't seem like a crass self-promoter. In this chapter, we look LinkedIn's varied uses for social marketing of both yourself and your company.

Getting Started

To understand the potential marketing value of LinkedIn, as shown in Figure 11-1, you can view it in two distinct ways: as a marketing vehicle for your own career, and as a marketing tool to understand and connect with the audience to which you market.

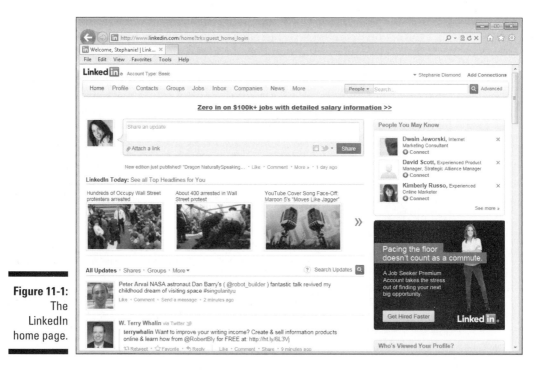

Figure 11-1: The LinkedIn home page.

It's safe to assume that everyone on LinkedIn is sold on the idea of networking. They know the value of a connection that can take you where you need to go. This means that you can connect with people knowing that you don't need to convince them that sharing contacts or advice is valuable.

On the other hand, the fact that they understand this value means that you can't use connections frivolously. At no time should you connect with someone without the understanding that you or your contacts could also be of value to them.

LinkedIn gives you the option to start with a free account. This account has lots of great features. If you are just getting started, you may want to join without making any additional financial commitment. You can decide if you need additional premium features after you get the lay of the land.

If you have used LinkedIn for a while or know that you will be using your account for something specific like an immediate job search, you may want to consider joining at a premium level. (See the section called "Finding a Job" later in this chapter.) What's in the premium subscription levels?

A few of the most useful features are

- ✔ **InMail:** This premium feature allows you to e-mail anyone on LinkedIn regardless of whether they are in your network. A free account lets you access only your immediate network. With InMail, you can e-mail anyone on LinkedIn. *Note:* If you do not get a response from the person to whom you sent the e-mail, they are not counted toward your monthly limit. The Business premium account allows 3 InMails per month; the Business Plus premium account allows 10 InMails per month; the Executive premium account allows 25 InMails per month.

- ✔ **Access to more profiles when you search:** A premium account allows you to see more profiles than you would if you had a free account. This increases the likelihood you will find the right person to connect with.

- ✔ **Search filters:** You can apply a variety of filters to your search so that you can zero in on the right target. For example, you can search for people who work for a certain size company or target only the Fortune 1000.

- ✔ **Expanded profiles:** When you see profiles, you see a more expanded profile of the people in which you are interested. You will also see everyone on LinkedIn who fits the criteria, not just those limited to your own network.

- ✔ **Who Viewed My Profile:** This feature of the free account allows you to see who viewed your profile. The list is restricted to a few names and profiles. With a premium account, you can see everyone who is interested in you and how they found you.

How much does all of this cost you? You have the following payment options:

- ✔ **Business:** This is the first tier. If you choose to prepay for the annual subscription, it is $239.40 (at the rate of $19.95 per month). The monthly rate is $24.95.

- ✔ **Business Plus:** At this tier, you prepay $479.40 annually (at the rate of $39.95 per month). The monthly rate is $49.95.

- ✔ **Executive:** At the highest tier, you prepay $899.40 annually (at the rate of $74.95 per month). The monthly rate is $99.95.

To see how many of each feature you can access at each tier, see the subscription chart at www.linkedin.com/subscriptionv2?displayProducts=& trk=home_level.

If you are more than a casual user of LinkedIn, you may want to try a premium account. The premium levels specifically for job seekers are discussed later in this chapter in the section "Finding a Job."

Creating a New Profile

Whether you are planning to use LinkedIn for personal career networking or consumer research, you are talking to a group of people who are focused almost solely on professional activities. Therefore, the most important first step is to look at your overall business strategy to see which social media marketing goals can be met by LinkedIn.

After you know your goals, you need to determine how to present yourself. This presentation is done by setting up a profile. You can set up only one profile on LinkedIn, so it needs to work for you in a variety of ways.

You also have the option of setting up a company page, but we recommend that unless you are specifically setting up a company page with several employees, you wait until you are more familiar with LinkedIn to do it. You want to be familiar with how things are done on LinkedIn before you promote yourself. If you have several employees who will be active online and need to get started right away, by all means do it.

Setting up your profile is deceptively easy. The quality of your LinkedIn profile is all-important. As with any career-related activity, you will be judged on a variety of measures, including the description of your previous successes and your willingness to help to others achieve their goals.

We recommend that you start with a profile to support the main goals you have and then revise as you go along. For example, if you are looking for a job, your profile contains very different content from that of a business owner doing market research. We cover these differences in the rest of the chapter.

Preparing a content strategy

You've probably heard a good deal about the concept of content strategy. It boils down to evaluating what content you have and what you need to meet a specific marketing goal. Content can be articles, product descriptions, videos, audio interviews, or any material that informs people about you or your business.

To illustrate, one of your LinkedIn goals might be to find new consulting clients. If this is the case, you want to review all the content you have created that show off your consulting expertise. Then you can start to share them on your profile. You would also consider going to LinkedIn Answers and begin to develop a following by writing the answers to questions. (See the section "Using LinkedIn Answers" later in this chapter). You can then repurpose this written content in other channels like your newsletter or blog.

Begin by doing an inventory of your e-books, posts, proposals, and so on, and determine what content you can use to let colleagues learn about you on LinkedIn. Then make an editorial schedule for yourself so that you can create any new things you need in a timely manner. Usually, if you don't schedule a specific time to do it, you won't. For inspiration, look at other people's profiles, and see what they have posted.

Covering what matters first

Your profile continues to evolve as you meet new people, join more groups, and attend events. You can't do everything all at once in the beginning. Consider the following tips when you are starting out:

- ✔ **Keywords matter.**

  We put keywords at the top of the list because as you put together your profile, you want to make sure that you include keywords that can be used to find you. You probably have some keywords that you already use for your websites and other channels. Make sure to include some of those, but also think through the goal of this profile and include any new keywords that will move you toward the top of the search results.

- ✔ **List the professional name by you wish to be known.**

  This is the name you use in your industry. You want colleagues and potential connections to find you. Don't use a nickname unless you use it professionally.

  LinkedIn only lets you create one profile, so if you own a business, decide ahead of time if you are going to use your own name or your business name. We recommend that you use your own name in case you close your business or want to change direction.

✔ **Use a real headline, not just a title.**

This section introduces your brand. If someone were to give you a wonderful introduction, it would include this content. If you are a best-selling author or award-winning salesperson, or have some special designation, this is the place to use it (for example, Jane Smith, Award Winning Salesperson).

✔ **Provide a summary that highlights your uniqueness.**

Here you detail the contents of your headline. Think of this as the follow-up to the headline. Imagine you are speaking right after the person who introduced you. Explain who you are and what makes you different among a sea of other members. Don't be modest.

✔ **Think carefully about how you list your positions — current and past.**

Display what you are doing now and any significant positions you previously held. This is not a detailed résumé. If you are seeking a new job, see the section later in this chapter called "Finding a Job."

✔ **Supply a professional photo.**

This is a key item. People don't like to admit it, but they like to be able to picture the person which with they're connecting. It's not a beauty contest. Get a professional photo with appropriate attire. Save the pose with your favorite pooch for Facebook.

✔ **Use links other than just websites.**

Don't be too literal. You can put in any link that you want to send people to. It doesn't have to be your main website. Just make sure that they are relevant and polish your brand.

✔ **Look at the ways in which you can list your achievements.**

The possible sections available include Education, Certifications, Patents, Languages, Honors and Awards, Organizations, Projects, and Publications and Test Scores. Use any of these that are pertinent. You have wide latitude here to really showcase your talents.

✔ **Make it a point to add some apps at the beginning.**

Apps are program add-ins that allow you to expand your reach. They are discussed in detail in the next section, "Using apps to enhance your profile." They are valuable because they allow you to link seamlessly with other programs.

✔ **Ask for recommendations.**

LinkedIn provides a recommendations tool that you can use to solicit comments from people who have been impressed by you. This could include a co-worker, manager, or client. Obviously, you want to have great recommendations, but don't go crazy at the start. Perfunctory recommendations from your friends aren't all that valuable. If someone has some real value to add, ask for their recommendation when you get started. This section will grow organically as your colleagues want to commend you (and have you commend them for a job well done).

✔ **Start making connections.**

Connections are at the heart of LinkedIn's success. You are here to build your network. Remember that these connections are people who will help you reach your goals, so make them meaningful. Don't be in a race to see how many connections you can get. After you reach 500 connections, LinkedIn lists your connections as *500+*. See more detail in "Finding connections" later in this chapter.

Using apps to enhance your profile

You will quickly benefit from choosing some of the add-in apps LinkedIn makes available to you, as shown in Figure 11-2. They can be found in the main tab, More⇨Get More Applications, or you can go to the URL `www.linkedin.com/static?key=application_directory`.

Following are five apps you might consider when you get started:

✔ **Blogs:** You can easily establish links to your blog (WordPress or TypePad). These apps instantly give you ongoing updates that you can share with your connections. This doubles the value of the content you create elsewhere by sharing it with a new audience.

✔ **Twitter:** If you maintain a lively Twitter account, you can share the content here as well. By blending a stream of content from these channels, along with specific information you choose for the status update box, as seen in Figure 11-3, you will have a very active stream.

✔ **SlideShare or Google Presentation:** You can provide a link to some of your best content using the SlideShare or Google Presentation links. These are services that allow you upload slides of a presentation you have developed. It's a great way for a new audience of professionals to view your work.

✔ **Polls:** The Polls application is popular because it allows you to add poll functionality to your profile. This is great if you want to do some market research or get a conversation going about a potential new product.

✔ **Events:** The Events app provides the ability to promote your upcoming event to all your connections. If one of your contacts signs up for the event, this fact is noted on all of their contacts' profiles. This is real marketing power. People who might never have known about your webinar or other event are made aware of it, and they can sign up too. It's an implicit endorsement.

Figure 11-2:
The
Applications
directory.

Update Status box

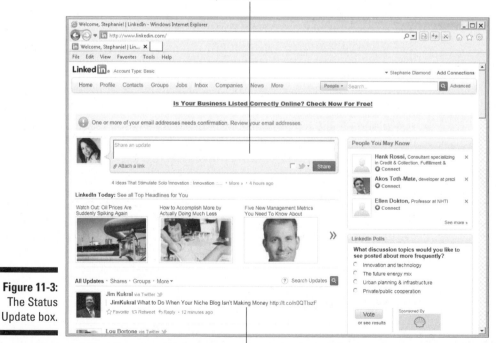

Figure 11-3:
The Status
Update box.

Status update in stream

Finding connections

LinkedIn makes it easy to get started finding new connections. One way to start is to look at the main navigation tab, Contacts ⇨Add Connections, as shown in Figure 11-4. You have several options to choose from. You can find colleagues from your various e-mail programs like Outlook, classmates from your educational institutions, or people you may know from nonprofits or clubs.

As you are presented with lists of these contacts, go through and choose the ones you want. Be certain to deselect the Share All check box so that you do not send invitations to people who don't belong in your network but are on your e-mail lists.

Choosing to advertise

Unlike with other social media platforms, advertising on LinkedIn involves little controversy. Perhaps because it's business-oriented, the idea of advertising doesn't seem as intrusive. When you are on the site, ads can be found on the following pages: Home, Profile, Inbox, Search Results, and Groups.

Contacts tab

Figure 11-4: The Contacts tab.

LinkedIn does a good job of helping you segment your ad targets, so it's important to know who you're targeting. We used a recent survey of LinkedIn demographics posted on SlideShare by Amodiovalerio Verde, (`www.slideshare.net/amover/linked-in-demographics-statistics-july-2011`) to show you a representative sample of ad potential. His source was the LinkedIn Ad Platform and was compiled on July 13, 2011.

You can segment your ad by

- **Industry:** There is a large list of worldwide industries to choose from. The report shows that the top five industries represented are high tech at 15.3 percent, finance at 12.9 percent, manufacturing at 9.8 percent, medical at 8.6 percent, and corporate at 8.2 percent.

- **Seniority:** This refers to job seniority, with 3.5 percent of the members identifying themselves as holding C-suite jobs. (A *C-suite job* refers to a job with a *C* in the title, like CEO, CFO, or COO.)

- **Geography:** The entire world is represented. North America is the largest group, with more than 54.3 million LinkedIn members residing there.

- **Job function:** The top five job functions reported are entrepreneur at 11.7 percent, sales at 10 percent, academics at 9 percent, administrative at 9 percent, and information technology at 6.8 percent.

- **Age:** In North America, 40 percent of the members are between the ages of 35 and 54.

- **Gender:** LinkedIn skews slightly male.

Carefully go over the details of ad spending. The ad itself is not unlike the one you might create for Google. If you decide to try it, look at several of them and see what's possible. Like any other ad platform, the costs can mount up unless you set goals and limits.

Participating in Groups

LinkedIn members sometimes overlook the value of joining groups. They focus on one specific activity, like finding a job, and forget that LinkedIn has the added value of connecting them with second- and third-degree contacts (people who are separated from you by one or two other people). The most powerful use of groups is to find people who you would never have the chance to meet in person. Joining a group they're in makes the introduction easier.

Benefitting from joining groups

You have several choices about how you want to participate in groups. One option is to join several groups right away to get introduced to those with similar interests. If you prefer, you can join one group and see how you like it. You are allowed to join a total of 50 groups. That sounds like a lot, but remember that you may have several goals for joining. Some benefits of joining groups are

- ✔ **Finding members with similar experiences:** You can join a group of those who have worked at the same company you have or are alumni of the same school.

- ✔ **Extending your knowledge of a company in which you are interested:** If you're thinking about working for a particular company, you can find other employees to connect with.

- ✔ **Connecting with members who are interested in the same charitable activities:** Nonprofit and charitable groups are in abundance. You can find like-minded members easily.

- ✔ **Establishing yourself as an expert in your field:** You can choose to take a leadership role in a group or make your feelings known.

- ✔ **Understanding the trends in your industry:** You can stay informed about important issues and developments.

- ✔ **Determining who the industry leaders are:** By virtue of their popularity and activities, you can learn from industry leaders who are active.

- ✔ **Connecting with and participating in discussions:** You can do a lot of consumer research in these groups if you take the time to read and listen.

- ✔ **Finding partners for joint venture activities:** If you're looking for investors, you may want to extend your feelers out in the group without having to give away too much information.

- ✔ **Discovering new clients:** People who are impressed with your breadth of knowledge on a topic can seek you out for consultation.

Starting your own group

If you have determined that starting your own group will help you meet your business goals, LinkedIn provides a great framework to do so. The most important thing you should consider before starting is whether you have the time and enthusiasm to be the leader. Managing a group takes work. If you start a group and then let it falter, it reflects badly on your professionalism.

With more than 120 million people as potential members, you can develop a solid group fairly quickly, but it's your responsibility to keep it lively and active.

Imagine yourself as the host of a party that needs your attention to be a success. This is particularly true for small business owners who wear all the hats in their organization. Picture yourself running this group a year from now and see how that fits into your plans.

Rather than hoping that everyone will police their own groups, LinkedIn has set some guidelines. They include the following:

✓ **You can only send one e-mail a week to members of your group.**

You can envision the amount of e-mail that could be generated by a group leader eager to connect (and sell things) to his members. Limiting e-mail communications helps everyone control the information flow.

✓ **The group must either be open or closed (by invitation only).**

You can choose to have invitation-only group or an open one, as shown in Figure 11-5. If you choose a closed group, members must be approved by the group leader and are the only ones who can see and participate in discussions.

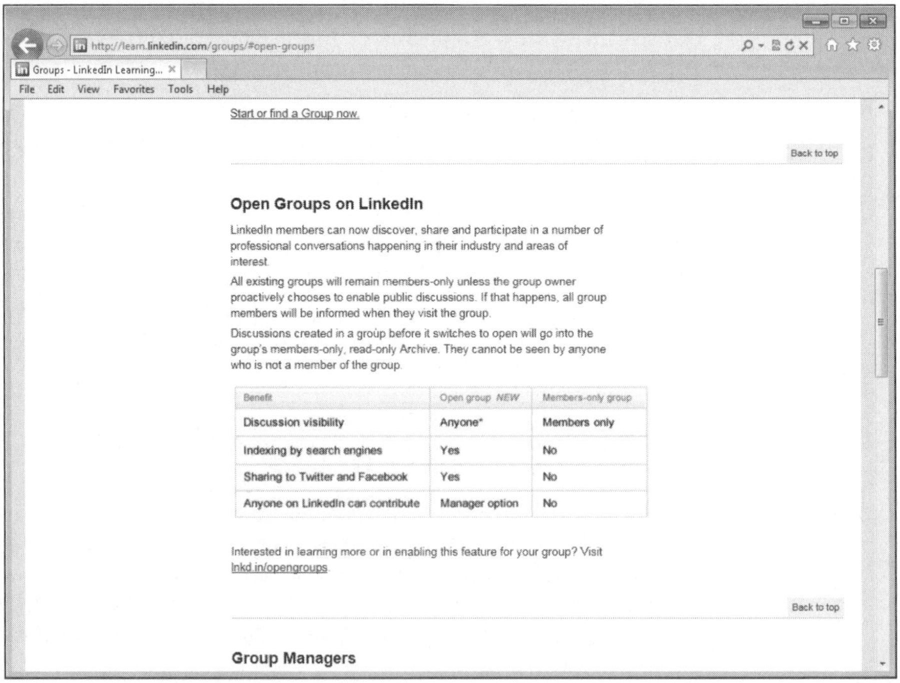

Figure 11-5: Choosing an open or closed group.

TIP

If you choose to have an open group, anyone can join. You should be aware that the discussions generated in an open group can be seen by anyone on LinkedIn, not just group members. In addition, the content can be shared on Facebook and Twitter.

Leaders of open groups can decide whether everyone on LinkedIn can participate in discussions or just be able to view them.

✔ **The group leader can allow members to invite people to join the group.**

As the group leader, you can allow members to seek out new members for the group by sending them invitations. If they accept an invitation from another member, they are instantly accepted.

Leading a successful group

What constitutes a successful group on LinkedIn? It's one that has value for both you and your members. You may hope to build a personal empire from your LinkedIn group, but the real success comes when your members act like a community. The value of the group comes from the power of the network. As members bring in others from their own network, the power grows. Here are some tactics that will help your group be a success:

✔ **Use your weekly e-mail.** You are allowed to send only one e-mail a week, so make it count. Think of it as the newsletter you might send to your website mailing list. Provide value and help members discover each other.

✔ **Hold the line on promotions.** As the leader, you are responsible for making sure that other members aren't overpromoting and ruining the experience. Nothing is worse that feeling like you are being taken advantage of by other group members.

✔ **Encourage comments and discussions.** The shared discussions are part of the valuable content your group builds. If you choose an open group, it can be shared on Facebook and LinkedIn. Monitor the groups and stir up some lively discussions.

✔ **Use events.** As we mentioned previously, LinkedIn has a great event tool. Create some virtual events and have members speak. Get everyone talking about new events. If enough people are interested in the idea, you can hold an in-person conference.

✔ **Interest the media.** One of your goals for the group should be to help the media find you. Publicity benefits the entire group. Think about having your members create an e-book or manifesto about your topic and let the media know about it. Some social media press releases could also do the trick.

Using LinkedIn Answers

To become a stand-out thought leader on LinkedIn, you'll want to share your advice. One of the best ways to do that is to use LinkedIn Answers. It can be found in the main navigation on the home page when you click the More tab, as shown in Figure 11-6. LinkedIn users post questions that require a level of expertise to answer. If you provide that answer, you can be perceived as an expert. Demonstrating your expertise is a great way to provide value and get noticed.

Answers also has additional value to a social media marketer. For example, you can get the following benefits:

✔ **Discovering content for blog posts, e-books, and slideshows:** The best way to create content is to answer questions. Not only will you develop material that people are interested in, but you can also see how helpful your answers really are. If they are not understood or require more information, that's great feedback for you. Then you can turn them into posts or other media with the knowledge that they have value.

Answers

Figure 11-6: LinkedIn Answers.

✔ **Uncovering trends by mining the questions people are asking:** If you start to notice a new concept cropping up, you may have uncovered a new trend. Keep your eyes open and read widely in your area of interest.

✔ **Locating potential joint venture partners:** If you are looking for an expert in a particular area, you can use Answers to find other thought leaders who may want to partner with you (or invest).

✔ **Finding a technical expert:** Locating a technical expert you understand and trust can be risky business online. If you find someone who answers your technical questions and can act as a freelancer or consultant, you have saved yourself a lot of time and money.

✔ **Letting new clients find you:** A great byproduct of showing off your skills is that someone with a budget to buy your products or hire you could be listening. Be generous with your expertise and let people get to know you. They'll be more likely to consider working with you.

Finding a Job

For job seekers, checking out LinkedIn is must. The basics are free and employers are actively looking. If you have diligently read and acted on the preceding sections, you should be ready to hit the ground running for your job search. You have a great profile, lots of important contacts, and an understanding of the various groups dedicated to your industry. So what else should you do to market yourself? Following are some ideas you can try when you are actively looking for a job:

✔ **Look at your profile as an employer would.**

If you have been on LinkedIn for a while and you are starting a job search, you want to re-evaluate your profile as an employer would. If you feel that an actual résumé style is required, you can check out Resume Builder at `http://resume.linkedinlabs.com`. This App helps you take your profile and build a good-looking résumé. Review it carefully to make sure that the chronological order is accurate and matches your profile. If you seek a design job, you can also check out an app in the directory called Creative Portfolio Display by Behance. It makes it easy to show off multimedia content you have created.

✔ **Create a unique presentation.**

In addition to anything you have done with your résumé to make it look better, you want to think about showcasing a presentation you've done. Programs such as Prezi can be used to develop something unique. You can also link to SlideShare from the Apps Directory or post a video. It's worth repurposing your best work and showing it off. You need a way to stand out and this will help.

✔ **Re-examine your keywords.**

You may have chosen general keywords when you first signed up. Now that you know specifically what type of job you are searching for, add keywords that will help you get found by your preferred employers.

✔ **Create a list of companies you would like to work for.**

Even if you don't have a specific company you are targeting, it will help to make a list of potential companies. Do some research on what jobs they have open and where you might fit in. It will give you ideas about how to improve your profile. If you do have a target list, look for someone in the company you might be able to approach to discuss the company.

✔ **Target your recommendations.**

If you've been reticent about asking for recommendations, now is the time to actively seek out people whose endorsement speaks directly to the job you want. LinkedIn makes it easy to add a recommendation, so it's not an onerous request.

✔ **Mine your network.**

Look at the second- and third-degree contacts in your network and see if you want to ask for introductions. That's where the power of LinkedIn is really demonstrated. Get started immediately because this could take some time. Not everyone has the same sense of urgency that you do.

✔ **Include other channel links.**

Don't forget that there is a whole wide world of other online channels that you are connected to. Make sure to showcase a website or show that you have an active Twitter following.

✔ **Consider purchasing Job Seeker Premium services.**

LinkedIn provides special subscription premium tiers for job hunters, as shown in Figure 11-7. If you are considering this, you may want to start with a month-to-month subscription to see if it works for you. If you see the job hunt is slow, you can always move to an annual subscription.

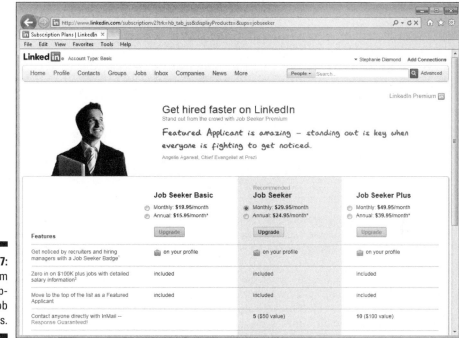

Figure 11-7:
Premium
subscrip-
tions for job
seekers.

How much will you have to pay for premium job seeker services? You have the following payment options:

- **Job Seeker Basic:** This is the first tier. If you choose to prepay for the annual subscription, it is $191.40 (or $15.95 per month). You pay $19.95 go from month to month.

- **Job Seeker:** At this tier, you prepay $299.40 annually (at the rate of $24.95 per month). You pay $29.95 to go from month to month.

- **Job Seeker Plus:** At the highest tier, you prepay $479.40 (at the rate of $39.95 per month). You pay $49.95 to choose a monthly subscription.

  To see how many of each feature you can access at each tier, see the subscription chart at `www.linkedin.com/subscriptionv2?display Products=&trk=hb_tab_jss&ups=jobseeker`.

A few of the most helpful features included in the premium accounts are as follows:

- ✔ **Job Seeker Badge:** Your profile has this visual aid next to your profile if you choose to display it. It helps employers quickly spot you. You can choose to display your badge (or not) in Settings, which is in the pull-down menu you see when you click your name in the upper right of the home page. The default choice is Off.

- ✔ **See real salary information:** You are able to zero in on your desired level and see real details from employers.

- ✔ **InMail:** As mentioned previously in the section "Getting Started," depending on the premium level you choose, you can contact a set number of members directly.

- ✔ **Who's Viewed My Profile:** As we noted previously, this feature allows you to see who viewed your profile. With a premium account, you can see everyone who is interested in you and how they found you.

The key to finding a job on LinkedIn is to work the power of your network. Not only can you find almost anyone in the industry or companies you target, but you can also market yourself in the best possible light. Remember that recruiters and employers use LinkedIn on a regular basis. If you make the effort, you could be in the right place at the right time. Good luck!

Chapter 12

Viewing Google through a Different Lens

*B*arely a year ago, a chapter covering Google wouldn't have been needed in a book on social media marketing. But because Google has done so much in the last year and has plans to do so much more in the next, a chapter on Google is indeed now warranted.

Google+ launched in June 2011. Brand pages were added to the platform in November. Google created a social music service and designed a Google button for usage on other websites and for integrating various social features into Google Search. Arguably, Google's social ambitions are much greater than its realities today (Google+, for example, only has approximately 40 million users compared to Facebook's 800 million), but that doesn't mean the future may not look different.

Looking at Google's Social Strategy

To know how to harness the Google web ecosystem for social media marketing, you need to first understand the core of Google's own social strategy. Fundamentally, Google is still a search platform and the most visited website on the Internet. The vast majority of its revenues and traffic comes from Google Search. That is unlikely to change in the near term. But over the last few years, the rise of Facebook has seriously threatened Google's online dominance. More and more people look to their friends on platforms such as Facebook when they're seeking information, whether it be product information or restaurant recommendations — in many cases, even before doing a Google search.

Google is responding to this threat in two different ways. First, they've tried repeatedly to create social networks to compete with Facebook — Orkut, which took off only in Brazil and India, and then Google Buzz, which recently shut down. Now there's Google+, as shown in Figure 12-1, which shows great potential. At the time of this writing, Google+ has 62 million users and is growing by leaps and bounds since its introduction.

Second, Google has decided to make every other part of the Google ecosystem more social. Whether it is Google Search or Google Music or even Google Apps, they are all getting more and more social by the minute. Both of these approaches present unique social media marketing opportunities for marketers.

Figure 12-1:
The sign-up
page for
Google+.

Grasping the Google+ Fundamentals

Google+ is a social network for anyone and everyone on the Internet. Launched in June 2011, on its surface, the social network seems very similar to Facebook. However, it does indeed have some architectural differences that have served to attract users to it.

Following are the core features of Google+, as shown in Figure 12-2:

Profile

Photos   Circles

Stream

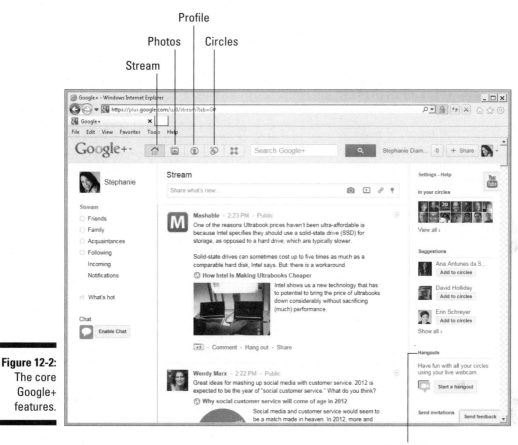

Figure 12-2:
The core
Google+
features.

Hangouts

✔ **Google Stream:** This is the home page you see when you log in to
Google+. It shows you all the posts by people in your circles. Just as
with Facebook, you can post a message to your stream. This can be
from your personal account or from a brand page. But better still, after
you type the text (or upload the photograph or video), you can choose
which circles or which people in those circles to share content with. In
this fashion, you can tightly manage who gets to see what pieces of your
content.

✔ **Google+ Photos:** Finally, Google has integrated photos more meaningfully into its web ecosystem. Clicking the Google+ photos icon takes
you to a photo page that is compelling and valuable both for users and
brands. The Google+ Photos philosophy is that the lens from which
you view other people's photographs should be the same lens through

which you view the content stream. On the Google+ Photos page, you can choose to view photos in the following categories: photos from your circles, photos from your phone, photos of you, photos from your posts, and your albums (integrating the Google Picasa application).

✔ **Google+ Profiles:** Every user on Google+ has a profile page that is similar to the Facebook profile page. All your activity appears on it, including the pages that you may have "+1'd" in the past. When you click the +1 button (known as the Google Plus One button) next to some content, you are sharing content with your Google circles. It's similar to the Like button on Facebook. You can select any kind of media (either your own or others) and let people know about it. You can add a photograph, share some information about yourself, upload photographs and videos, and allow others to send you e-mails and messages from this page. The profile page also shows how many people are in your circles and how many circles you are in.

✔ **Google circles:** Integral to Google+ is the concept of circles, which is the categorization mechanism for people whom you connect with on the platform. They are groups of friends that you organize by topic. Topics can be as straightforward as friends, co-workers, and family, or as rarified as stamp collectors, Justin Bieber fans, and tennis players. On the circles page, you can add friends to any number of circles. Then when viewing your news feed in Google+, you can limit the views by particular circles.

As you set yourself up in Google+, create professional circles of people who matter to you and your company. Whether from your personal account or from your Google+ brand page (more on that in the section "Google brand pages" later), you want to create a circle for co-workers, influencers, competitors, and industry analysts. In fact, you could use the same categorization for your circles as your PR team does for its tracking documents. These circles help you keep track of what people are saying. Circles provide you with meaningful opportunities to develop relationships by participating in their conversations.

✔ **Google+ Sparks:** This is a simpler and less integral feature to Google+. It helps you find content based on your own interests. Think of it as something similar to Google Reader, which lets you view blog posts that you care about in one simple interface. The additional benefit with Sparks is that it provides content recommendations for you. Use Google Sparks to follow topics that are of interest to you professionally or that matter to your company.

It's a bit difficult to find Sparks unless you know where to look. To find Sparks, do a search in Google+ from your stream. When the search comes up, click the Everything pull down menu and you'll see Sparks as one of the choices. Click on it and peruse the list as shown in Figure 12-3.

Figure 12-3:
Sparks and
Hangouts.

✔ **Google+ Hangouts:** This is probably one of the more unique and fun features of Google+. Hangouts are like virtual rooms that let you run video chats with people who are in your circles. It is a focused video chat with friends, family, co-workers, or business contacts. Because Hangouts are triggered through circles, it is easy to find the group you want to talk to and then to set up a Google Hangout (see Figure 12-3).

You can use Google Hangouts to have business conversations with other people in your company or even suppliers, business partners, or customers. If your brand is on Google+, Hangouts are a great way to socialize with customers or to run online events with them. For example, you can announce products on Google Hangouts and invite all your customers, business partners, suppliers, and employees to participate.

✔ **Google+ Huddles:** Huddles, another valuable feature of Google+, enables you to run group messaging with people in a given circle. So just as Hangouts lets you run live video chat sessions with them, Huddles allows you to talk to them via group messaging. Google Huddles is currently only available for the iPhone and Android devices. You cannot access it from a web browser. Arguably, this tool has no direct implications for marketers as yet, but it is a useful collaboration tool among marketers within an organization.

Google brand pages

On November 7 of 2011, Google launched brand pages on Google+. Although in the prelaunch, a few brands such Ford established their presences on Google+, as shown in Figure 12-4, November 7 marked the official launch, allowing all brands to participate.

These pages are similar to the user pages on Google+ and include features like circles, Streams, Sparks, Hangouts, and Huddles but have some key differences. These differences are designed to allow for the nuances of social media marketing and also to prevent brands from "overmarketing" on the social media platform.

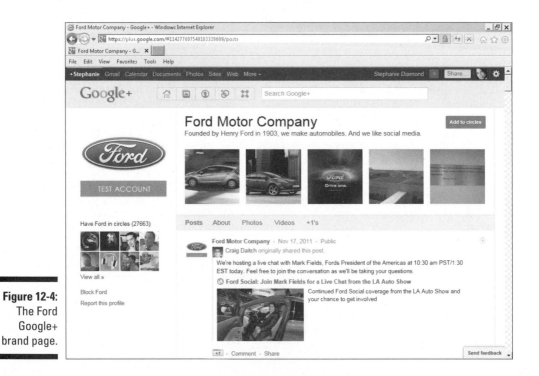

Figure 12-4:
The Ford
Google+
brand page.

Following are the key differences with Google+ brand pages and what they mean for you:

✔ **Adding users to circles requires permission.**

A Google+ brand page cannot add a user to a circle unless that user has already added to the page to one of his circles. This is very important because it prevents a brand from sending you messages until you have explicitly added the brand page to one of your circles and are open to receiving content from that brand. In other words, brands have to earn their place in a user's stream before they can start pushing messages into it.

✔ **Content is public.**

In contrast to personal profiles, pages on Google+ are set to public by default. This means that not only can the people who have the brand in a circle view the content, but anyone who visits the page can too. Most brands want more people to see their content, so this default setting serves everyone well. It also gives individuals an opportunity to scan the content being published by the brand before choosing to add the page to one of its own circles. The default setting can be changed by the brand administrator.

✔ **Pages have +1 and Add to Circles buttons.**

Individual user pages only have the Add to Circles button in the top right corner. Brand pages allow you to +1 the page or content on it as well. The +1 button is something that Google is trying to push out across the entire Internet. When you +1 a piece of content, it improves that content's rankings in the Google search engine. And when you +1 a page on Google+, it is the same result as when you do so on an external website. This is a seemingly small feature but a very important one.

✔ **It is integrated with search.**

Google is working hard to integrate Google+ with Google Search. If you search for a brand and add the plus sign (+) symbol in the search box before the name of the brand, in the search results, you'll be given the opportunity to add the page to a circle immediately. In fact, Google is testing this currently and some users are taken directly to the Google+ brand page.

Tips and tricks for Google+

It's still the early days for Google+. We have yet to see how the platform will evolve and become really valuable for marketers. Only time will tell. However, here are some tips and tricks to consider so that you are prepared for the many enhancements to Google+ that we know are coming:

✔ **Set up shop on Google+ now.** There's no question that the brands who set up shop early on Google+ are the ones who are able to attract the most people to their brands on the platform. This was the case with Facebook in its early days (some of the largest pages are still the oldest ones). The same applies to Google+. In fact, we've already seen that the brands that were part of the Google+ launch already have significantly more people in their circles than the brands that joined later.

✔ **Write once, publish everywhere doesn't work.** Before you start publishing extensively on Google+, take the time to familiarize yourself with the platform and how individuals are using it. You'll notice that it is often used as a medium for more serious conversations. Although this may change in time, the threaded nature of conversations on it and the ability to organize Hangouts, not to mention the early composition of people on the platform, are making it a more serious platform than Facebook (at least for now). As a result, don't automatically republish content designed for Facebook on Google+. Instead, establish a distinct Google+ content strategy.

✔ **Focus on search engine optimization.** One of the hidden benefits of participating as a brand on Google+ is the search engine optimization advantages that come with it. Google+ is not a stand-alone social network. It is part of a broader Google ecosystem that has information discovery at its core. As a result, every link you post on Google+ as a brand that's then clicked as a +1 on Google+ gets better optimized for search engines. That alone is a compelling reason to be an early participant on Google+.

✔ **The +1 that you see in Google+ requires attention.** Not only do the +1 button clicks impact search engine results, but in time, they will also have a direct influence on paid search and display ads running on Google. If Google has its way, these buttons will be as pervasive across the Internet as the Facebook Like buttons. This means that when you redesign your website, you'll want to include those Google+ buttons. And even though having a brand page may not directly drive the increased usage of the button (your content and your brand being clicked as a +1 a lot more), having the community can certainly serve as a strong foundation.

Learning from the examples of others

The best way to learn what to do and what not to do on Google+ is to pay attention to what other brands are doing. See how often they post, what they post, and how their content sharing on Google+ jives with their Facebook strategies. Pay attention to user activity on their pages.

Some of the early brands on Google+ to pay attention to are the following:

- All-American Rejects
- Anderson Cooper 360
- Angry Birds
- Barcelona Football Club
- Burberry
- Dallas Cowboys
- Pepsi
- Phoenix Suns
- Save the Children
- Toyota

As you can see, they are all kinds of brands, and you can probably learn something different from each one. Figure 12-5 shows the Save the Children brand page on Google+.

Figure 12-5:
The Save
the Children
brand page
on Google+.

Listening to Google and Music

In the last year, Google has launched a Music service to take on iTunes and the Apple ecosystem that extends to all the Apple devices and platforms. Google needed to do this so that its Android mobile operating system could be competitive with the Apple iPhone. In this section, we cover its core service and sharing functionality that will have social media marketing implications:

The Google Music platform has the following key components:

- ✔ **You can upload all your songs to the Google Music service.** It can hold up to 20,000 songs for free (this piece is often referred to as the *cloud music locker service*). It can take up to a week to upload if you have a lot of songs.

- ✔ **The songs can be accessed in several ways.** They can be accessed on any Google Android device or via the Google Music website at URL `https://music.google.com/music/`

- ✔ **You can get recommendations for other songs.** These recommendations are based on what you already have in the locker and with what frequency you are listening to particular music. The Android Market also lets you buy songs that when bought are available on all the platforms too.

- ✔ **All the music that you buy in the Google Android Market can be shared.** The most interesting piece of the Google Music platform is the sharing functionality that you can enable. The way it works is simple — when you buy some music, you can choose to share it with your Google+ circles. After you've chosen which circles to share it with, your purchased content appears in their Google+ streams, where they can listen to the tracks for free (one listen per track). You can imagine that as the core Google+ functionality improves, so too will the ways in which Google+ integrates with it.

What does Google's entre into social media mean for social media marketing? Just think about the possibilities for a moment. As a brand, you can not only share content with certain members of your customer base (through specific circles), but arguably you can start sharing specific music too. If you're a brand that plays in pop culture and for whose customers music matters, this could be a really interesting way to attract attention to your brand and build loyalty around it. Needless to say, doing this right means doing it in a way that makes sense for your brand and for your customers.

Chapter 13

Marketing via Niche Networks and Online Communities

*T*hroughout this book, we discuss social media marketing on the major social platforms: what you can do on the paid side of the equation as well as on the unpaid or earned media end. Still, much more social activity is happening online beyond Facebook, YouTube, LinkedIn, and Twitter, and you need to account for it. Industry insiders believe that in the coming years, greater cohesion will happen as user-generated content flows more seamlessly between the major social platforms and the rest of the Internet.

In this chapter, we discuss the social platforms beyond Facebook, YouTube, LinkedIn, and Twitter. We introduce these other social platforms, help you identify which ones are most appropriate for your marketing needs, and guide you through the process of determining how best to market on them.

Exploring the Niche Social Networks

So what are these niche social platforms that we're talking about? Table 13-1 outlines the top 15 social networking platforms as of December 2011 according to eBizMBA, a marketing research company. Keep in mind that although this categorization uses the term *social networks* very loosely, it still excludes user-generated content (UGC) video sites such as YouTube. Table 13-1 displays the see the Alexa rank of and number of unique visitors to the 15 most popular social networking platforms. The Alexa rank is a three-month measure of such things as page views and visitors to give you an idea of the most viewed sites online.

Table 13-1	The Top 15 Most Popular Social Networking Sites	
Social Networking Platform	**August 2011 Unique Visitors (000)**	**Alexa Rank**
Facebook	700,000	2
Twitter	200,000	9
LinkedIn	100,000	17
MySpace	80,500	79
Ning	60,000	128
Google +	32,000	n/a
Tagged	25,000	141
orkut	15,500	93
hi5	11,500	62
myYearbook	7,450	1,036
Meetup	7,200	528
Badoo	7,100	125
bebo	7,000	588
mylife	5,400	1,789
Friendster	4,900	301

Arguably, by studying the monthly unique visitors and Alexa rank, you may wonder whether calling them *niche* platforms is even appropriate. They still have millions of unique visitors each month and are growing at a relatively brisk pace. For many people, niche social platforms are more valuable and personal than Facebook, Twitter, LinkedIn, or YouTube.

Here's why we categorize these as niche platforms: Their size pales in comparison to that of the four major social platforms you see at the top of the list. These networks are typically more narrowly focused (Multiply is for meeting new people, and Friendster for gaming), and in some cases, they serve as platforms only for the aggregation and distribution of social media and are less focused on the social graph.

But here's a tricky fact: When you look at the major social platforms through the lens of your target customers, you may discover that they're not spending as much time on them as you expect. It is even possible that their time spent on a niche platform or cumulatively on several niche platforms exceeds time spent on the major platforms. It becomes apparent that you need to be focusing as much attention on these niche platforms (even though there are many more of them) as you do on Facebook, Twitter, LinkedIn, and YouTube.

Finding the Right Social Platforms

If we were to start a new business, it would probably be a business that, through some magic formula, would tell marketers which social platforms their specific customers are spending most of their time on in a given month, with guidance on how to reach them. It would probably make a fortune for the simple reason that it's hard to find these customers beyond the major social platforms.

It's easy to learn the paid and unpaid marketing solutions on the second rung social platforms (those listed in Table 13-1). What about the rest? How do you, as a marketer beginning to apply social media marketing, know where your customers are spending their time? Making your job even harder is the fact that you can't just focus on the social networks: You need to look more broadly at the video websites, the mainstream media websites, the blogger networks, and social media publishing tools that are all beginning to incorporate social functionality.

To help you identify the social platforms, we're going to share a four-step process for identifying the right social platforms on which to find your customers. But before we do that, we'd like to classify the social platforms into a more meaningful segmentation.

Classifying the social platforms

As of this writing, there are four major social platforms:

- ✔ Facebook
- ✔ Twitter
- ✔ LinkedIn
- ✔ YouTube

We classify them as the four major platforms based on their overall size and the growth rate. When you're marketing to a mass-market audience, you simply cannot ignore these platforms.

It's just a matter of time before the major media and entertainment sites incorporate so much social functionality that they'll be considered social platforms too. In fact, the *Wall Street Journal* already includes a community section (it's still free), and *Bloomberg Businessweek* runs Business Exchange (http://bx.businessweek.com), an online community to share relevant content among like-minded professionals.

Next come the *niche social platforms*. These are the ones that have a narrower focus, whether that's driven by the subject matter, the audience reached (Facebook, for example, only reached college students once upon a time), their overall size, or their core focus. CafeMom and deviantART are good examples. These platforms succeed by defining a sharp niche and owning it.

The *social platform infrastructure providers* are a separate category too. These infrastructure providers allow users to create their own social networks or blogging environments on them. Ning (`www.ning.com`) and Gather (`www.gather.com`) are among the most well known of these platforms, allowing people to set up social networks that behave similar to the way MySpace or Facebook behaves, with member pages, community areas, and activity streams. WordPress (`www.wordpress.com`) and Blogger (`www.blogger.com`) are other successful infrastructure providers too.

Finally, you have the *blogosphere*. Blogs rarely have any formal or technical relationship with each other, but they behave cohesively from time to time thanks to trackbacks, commenting, and the reciprocal linking that goes on between them. According to the 2011 Technorati State of the Blogosphere report, blogs are the most trusted source for brand, product, or service information.

You need to look for your customers on the major social platforms, the niche social platforms, the social infrastructure providers, and across the blogosphere, too.

Understanding your customers

To discover where your customers are spending their time online, you need to begin by understanding them better. Depending upon their *socio-technographics* (which means how your customers engage on the social platforms), they might be spending a lot of time on the major social platforms or very little. The first step in understanding them is to determine their participation levels in the social web.

The freely available online Forrester Social Technology Profile Tool allows you to profile your customers' social computing behavior. All you have to do is select the age range, country, and gender of the people you want to research. The tool then returns an analysis of your customers, dividing them up into creators, critics, collectors, joiners, spectators, and inactives. It is a useful starting point for understanding your customers. You can find the tool at `www.forrester.com/empowered/tool_consumer.html`.

Quantcast (www.quantcast.com/) is useful to understand the audience profile of someone using a social platform. Just type the website address of the social platform and the tool returns demographics information for that website. In some cases, it may even go deeper and include user segmentation responses as well.

The third form of research (and our favorite kind) is to actually talk to your customers. Conduct social media research to discover how they use the web, whether they socialize online, where that takes place, and how their friends and networks influence them. Even a small sample of users can yield a lot of valuable information about their online behaviors and the social platforms that they're engaging on. Often, the best way to do that is to ask interviewees to come in for the interviews with a few friends and observe them interact with each other. You can then supplement this in-person form of research with site surveys to get statistically significant results.

You can also research what consumers are saying online about the product, company, or brand. Using the research tools outlined in Chapter 25, you can understand where these conversations are taking place and how your customers think. Don't ignore peeking into these conversations — sometimes it's more insightful than any other form of research.

 Social behavior online is changing at a rapid pace, so consider putting an ongoing social research program in place. The ways your customers use the social web probably change every three to six months. You want to be ahead of those changes, so ongoing research is important.

Researching the platforms

Just as it is extremely important to understand your customers and where they're spending their time online, and with whom, it's extremely important to research the social dynamics of the various social platforms. It's no use proposing a social influence marketing strategy that covers YouTube if you don't really know how marketers can and are allowed to use YouTube. Nor will your marketing efforts be a success if those marketing efforts, even if YouTube allows them, are out of sync with how users expect to use that social platform.

We've discussed how you can market on the major social platforms, covering Facebook, Twitter, LinkedIn, and YouTube, but there's more to the social web than those platforms. Knowing what is permissible and appropriate for the other social platforms can be tricky. There aren't any hard and fast rules, and the advertising industry is continuing to establish guidelines, advertising formats, and best practices.

Keep an eye on the Social Media Committee of the Interactive Advertising Bureau (www.iab.net/member_center/councils_committees_working_groups/committees/social_media_committee), which has defined best practices for advertising in social media. Also watch the Social Media Advertising Consortium (www.smac.org), as shown in Figure 13-1, which includes representatives from agencies, brands, and publishers. They have defined standards for ad units, a common vocabulary, and best practices.

Although marketing tactics on the social platforms are still developing, a few practices and standards are emerging. These can be classified as follows:

✔ **Traditional display advertising:** Think of these as display banners that you see elsewhere across the Internet. These banner ads generally have cookie-based behavioral and other forms of targeting overlaid on top of them. They're sold and measured as traditional display banners are (primarily through CPMs, or cost per impressions, and CTRs, or click-through rates).

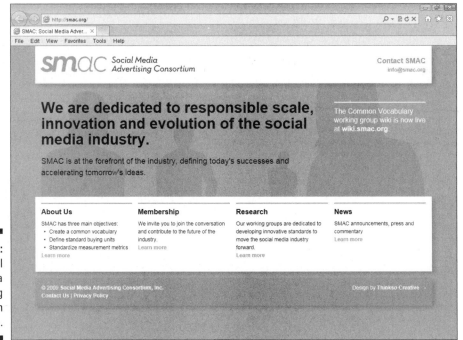

Figure 13-1:
The Social
Media
Advertising
Consortium
home page.

✔ **Social advertisements:** These ad formats bring a person's social graph into the ad unit itself, encouraging engagement (imagine if you saw a friend's photograph in an advertisement) or pushing similar advertisements to friends of a person who clicked a specific advertisement. Sometimes these social advertisements include user-generated content and are targeted based on browsing patterns of friends in a network.

✔ **Sponsorships:** Drawing inspiration from the advertorials of print publishing, these ad formats encourage bloggers specifically to discuss certain topics. You can establish specific rules governing what can be blogged about, but the bloggers have a lot of freedom too. When you see these posts, they're typically marked as sponsored ones. Sponsorships are becoming more popular on Twitter, too, although keep in mind that some bloggers find pay per post formats and incentives distasteful.

✔ **Influencer marketing:** Social platforms like CafeMom give you access to influencers who are given assignments to perform and then discuss the results on their blogs or their social platforms. For example, Kohl's gave CafeMom influencers gift cards and opportunities to explore their favorite colors at Kohl's stores. Each mom then returned to the site and wrote about their shopping experiences.

✔ **Widgets and applications:** Several social platforms allow the creation, launch, and seeding of widgets and applications on their platforms. You can either sponsor popular widgets or create new utilitarian or entertainment ones that fulfill a specific purpose for the users and have a tie-in with a brand. When launched, these widgets are promoted by the social platform and typically include a media buy as well. Sponsored music players on MySpace and myYearbook (`www.myyearbook.com`), for example, are becoming quite common.

✔ **Brand pages:** Just as the major social platforms allow for the creation of brand pages, so too do the other social platforms. These may differ in functionality and purpose based on the platform, but they're all virtual homes where you can promote your products, showcase your latest advertising, and launch promotions and contests. They can often include games, screen savers, desktop backgrounds, iconography, and the ability to recruit fans.

✔ **Gifting:** Mimicking Facebook's extremely successful gifting program, more and more niche social platforms offer gifting-related advertising. You can offer users gifts, such as a virtual birthday cake or chocolates that they can share with their friends. The gifts are extremely viral, and the advertising buy runs out once the gifts have.

✔ **Other promotional opportunities:** Most niche social platforms offer other similar related branding opportunities. These include sponsoring different parts of the social platform, sponsoring applications, polls, and contests. Other opportunities include pairing members together to accomplish tasks, sharing database information for remarketing and customer research purposes, and social merchandising.

Advertising formats for the social web are always in a state of flux. New ad formats are emerging just as old ones are being retired. The rules for advertising on the Internet are changing too as a result. The advertising formats by definition cannot be totally comprehensive.

If you're looking for guidance on blogger outreach and are worried about harassing bloggers and losing their support, take a look at the Ogilvy PR Blogger Outreach Code of Ethics (`http://blog.ogilvypr.com/2007/10/the-ogilvy-pr-blogger-outreach-code-of-ethics/`). It includes some excellent recommendations.

RFPing the vendors

After you've decided which social platforms are appropriate for your target audience and have a sense of what can be accomplished on them, consider issuing requests for proposals (RFPs). RFPs are created to gather bids from potential vendors. They detail what is expected and how it should be delivered. It may become a time-consuming effort, but it helps you in the long run. The RFPs matter if the cost of your marketing effort is going to exceed $7,500. If you're planning on spending less on your marketing efforts, it may be better to use the cheaper, less sophisticated self-service tools provided by the major social platforms. Here are some pointers to consider when issuing RFPs:

✔ **Describe your objectives explicitly.**

The social platforms are vying for your business. The more explicit and specific you can be about your marketing and campaign objectives, the more the social platforms can provide a response that meets your needs. Don't shy away from telling them exactly what they need to know. This means describing your audiences in incredible detail too. You're fundamentally looking to match your audiences with theirs and build engagement around it. Some social platforms are invariably a better fit than others.

✔ **Be clear about your benchmarks for success.**

The social platforms need to understand how you're going to measure the success of your marketing efforts. It's important to be very clear about those benchmarks because you'll probably be holding the platforms to them as well. Most social platforms (as well as other publishers on the Internet) want to know how they're going to be measured before participating in an RFP. Accordingly, a few of them may even choose to drop out of the process if they believe they can't achieve the expected measurements. They're always more interested in a long-term mutually beneficial relationship than a one-off partnership that hurts their credibility.

✔ **Recognize that you're getting free advice.**

When you're issuing a request for proposals, you're asking the social platforms to prove why they're the right places for you to market. But not only are you getting their credentials, you are also getting a lot of great ideas. As a result, it's important to be completely fair and transparent during the RFP process. Even if you do not choose a specific platform, you're going to learn a lot from them while going through the RFP process. Furthermore, they'd have put a lot of time and effort into responding to the proposal. You owe it to them to be transparent, clear, and appreciative of their efforts. Providing feedback on why you didn't choose them when you can is also important.

✔ **Beware that you can be limited by who you RFP.**

When issuing RFPs, it's easy to forget that you're limiting yourself by whom you ask to participate in the RFP process. Therefore, choose who you invite to participate in the RFP process carefully. Make sure that you're casting a wide net and are including all the different types of platforms that may be able to help you achieve your marketing objectives.

For example, social platform vendors that provide appvertising solutions on Facebook, like Buddy Media (www.buddymedia.com) or Context Optional (www.contextoptional.com), may get left off the RFP process because they're neither social platforms nor social platform infrastructure providers. They sit somewhere in between. The same applies to a social gaming company like Playfish (www.playfish.com), which provides some exciting opportunities for advertisers reaching specific audiences.

Evaluating and planning strategically

Planning is, of course, the most important step. As you plan your SMM campaign on a niche platform, you want to make sure that you're reaching the audiences that you want to and are engaging with them in an authentic, transparent, and meaningful fashion. Choosing the niche platform is always part art and part science. We've spent time discussing the science part of the question — how you find where your audiences are, what they're doing, and what tactics are most appropriate.

Now we want to look at the art piece of the equation. This means having an intuitive sense for the following items:

- **Knowing which social platforms can extend or strengthen your brand.**

  You don't want your brand to be tightly associated with a social platform that has a mixed reputation.

- **Having a sense of which social platforms are on the verge of breaking out and growing in size and scale.**

  Victoria's Secret Pink practiced SMM on Facebook in its early days and those efforts have paid off today. What's the next Facebook?

- **Being able to separate the wheat from the chaff.**

  This matters especially with the niche social platforms. Because hundreds of them are out there, many of which have a lot of traffic, knowing which ones have meaningful social engagement and can help you achieve your marketing objectives can be tricky.

- **Thinking beyond audiences and reach.**

  Traditional advertising online has always focused on audiences and where they are. But with social influence marketing, you have to think in terms of the influencers and the exponential value of their participation and engagement. Don't just use the traditional display banner metrics.

- **Being in it for the long run and not getting impatient.**

  Social media marketing requires patience: the patience to build relationships, to test, to learn and optimize, and to think beyond the confines of a campaign. These philosophies apply all the more when you're practicing SMM on the niche platforms. They may not give you the results that you want on the first day or the first month or the first quarter, but they've proved to showcase strong results over the long term.

> ✔ **Thinking holistically and strategically.**
>
> Most important, think holistically about your social media marketing efforts. Think about how you want your marketing efforts on the niche platforms to work with those on the major social platforms and on your own website too. Don't treat them all as separate, disjointed marketing efforts. They need to work together. And ideally, these marketing efforts should also be coordinated with offline marketing efforts too, where one feeds the other.

Moving Beyond the Platforms and the Blogosphere

A discussion about marketing in the social web would be incomplete without addressing the role that companies, which create new advertising opportunities on the social platforms, play. For lack of a better name, we call them *social platform enhancers*. They're not social platforms and do not have their own audiences. Nor are they advertising agencies or public relations firms that can help you market on the social platforms. Some of them function as advertising networks that sit on top of the social platforms, whereas others are more similar to software companies that build applications and widgets for the social platforms and the blogosphere. Regardless of how they fit into the social ecosystem, they play an important role and you can harness them for marketing purposes. In the next few sections, we discuss a few of the types of social platform enhancers.

Social advertising network

The first type of platform enhancer is the advertising network. Many of the most successful applications on Facebook belong to networks of applications that solicit advertising in a unified fashion by aggregating audiences. Sometimes the network is just one application developer who owns and manages a series of extremely popular applications. In other cases, several application providers band together to form a network and solicit advertising. RockYou (www.rockyou.com), shown in Figure 13-2, Skillpodmedia.com (www.skillpodmedia.com), and Slide (www.slide.com) are the leading advertising networks that reside within Facebook and MySpace. Their Facebook and MySpace applications serve as a home for brand advertising. Through them, you can place branded ads, application promotions, and integrated sponsorships next to specific applications on those social platforms.

Figure 13-2:
The
RockYou
home page.

Appvertisement providers

In conjunction with the advertising network are the platform enhancers who build appvertisements for brands. These *appvertisements* combine the best of advertisements with useful or entertaining applications, hence the name *appvertisement*. These appvertisements harness a person's social graph and are designed to provide meaningful value to users, often by having them contribute and personalize the application. This can be in the form of entertainment, information, or a utility that can sit within a social environment like a Facebook profile page. They're designed to be social in nature, encouraging people to install the application and have their friends install it too. These appvertisement providers work with your advertising agency to define and build the appvertisement and then guarantee a certain number of paid installations by leveraging the social advertising networks. Gigya (`www.gigya.com`), Buddy Media (`www.buddymedia.com`), and Context Optional (`www.contextoptional.com`) are all examples of appvertisement providers.

Blogger networks

It's hard to measure exactly how many active blogs are out there, but sources put that number at over 20 million. Probably not more than 10,000 have significant traffic. But even reaching these bloggers can be challenging. It's a question of scale. As a marketer, you certainly don't have time to reach out to 10,000 bloggers yourself. This is where blogger networks enter the picture. Every day, more and more bloggers are organizing into blogger networks that represent them. The representatives align marketers with the appropriate blogs, promote the blogger network, manage the relationships with the bloggers, and handle all advertiser relations. Many blogger networks also have dashboards that allow you to choose different advertising options by selecting audiences, specific topics, and blogs through which you want to market. The most important blogger network is probably Federated Media Publishing (www.federatedmedia.net), which represents probably 200–300 of the most influential blogs covering most topics. BlogHer (www.blogher.com) is another important blogger network, representing women bloggers. Six Apart (www.sixapart.com) also has a very active blogger network, as does WordPress (www.WordPress.com). In the case of Six Apart, as with Technorati and WordPress, their blogger networks represent blogs that reside on their own platforms. Other blogger networks include Twelvefold Media (www.twelvefold.com) and 20 Something Bloggers (www.20sb.net).

Taking Care of the Unpaid Media Basics

No marketing effort on the niche platforms is complete if you ignore all the possibilities on the unpaid side of the equation too. The social platforms, which depend on advertising as revenue, may not always be keen for you to deploy these tactics.

In the following sections, we discuss some tactics to consider in the unpaid realm.

These platforms afford the opportunity, and as long as you're not disrupting the platforms, breaking any privacy rules, or irritating the users on them, these tactics are fair game.

Wikipedia

You should always research how your company or brand is represented on Wikipedia (www.wikipedia.org), which is the free encyclopedia that anybody can edit. When you do find your company page, don't pepper it with marketing-speak. The page will just be reedited to the original version. Instead, read the page carefully and correct any misrepresentations. Shy away from promoting your company or products. Instead, point to complimentary articles. In fact, most social media professionals believe that you should never edit your own Wikipedia page because it may be considered a clear conflict of interest. Those professionals encourage brands to only comment on the discussion tab.

Flickr

This Flickr photo sharing website (www.flickr.com), shown in Figure 13-3, is starting to act and feel more and more like a social network. You'll want to search for your brand and company name on it to see what photographs are associated with your company. If photographs have been uploaded by someone else and tagged with your company name, you just have to live with them. However, you can also publish your own corporate and product imagery so that users know your own digital photography. We recommend setting up an official company account to share photographs, run contests, and encourage others to publish photographs, too.

Delicious

This bookmarking site (www.delicious.com) is extremely popular: Consumers use it to store their website bookmarks and to find other useful websites. All that you have to do here is make sure that your corporate website and any brand or product sites that you may have are bookmarked and tagged with your company name.

Digg

Here's another site (www.digg.com) that looks and feels like a social network but isn't. Digg is fundamentally a user-powered news aggregator. Each time you have an interesting piece of news to share about your company or product, publish it to Digg. Depending upon its newsworthiness, it may get voted to the top of a category, giving you an immense amount of free publicity.

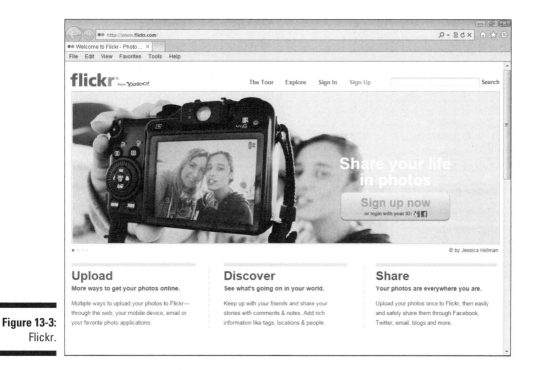

Figure 13-3:
Flickr.

Message boards

Regardless of how you use the social platforms, you'll want to know what conversations are happening on the message boards about your company and brand. The best way to do this is to use a service like Boardreader (www.boardreader.com) to scan the message boards for mentions of your company or brand. Here again, how you participate depends on the specific message board, the type of discussion, and whether you have to deal with a factual error, slander, or just category information. You'll have to make the judgment call for yourself.

Chapter 14

Accounting for the Influencers

*I*n Chapter 1, we briefly introduce the social influencers and how they affect purchasing decisions. In this chapter, we discuss social influencers in greater detail and explain why they matter, how you can reach them, and what best practices to deploy in the process of doing so. We focus on the social influencers who reside within the social graphs of your customers and how you can account for them in all your marketing efforts. Some of the concepts in this chapter rightly seem to draw inspiration from influencer marketing, with its roots in the public relations world, whereas other concepts will feel very different.

How influencers are defined is a controversial subject among marketers. Some marketers focus on what they consider to be key influencers, whereas others place more emphasis on everyday influencers. Back in Chapter 1, we introduce the three types of social influencers, which we believe accounts for all the types of influence taking place around a customer. Here's a quick recap:

▶ **Expert influencers** are considered authorities in the specific domain or are people whom others depend upon for information advice. They do a lot to build awareness and affect purchasing decisions at the consideration stage. One example of an expert influencer is a subject matter expert.

▶ **Referent influencers** are in a friend's social graph, but they may not be tightly connected with the user. One example of a referent influencer is your work colleagues.

> ✔ **Positional influencers** are that inner circle around the user and often have to live with the choices of the purchasing decision. One example of positional influencers is your family members.

We're now going to delve into the social influencer categories, starting with the expert influencers.

Knowing the Expert Influencers

The *Word of Mouth Marketing Influencer Handbook* explains that there are five types of influencers who you need to account for. When you think of expert influencers, be sure to cover these five types:

✔ People in formal positions of authority

✔ Individuals or institutions that are recognized as subject matter experts

✔ Media elites (journalists, commentators, and talk show hosts)

✔ Cultural elites (celebrities, artists, and musicians)

✔ Socially connected individuals (neighborhood leaders, members of community groups, online networks, and business networkers)

You can find out more about the Word of Mouth Marketing Association, shown in Figure 14-1, at www.womma.org.

Figure 14-1: The Word of Mouth Marketing Association.

As you scan the preceding list, you may be asking yourself the following questions:

- ✔ **Is your PR department nurturing the relationships with these expert influencers online via all the social platforms on which these expert influencers have set up presences?**

   Your public relations department is probably concerned with these expert influencers and is already developing relationships with them. That's good news, and it should be encouraged. It's not enough to know what the expert influencers are doing and saying in the physical world — you need to track their activity, commentary, and points of view online too. And most important, you need to build relationships with these influencers online as well.

- ✔ **Is it even possible to develop a relationship with these expert influencers online? Will they even care what you think?**

   You may wonder whether you *do* even need to track their online activities. If you're a marketer in a small business or maybe chief executive officer of a small business that doesn't have a formal marketing department, you may wonder whether they will even respond to your tweets, personal Facebook friend requests, and prodding e-mails. Those are all valid questions.

- ✔ **Are you pursuing the wrong list of influencers?**

   The final thing you may ask yourself is whether you even have the right list of expert influencers. Thanks to the excesses of several mammoth corporations, we now live in an age where trust in formal authority is at an all-time low. An April 2009 article in *The Economist* emphasized that consumers are increasingly distrusting big business and are turning to each other for advice. The experts that your consumers depended upon when making purchasing decisions may not be the very same experts that they are looking toward today.

What does all this mean? Quite simply, it means that you must begin by analyzing who are the expert influencers affecting brand affinity and purchasing decisions for your target markets. They may be all the people that your PR department is currently tracking, but that list of people may have changed too.

In the final analysis, you need to know the following:

- ✔ Who these expert influencers are
- ✔ Where they are active online
- ✔ Whether it is feasible to even develop a relationship with them on the social platforms in which they are participating
- ✔ How much influence they actually have

Recognizing the importance of influence

Can influence really be that important? Most studies say yes. Research studying the influence of people who regularly review products was done by University of Rhode Island business professor Kathleen Ferris-Costa. She found that these reviewers were 50 percent more likely to influence purchases. To support this finding, the Cone Report (a PR firm) found that 55 percent of all consumers go online to read user reviews.

How about social networks? Are people on these networks really influenced? The research firm Exact Target found that 90 percent of Facebook users trust the recommendations of their Facebook friends. That's evidence of real influence.

 Other departments within your company may already have relationships with the expert influencers that they have nurtured over a long period of time. That's a good thing. Find out whether existing relationships are in place before knocking on the doors of the expert influencers. They certainly don't want to be harassed by multiple people from one company.

Reaching the Expert Influencers

Different strategies exist for reaching and activating the expert influencers. How you reach them varies based on who they are, what you want them to accomplish, and where you think you have the best chance of establishing a relationship with them.

You may want to consider the following tactics:

- **Introduce yourself to them at conferences.** Most people at business conferences respond to a face-to-face introduction. Make use of that but beware of seeming too intrusive.

- **Reply to their tweets.** Responses to a tweet are expected. Just don't assume too much, too soon.

- **Comment on their blog posts.** A thoughtful reply to a post may get you more positive attention than you expect.

- **Friend them in Facebook.** You may not get their complete attention if you have a personal profile page, but you may at least get on their radar screen.

The good news is that influencers like to influence, and as long as you have a promising value proposition, they will at the very least listen to you.

Keep in mind that nurturing expert influencers is an investment in the long term, and you may not always get the response you want from them immediately. Also remember that influencers draw their strength and importance from being unbiased, independent, and credible. Don't ask them to compromise that position.

Expert influencers like to be in the know. Provide them with exclusive sneak peeks, and they'll be grateful for the opportunity to see and talk about your product before anyone else does. You can use that access to information to deepen your relationship with them.

Reaching the expert influencers may be easy depending upon your industry, the size of your business, and the product you are selling. But for other marketers, that may not be the case. For example, if you're a marketer for a small business, reaching expert influencers is going to be even harder because these people may not be high-profile or visible. You'll have to really seek them out. Here are some tips for reaching expert influencers:

✔ **Ask your customers who they seek out for advice.**

Very little in marketing beats firsthand customer research, and the same applies to social influence marketing. You can identify and reach the expert influencers by asking your consumers who they are and where they spend their time.

✔ **Pay attention to the media.**

Keep an eye out for the experts who are quoted frequently by the media when your product or category is discussed. Also keep an eye out for who appears on television. Make a list of these experts and use that list as a basis to research their influence.

✔ **Look at your competitive environment.**

Your competitors, suppliers, and business partners probably seek out the experts just as you do. In many cases, these experts sit on the advisory boards of other companies that operate in your space. Understand who these people are. A lot of that information is freely available online.

✔ **Attend conferences and exhibitions.**

The expert influencers are often called upon to give keynote addresses to industry conferences, lead seminars, and pass judgment on new products and services at exhibitions. Pay attention to these people at those events.

✔ **Seek out the industry analysts.**

The analysts often have an outsize influence on customers in your product category. Their influence increases dramatically in the business-to-business space, where customers depend upon them for advice when making large-scale purchasing decisions. Pay attention to them and to what they have to say.

✔ **Evaluate their online footprint.**

Tools like Technorati (www.technorati.com), as shown in Figure 14-2, rank all blogs based on the number of inbound links to them. Search the rankings by your product category and see which independent blogs rank high. Those bloggers are expert influencers to develop a relationship with. Use other professional tools for the rankings, such as the Alexa scores (www.alexa.com), the Google PageRank, the number of RSS subscribers (often listed on the blog itself), and proprietary technology like the influencer identification ones from Collective Intellect (www.collectiveintellect.com).

✔ **Become an influencer yourself.**

Sometimes there's no better way to influence than to become an influencer yourself. Seek out leadership positions in your community and in your industry by joining trade groups and industry associations. Make it a goal to speak at conferences in your field. Using these tactics, you'll become an influencer and will get access to other influencers.

Figure 14-2:
The
Technorati
home page.

Tapping into the Referent Influencers

Until recently, there was no way to reach referent influencers. In fact, in conversations about influencers, no one mentioned referent influencers because they couldn't be identified and therefore were not even thought about. Marketers had no way of identifying them, tracking their behavior, or marketing to them specifically. For all practical purposes, they did not exist. That's now changed because consumers connect with their friends and make their social graphs available through the social networks.

Social graphs are commonly defined as the global mapping of everyone in the world and how they are related to each other. When I refer to an individual's *social graph,* I'm referring to who is mapped to that individual and how he relates to that individual. Referent influencers are people in your friendship circle, such as your high school friends or people you've become friendly with at work. You may be close to only a few of them, but you probably observe the activities of them all on your favorite social platform.

The holy grail of social influence marketing is increasingly considered the ability to identify which referent influencers are most powerful and have the highest impact on brand affinity and purchasing decisions. After you've identified them, the next question is, how does a marketer reach these referent influencers that surround their customers? They matter because it has been statistically proved that networked neighbors (or those consumers linked to prior customer) adopt the service or product at rates three to five times greater than baseline groups. The research also shows that these network neighbors impact purchasing decisions very directly too.

The referent influencers themselves break down into two categories, which we cover next, and it is important to differentiate between the two.

Anonymous referent influencers

These are everyday people who are extremely active on the social platforms and blog, upload, comment, rate, and share much more than other consumers who share their same demographics. By virtue of the volume of their activity on the various social platforms, the anonymous referent influencers carry weight. Your customers probably don't think of them as experts, but they do notice what these people are doing online.

Known referent influencers

These are the everyday people who reside specifically within the social graphs of your customers and are known to your customer. The best way to think about this group is to consider your high school class. Of the approximately 300 kids who may have been in the class, there were probably 10 or 15 who everyone else looked up to and followed. These are the cool kids who everyone wanted to be like even though they may not have known them well. These are the referent influencers.

Marketing to the referent influencers is all about knowing who they are, the weight they carry, whether they reside within your customer's social graph, and how to reach and activate them to influence your customer.

Reaching the Referent Influencers

Referent influencers are not easy to reach. Most social platforms do not allow marketers to mine the social graphs of their users, so identifying these people and reaching them can be challenging. As a result, it can be difficult to identify these referent influencers and activate them.

But there's good news too. Some enterprising advertising technology companies have been researching ways to reach these referent influencers without compromising the privacy of your customers or their circle of friends. Reaching the referent influencers through these methods is safe and reliable, although it does cost you money, with the amount depending on how many referent influencers you're trying to reach. In the next few sections, I discuss how these companies help you reach the referent influencers.

Not all tactics for reaching referent influencers need to be paid for. Your company's Facebook page can be a great place to build a community and encourage referent influencers to influence your customers by incentivizing them with competitions, coupons, and special offers. Your customers who like your Facebook page will probably bring their referent influencers to the page too if you give them incentives to do so.

Social graph analysis

Using database technologies, companies can crawl the major social networks in a similar fashion to the way the search engines crawl web pages. These companies can create a mapping of users and how they relate to each other on the major social platforms. They can also capture personality attributes of the users, the number of friends they have, how active they are on a social platform, and whether their friends respond to actions that they take. Companies in this space include RapLeaf (`www.rapleaf.com`) and LookUp Page (`www.lookuppage.com/`), which use metrics like friend count, social persuasion track record, and *influence context measurement* (meaning how the subject matter affects influence) to identify the influencers.

These advertising technology companies map your e-mail database against their social graph database to determine the overlapping customers and to identify the influential ones from the mix. That serves as a starting point for you to then market to the referent influencers and encourage them to talk about a brand.

A place to get started creating your own social graph is Google's Social Graph API, as shown in Figure 14-3, at `http://code.google.com/apis/social graph`. This lets you add social functionality to your own website, encouraging your friends and customers to join the mini-social network.

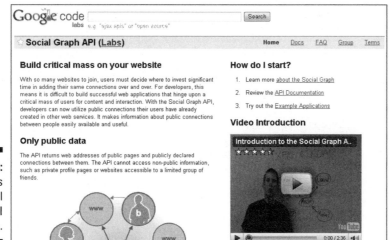

Figure 14-3:
Google's
Social
Graph API
page.

Cookie data

Other technology companies analyze cookie data to infer the relationships between people and target similar advertising to them both. If one set of users responds well to the advertisements, they then present the same advertisements to other similar people or to the friends of the original group in similar social networks, conversations, or websites as the original set of users. It allows for your advertising to reach anonymous referent influencers. Keep in mind here that this applies only if you have an advertising budget and are advertising online. Otherwise, you won't be able to take advantage of the cookie data. Two companies that focus on this are 33Across (www.33across.com) and m6d (www.m6d.com).

Website behavior

You can do a lot on your website to allow for the referent influencers to converge and positively influence each other. From the most basic of solutions, like implementing customer reviews, to creating discussion forums where customers can talk about issues of concern, your website can be a destination where people congregate and talk to each other. Recent developments like Facebook Connect, which we discuss in Chapter 7, address how you can more directly enable your prospective customers to bring their referent influencers to your website.

After you've identified these referent influencers, be sure to give them the best possible service if they're customers. Not only will you increase the sales from them, but you'll also increase sales among the people that they influence directly. As a recent Huffington Post article pointed out, American Express gives its influencers (who they identify by how much they spend) a distinct credit card with special benefits that include a concierge service and first-class upgrades.

Use this group to improve your products and services, too. They're typically people who have strong opinions, care about the products, and want to impact product design. Ask their opinions — or at the very least, share new products with them — before you do so with anyone else. Similarly, also consider giving them special discounts and coupons and cultivate their loyalty by marketing to them with additional care.

Tapping into the Positional Influencers

Finally, there are the positional influencers. These are the people who are closest to your customers and influence them the most at the point of purchase. Because they are the people who have to live with the purchasing decision, they are the most vested in it too. But they're not celebrities, so they're not always noticeable and can be the hardest to find. They're important, but marketing to them can be similarly difficult.

What makes tapping into the positional influencers harder still is the fact that how big a role they play in a purchasing decision varies dramatically by the purchase. For example, if you were to buy a desk for your home, your spouse or significant other (arguably the most important positional influencer in your life) would have a huge impact on the purchasing decision. Their opinion would heavily influence where you shop and what you choose. On the other hand, if you were purchasing a laptop for professional use, they would play a much smaller role in the purchasing decision. This is because the choice doesn't impact them significantly and the product isn't of interest to them even though it's a high-consideration purchase.

Without a doubt, positional influencers are important. Identifying them can be challenging, as can developing an understanding of the weight they may carry.

Sometimes it may be hard to separate the referent influencers from the positional influencers, especially when you're marketing on a social platform. In those cases, it doesn't matter as much. What matters is that you should give your customers incentives to bring their influencers to you so that you can market to them as well. Focus on that, and the right influencers will be influenced, and then they'll do the influencing for you!

The following sections cover tips to allow for positional influencers to play the role they normally do best.

Understanding the circles of influence around your customers

Most important is to understand who will be most impacted by the purchasing decisions of your customers. That alone will tell you who the positional influencers are and how important their influence is. For example, with first-time car purchases, family members are very important positional influencers because they'll be riding in the car and, in some cases, driving it too.

Letting consumers shape and share the experience

It may be hard for you to reach those positional influencers, but your customers will reach them for you. Make sure that your e-commerce website or even your campaign-centric microsite allows for the sharing of content and posting to Facebook and other social platforms. Let the consumers shape and share the experiences in any format that they want. Make it easy for customers to pluck information off your website and carry it elsewhere and to their positional influencers.

Articulating your product benefits for multiple audiences

You probably always assume that you're selling a product to your target customer, ignoring the fact that social influencers play a big role in the purchasing decision. If you know who the influencers are, articulate your product benefits so that they resonate with the influencers too. To go back to car purchases once more: If you're selling a car to a college student demographic, tout the safety benefits because the students' parents will most probably be involved in the purchasing decision. Don't ignore them.

Fishing where the fish are

This is becoming a cliché in social media marketing, but the point holds strongest in the context of positional influencers. As these influencers are the hardest to find yourself, you need to make sure that you're marketing and selling your products where these positional influencers probably influence your customers. So it goes without saying that you need to have a deep presence on all the social platforms where your customers and their influencers are congregating. But it also means that you need to design your website or your presence on the social platforms to encourage your customers to reach out to those positional influencers. You need to include the basic Share This functionality that lets a user take product information from your website and socialize it with her influencers. You can start by allowing users to share your website info with Add This, as shown in Figure 14-4, at www.addthis.com.

Giving badges and promotions

As consumers, we buy products for many different reasons. The product purchase can be a necessity, a comfort, or a luxury. It can also be a status symbol or a statement about your own identity. Whatever it may be, you want to make sure that you give your customers a way to promote their purchase among their peer group. You want them to be able to tell their referent and positional influencers what they've purchased and how it'll benefit them. As a result, it is important to allow for additional *badging* (as shown in Figure 14-5), which is the ability for your customer to announce his affinity with your product by placing a badge of it on his blog, social network profile, or website.

Figure 14-4: Add This functionality in use on a blog.

Share button

Twitter badge

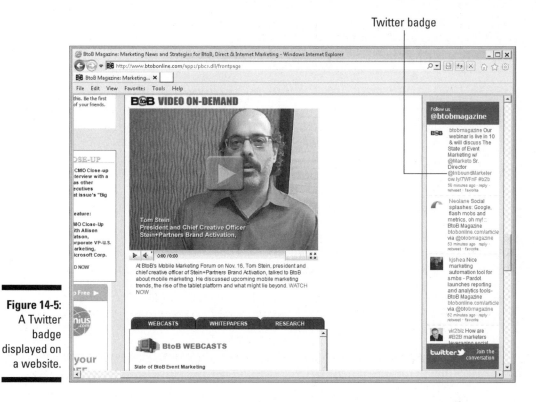

Figure 14-5:
A Twitter
badge
displayed on
a website.

Offering friends and family incentives

When talking about social influencers and the role they play in brand affinity and purchasing decisions, it is easy to forget that many marketers have been practicing these concepts in the physical world for decades. One of the most popular examples of reaching out to social influencers is in the form of "friends and family" incentives. For example, AT&T has introduced a special family plan for its mobile phone service. If your whole family uses the service, you get discounts on the monthly plan. The best way to engage the positional influencers around your customers is to have your customers engage them for you. You get them to engage the positional influencers by giving them incentives to do so or by converting the purchasing decision into a group decision.

Translating Influence to the Offline World

For all the discussions about social influencers, we would be remiss if we didn't discuss how this concept ties into influence in the offline space. The online world is not completely separated from how influence works in the real world. The following sections include recommendations for how you can tap into social influencers to affect physical world purchasing decisions.

Putting your customer reviews in your stores

If you sell products in stores, consider putting the customer reviews that have been created by customers on your website next to the actual products in the physical stores. If there isn't space to place customer reviews, at least include the customer ratings. Staples is one company that has already started doing this. The result is that in-store sales of products with the customer ratings have increased. Along with the customer reviews, consider adding expert reviews and ratings. They do a lot to give your customers confidence about the purchasing decision and also help them choose between products.

Marrying social media marketing with events and PR

Here's a tip about social media marketing that's worth paying a lot of attention to: Marketers who tie together social media marketing initiatives with traditional events and surround them with PR tactics invariably have immense success. When you're trying to tap into social influencers, consider organizing an event that your customers can bring their social influencers to. Promote the event heavily on the social platforms, and use your presence on those platforms as a way to manage invitation lists, reminders, and post event communications. For example, send out invitations through Facebook and encourage your potential customers to RSVP through Facebook itself. You can also create a special hash tag (#) for your event so that when you're tweeting about your event, others will see it. It helps generate buzz for your company and encourages people to attend future events.

Measuring online buzz and offline influence

Even though it may not always be obvious, there's a very direct relationship between online buzz and offline influence. What is talked about on the social platforms often gets translated to real world conversations when people interact with each other at work, in the shopping malls, and at home. Consider tracking how your social media marketing activities translate into offline influence. How? By using surveys to track conversations about your brand before, during, and after a social media marketing campaign. If you're a large brand, you may want to use a market research firm to help you understand the ongoing buzz about your brand in the physical world.

Connecting influencers at meet-ups

We've talked about marrying events with social media marketing so that your potential customers expose their influencers to your brand too. You may want to run specific programs just for the influencers who play a significant role in impacting brand and purchasing decisions in your category. Whether they be expert, referent, or positional influencers, you may want to consider organizing programs that address them directly. Some of these can be real-world events too. Insurance companies put a lot of effort into developing relationships with parents of new drivers because they know they heavily impact the first car purchase. And because parents are always concerned about the well-being of their children, they're more likely to push for better auto insurance. Two services that you can use to create those events are Meetup (www.meetup.com) and House Party (www.houseparty.com), which enable companies to connect with local communities around their products or categories.

Treating your stores as cyber cafés

Bookstores like Barnes & Noble have blurred the lines between their physical stores and their online storefront. You can buy books online and return them in the store. You can get notifications about in-store events in your neighborhood through e-mail and customers can look up books online while they're in the stores. They also organize readings and book clubs and encourage customers to bring their friends to them and promote the events online too. Online or offline, these bookstores don't care: They encourage deeper interaction and encourage customers to bring their social influencers with them at every stage.

Putting Twitter on the big screen

Twitter is all the rage these days, and with good reason. The follow-follower dynamic and the 140-character limit lend themselves to frequent, short bursts of communication. But have you considered promoting your Twitter account in your physical stores? Or better still, have you considered having a live Twitter stream on a screen in each of your stores to show customers how you're answering the queries of others, responding to problems, promoting specific products, and deepening relationships with your community? Call it the Twitter influence, but the way in which you're interacting with your other customers on the social platforms can strongly influence a customer to purchase from you as well. Don't miss that opportunity.

Part IV

Old Marketing Is New Again with SMM

The 5th Wave — By Rich Tennant

"Woo!"

In this part . . .

*I*n Part IV, you learn how to transform your own Web site to allow for social media marketing. We also explain what it means to be an authentic and engaged advertiser — in other words, how to take your existing advertising efforts social and get more mileage out of them.

In Chapter 15, we give you recommendations on how to retool your corporate website to allow for social media marketing. In Chapter 16, we show how earned and paid media can help with your social media marketing efforts and how to leverage your SMM efforts with offline marketing efforts. Chapter 17 discusses how to tap into the mobile phone market to spread your SMM campaign. In Chapter 18, you find out how to get your employees practicing social media marketing in your own company. Chapter 19 goes in-depth on how to measure your campaign to find out how successful it was.

In Chapter 20, we discuss the fundamentals of social media governance. We also show you what models of governance you can choose to make applying them easier. Chapter 21 discusses how real-time marketing is making a big impact on SMM and how you can jump in.

Chapter 15

Practicing SMM on Your Website

Corporate websites have gone through many changes since their introduction. When Stephanie began working at AOL in 1994, the companies she worked with to create their AOL websites were initially concerned that having a website might be too big a step, but as they watched some of their adventurous competitors do it, they started to become a bit more comfortable.

Still, companies needed websites to be all things to all people. They had multiple audiences; sometimes needed to sell the product directly; and had to create a timeless, stable impression. The corporate site didn't cater just to prospective customers, but to existing customers, shareholders, members of the press, business partners, and suppliers, too. It needed to carry information and include functionality that met all their needs. What's more, the corporate website needed to reflect the company's brand; the company couldn't change its look and feel based on the whims of a specific campaign.

For this reason, the concept of microsites came to be. Companies built these mini websites to support display banner campaigns, and the microsites were time-bound and oriented toward specific events or audiences. These events could be Christmas shopping, Father's Day, or back-to-school promotions for teenagers. Creative uses for the display banners directly reflected on the microsite, which would typically contain information about the specific offers. After all, with companies spending so much money on the display banners, they needed to drive visitors who clicked the banners to a site that extended the experience of the banner. This strategy of separating the corporate website from the microsite and treating the microsite as an extension of the display banners worked for a long time. But then the social media revolution came, and it all began to change.

Websites have again become the hub of corporate activity. From this hub, you are sent to supporting social media sites that can hold contests, acquaint you with your local store, and provide you with the review information you need to make purchasing decisions.

In this chapter, we give you recommendations on how to retool your corporate website to allow for social media marketing, along with tips for opening your corporate website to the social web in a meaningful fashion.

Moving Toward the SMM-Focused Website

Today's consumers are not as easily impressed as they once were. They want more than a campaign; they want a committed and longer-term relationship with your company to which they give their time and money. And given that you spend so much money in advertising to your customers, it only makes sense to generate more than an impression or a single sale from your campaign. Yes, consumers will always want those short-term deals and the back-to-school offers, but they do want more.

When consumers click banner links today, they expect to be taken to a website that tells them everything about your product or brand that they're interested in. They want to be able to view your offer and make a purchase, but also navigate the rest of your website. These consumers want to be able to view what else you have for sale, learn more about your company, and share that information with their friends. Having a disjointed microsite experience separate from the corporate website makes it more difficult for them to accomplish their goals.

Today's consumers visiting your website don't want to just depend on your brand or company to tell them what to buy and whether the offer you're pushing at them is special. They want to draw that conclusion themselves with the assistance of their social influencers. So as you think about social media marketing on your website, first and foremost, consider moving away from designing and building microsites to support online advertising campaigns. Your consumers want more.

Making the Campaign and the Website Work Together

The best way to make the advertising campaign and your website work harmoniously in a social world is to link the two. You should also link with the various social platforms on which you have a presence. In the sections that follow, we tell you how you can create those links.

Treating your website as a hub not a destination

The first step in practicing SMM on your website is recognizing that it's a hub that fits into a larger digital ecosystem supporting your brand. This digital ecosystem includes your website; your display banners across the Internet; your presence on various social platforms; and the conversations about your brand on blogs, the social platforms, in online communities, and discussion forums. Your purpose shouldn't be to bring people to your website and entice them to stay on it as long as possible. That might contradict every traditional marketing principle, but it's true.

If someone wants to know everything about your company — good, bad, or ugly — he should feel that your website is the best *starting point* for him.

Design your website as a hub versus a destination and your website will immediately become more valuable to your customers. Even though this may mean that you'll be pointing your consumers to external sites, they'll always treat yours as a starting point in the future.

The Mars brand Skittles designed its website (www.skittles.com) so that every navigation item links to a different social platform. There is no more true Skittles website, only a home page (see Figure 15-1). You have the option of clicking on social media platform links, or you can scroll down and get involved in the activities right from the home page. For example, you can upload your own video or picture to the "rainbow" by clicking the Upload to the Rainbow link. While you move between all these social platforms, the Skittles navigation box stays in the background so that you can move between all the Skittles social pages very easily.

Linking prominently to your presence on social platforms

As long as customers interact with your brand, it matters little where they're interacting with it. For many consumers, the Internet is the social platform on which they share information, connect with their friends, develop business relationships, and get entertained. They're also interacting with brands on these social platforms. That's not a bad thing. Highlight your presence on these social platforms right on your website, too. If your customers want to interact with you on social platforms, allow them to do so by showing them how they can. For example, The Perfect Bass, a company that sells bass guitars (not fish), displays links to their other sites on their home page, as shown in Figure 15-2.

Figure 15-1:
The Skittles
website.

Depending on your business model and the strength of your brand, how prominently you link to the social platforms may differ. For example, if you're a luxury handbag brand that likes to entice customers by creating a feeling of mystique and exclusiveness, linking extensively to the social platforms may do more harm than good. However, if you're Coca-Cola and are keen to deeply immerse yourself in the pop culture, linking to social platforms where conversations are happening (potentially about events that Coke may sponsor) becomes important.

Promoting campaigns on your website home page

As we mention earlier in the chapter, your corporate website serves many audiences and has many purposes. But that shouldn't stop you from using the featured zone on your home page to promote a campaign. That's the first step in linking the campaigns with the website. This may be obvious to you, but many companies don't do this. The Perfect Bass displays its products for sale on its home page, as shown in Figure 15-3.

Figure 15-2: ThePerfect Bass.com displays its social media links.

Social media icons

Figure 15-3: Products for sale on ThePerfect Bass.com home page.

Product for sale

The benefit of doing this is that after you link the two, you're creating a reason to direct customers who have come to your website through your campaign to areas of your website where they can interact with each other. You've suddenly opened the door for social influence to take place.

If you're using featured zones on your home page to promote campaigns, be sure to update them frequently with new promotions. No one likes to see the same promotions again and again. It implies that the company is neglecting its website.

Encouraging deeper interaction through your website

Consumers who respond to your campaign want to learn more about the products or services you're selling them, and you can do more than just provide them with that information. Instead of just bringing them the information, you can connect them with other prospective or current customers by pointing them to a discussion area on your website (if you have one) or third-party review sites that discuss your product. You can also introduce a live-chat feature, whereby they can talk to you and other customers in real time.

More and more companies are building community functionality into their websites, where customers discuss potential products, critique existing ones, and exchange thoughts with one another. These communities go a long way in convincing a prospective customer to buy from you. The AV Club's Wrapped Up in Books section sponsors a live chat for customers to hang out in, as shown in Figure 15-4.

Asking customers to critique the campaign

Customers feel they own a bit of your company when they're loyal to your products. They want to have the inside scoop on your company, products, and advertising campaigns, too. The behind-the-scenes advertising campaign assets fuel their interest in the company. Make sure that your TV, print, and even digital advertisements are available for your fans to view on your website. Allow them to critique the campaign assets and provide feedback. It serves to build trust, enthusiasm, and ownership among them.

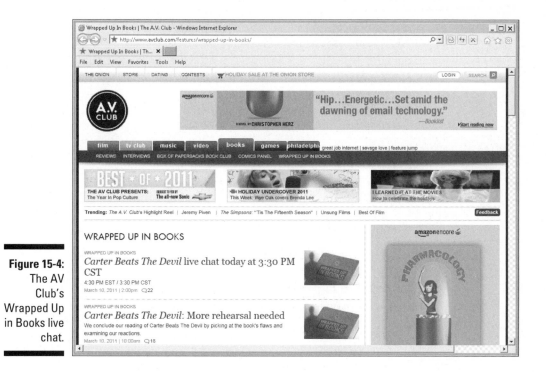

Figure 15-4:
The AV
Club's
Wrapped Up
in Books live
chat.

Rethinking Your Website

Practicing SMM philosophies on your website isn't only about approaching campaigns differently and tying them into your website more strategically. You can also rethink your whole website experience to enable more direct social influence to take place. Redesigning your website with the social influence elements can increase sales and deepen relationships with your core customers. In the following section, we give you some recommendations on how to do that for four important areas of your website.

All these recommendations may not be applicable to your website (some require you to sell online, for example), but even those are worth reading nevertheless.

Product pages

The most critical change you can make to product pages on your website is to include customer reviews. Nothing sells a product better than actual customer reviews and ratings of the products. The customer reviews provide the shopper with the perspective of other customers. They give your customers the inside scoop on your products — the ins and outs of them and why they're good or bad. Customer reviews are extremely popular. According to a 2010 eMarketer survey of U.S. Internet users who are moms, customer reviews on the video site EXPO are trusted nearly 12 times more than the manufacturer's description. An eConsultancy survey in July 2010 found that a high product rating increases the likelihood of purchase by 55 percent. Amazon is the most well-known example of a company that provides customer reviews, as shown in Figure 15-5.

You'll find that customer reviewers serve a couple of purposes:

✔ **They help sell products, no matter the review.**

Even though you may be worried that customer reviews may damn your products, they invariably convince customers to purchase, and they lead to more sales. Unflattering customer reviews may drive your customers away from certain products, but they also drive customers to peruse other products on your site, which could result in a purchase.

Figure 15-5:
Amazon customer reviews.

✔ **You get feedback about what does and doesn't work.**

The customer reviews also serve as a valuable feedback mechanism, telling you what products are liked and why certain products are purchased more than others. Many a marketer has learned valuable insights about missing features of their products by reading the customer reviews on their websites.

According to research by the e-tailing group in June 2008, of merchants who adopted customer reviews, 58 percent said improving customer experience was the most important reason for adding reviews to their sites, followed by building customer loyalty (47 percent), driving sales (42 percent), and maintaining a competitive advantage (37 percent).

There were similar findings from a case study done by Bazaarvoice in conjunction with CheapCaribbean.com. In July of 2010, CheapCaribbean.com added Bazaarvoice ratings and reviews to their site. They found that during the period August–September 2010, those who looked at the reviews converted to sales 123 percent more often than those who did not.

In addition to adding customer reviews on your website, you can incorporate them in other ways:

✔ **In your search engine advertisements:** Some retailers have found customer reviews and ratings to be so successful that they now include customer ratings in their search engine advertisements. Including the ratings in those advertisements has also increased the *click-through rate* (the number of clicks in an advertisement that drives users to the website) to their websites.

✔ **On your physical shelves:** Other companies, such as Staples, include customer ratings sourced from their website on the display shelves of their physical stores. Even when customers see the ratings in a physical store, they are influenced.

It's in the customer reviews and ratings that your customers truly influence each other. Allow for that social influence, and you'll probably see it building trust, increasing sales, and improving customer service.

News and events pages

News and events pages, which are often referred to as the press room, provide ample opportunity to allow for social influence with the injection of social features. The first step is to make all content in your press room portable so that journalists and others who use the page can easily pluck the content and publish it elsewhere on the web, in whatever format may suit them. This means enabling sharing functionality on all your press room pages. You want to make it really easy to share the content here.

It's also important to craft your press releases for the blogosophere, in which you'll find the people who can take and amplify your message better than anyone else. But to do so effectively, you need to publish the content in your press release area in a blogger-friendly format.

Making your content blogger friendly means publishing what is referred to as a *social media press release,* which is a press release that's optimized for bloggers, with excerpts and quotes at the top of the press release. From a social media press release, bloggers can also download images and resize them easily. Shift Communications publishes a template for social media press releases (as shown in Figure 15-6). You can find the complete Shift Communications Social Media Press Release template at `www.shiftcomm.com/downloads/smprtemplate.pdf`. It includes the following components:

- ✔ **Contact information:** Includes fields for the client contact, spokesperson, and agency contact information. Listed for each are their names, phone numbers, instant messenger addresses, websites, Skype usernames, and blog addresses.

- ✔ **News release headline:** This is the headline for the press release. It can also include a subheadline.

- ✔ **Core news facts:** Here, in bullet point form, you can list the core news facts for your press release. Be aware that you should use this to list facts only. Hyperbole is not recommended.

- ✔ **Links and RSS feeds:** Next you need to set up a link and RSS feed to a Delicious page (`www.delicious.com`). That page needs to directly offer hyperlinks to relevant historical, trend, market, product, and competitive sources.

- ✔ **Multimedia:** Below that come the photo, MP3, podcast, graphic, and video links, as required. This can also include links to white papers.

- ✔ **Preapproved quotes:** Place preapproved quotes from management, analysts, customers, and partners here.

- ✔ **Links to relevant coverage:** It's important to link to existing coverage of the story, as it's invaluable for any journalist or blogger.

- ✔ **Boilerplate statements:** The template includes a place for these, but as you can see, their importance is significantly reduced.

- ✔ **Tagging and tracking links:** You can include Technorati tags, Delicious links, and other RSS feeds here.

Publishing press releases on your website (and through the wires) in this format makes them blogger-friendly. And as the line between mainstream journalists and bloggers blurs, these press releases become more and more valuable.

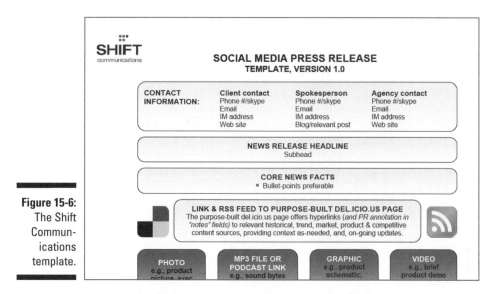

Figure 15-6:
The Shift
Commun-
ications
template.

About Us and Contact Us pages

The About Us pages of a website have traditionally included management team profiles, investor information, company history, contact and address information, company values, and fact sheets. Those sections are extremely important, and you can make them all the more so by injecting social features. For example, include links to the blogs and Twitter profiles of the management team along with the traditional profiles.

The chief executive officer of your company may want to include a YouTube clip of himself sharing his vision for the company and how the company can serve customers. The company history page can link to external websites that explain more about the company's history, and the fact sheet can include quotes and factoids from third-party providers and individual experts. On these pages, you can feature expert influencers who endorse the company. See Chapter 14 for more information on the expert influencers.

The Contact Us page requires special attention. It mustn't be a page that lists only telephone numbers, e-mail addresses, and locations. In today's world, customers assume *Contact Us* means that they can talk to an employee right away about a problem. Include live chat technology on the Contact Us page (if your company sells a consumer product) and also link to your company's Twitter feed. Figure 15-7 shows how to contact CafeMom, which has links to Facebook, Twitter, its mobile site and traditional contact info such as its e-mail address.

Figure 15-7:
Contact
CafeMom.

Contact CafeMom

The Twitter feed matters because the customer may want to engage in a conversation with someone in your company directly then and there. What better place than Twitter, where you can invariably make a statement that you're authentic and transparent?

Another potential solution for the contact us page is to enable customers to provide product and business ideas to your company. Call it crowdsourcing, but customers often don't mind giving free advice to companies. The My Starbucks Idea site (www.mystarbucksidea.com), as shown in Figure 15-8, solicits feedback from customers and has been extremely successful. In the last two years, it's received thousands of ideas from customers about every part of its business.

On the site, customers can comment on the ideas submitted and rate them, pushing the best ones to the top. The most successful ideas are implemented by Starbucks in some form or the other. It is a win-win situation already. The customers feel empowered to provide constructive feedback, their voices are heard, and the company benefits from the fabulous ideas. Another good example of crowdsourcing is the Dell IdeaStorm (www.ideastorm.com), which encourages customers to post ideas about Dell products and services.

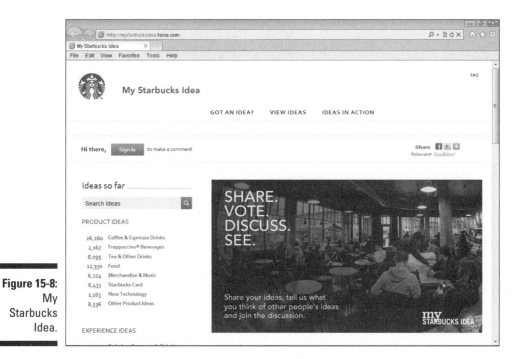

Figure 15-8:
My
Starbucks
Idea.

Private online communities

Every day, more companies are building customer communities for the purposes of conducting customer research and soliciting feedback on product concepts. These customer communities (accessible via your website) are typically closed communities with only select customers participating by invitation. Customers are recruited either through third-party vendors or by mining customer databases for brand advocates who have strong, thoughtful opinions on the products. Marketers use these customers to road-test product concepts and marketing messages and provide feedback on everything from shopping experiences to customer service. These communities typically include live chat, discussion boards, polls, and multimedia sharing. You'll typically give customers special benefits for participating, such as discount coupons, quicker access to new products, and passes to special events and promotions. Rarely do companies directly pay customers for their participation. Communispace (www.communispace.com) and Passenger (www.thinkpassenger.com) are two leading technology providers of private online communities.

By listening to your customers through these customer research communities, you get important real-time intelligence on shifting patterns of behavior and trends, identify new product ideas and improve existing ones, deepen loyalty by your ability to listen, and invariably develop brand evangelists who can help promote your new products and launches. Think of these private online communities as free focus groups that are with you 365 days of the year, and you'll start to realize how beneficial they can be. Companies — including JC Penney, Mercedes Benz USA, Mattel, Adidas, and Microsoft — use private online communities to test products, learn how to respond to a PR crisis, and launch new initiatives. In fact, Mattel's The Playground, which is a private community of 500 moms, was extremely valuable when the company had a series of product recalls of popular toys in 2007. The company used the group as a sounding board for recommendations on how best to handle the PR crisis. The result was that even though they had a damaging product recall, fourth quarter sales were up 6 percent. This is largely because those 500 moms in the private online community gave Mattel insightful advice on how to respond to the crisis.

In fact, many believe that these private online communities are more valuable than any traditional form of market research. You can use this feedback to support the launch of a new product and create a body of social influencers, who can be provided with the tools with which to promote the launch. In other cases, you can use this community as a way to deepen existing relationships with your customers.

Facebook Social Plug-ins

Practicing SMM on your website doesn't just mean opening it up to the social web by making the content more pluckable and including tools that enable consumers to share the content more easily. It also means making your own website truly social by bringing your customers' social graphs to your website.

With the advent of technologies like Facebook's s social plug-ins (shown in Figure 15-9), OpenSocial, and Microsoft's own data portability initiatives, it's now possible to bring a consumer's social graph to your website. For example, you can include the login information for Facebook on your website using a plug-in. Upon login, the user's friends list also appears on your website. You can then share their activity for your user. In other words, your website becomes a location where a consumer can see and participate with his existing network of friends as he makes brand affinity and purchasing decisions.

Through these technologies, any third-party website (including yours) can take a customer's profile data — including age, gender, region, and interests — from his profile on a social platform and match them to any action, such as purchasing, commenting, or reviewing. If you're a user logging in to a website, you can, for example, see user-generated content prioritized to display your friends first, followed by other people in your region, of your age, and with your interests.

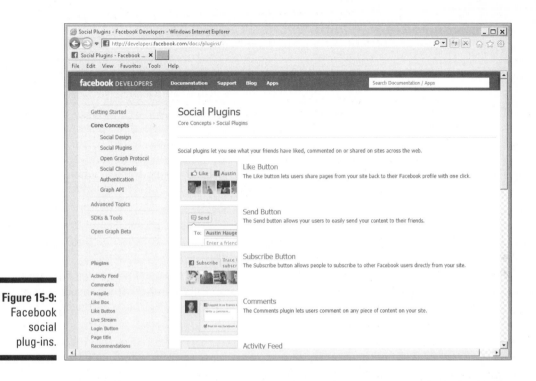

Figure 15-9:
Facebook
social
plug-ins.

Probably the most famous example of portable social graphs is what CNN did on Inauguration Day in 2009, in partnership with Facebook and using the Facebook Connect technology. Users were able to watch a live video feed of President Obama's inaugural address on their computers via the CNN.com website. But more than just that, they could comment on his speech and, in near real time, see comments by other people in their social graph taking place on the CNN.com website. Now think about that for a moment. You're watching this live feed, and next to it, there's a window open that is display-ing a streaming list of comments from all your friends. The website knows that they are your friends because you've connected with them through Facebook. You, in turn, can add comments that are seen just by other friends who are watching the inauguration on the CNN.com website, too.

Influencing conversations and getting your brand inserted into conversations has always been difficult and expensive for marketers. But now, with tech-nologies like Facebook Connect, if you can give people reason to talk, you don't have to build a brand-new community from scratch, nor do you have to limit your social efforts to Facebook or Twitter. You can design an experi-ence whereby consumers are encouraged to bring their social graphs to your website and interact with their friends on your website and on your terms. You can use their profile data and the behavior on your website to make the experience more personal and meaningful, too. But this truly represents one of the most powerful concepts in social media marketing: The technology lets you create experiences that let consumers influence each other in a natural fashion with low (or virtually nonexistent) barrier to entry.

Without a doubt, Facebook Connect is one of the most advanced technologies you can use to enable social interaction via social graphs on your website. Given that Facebook is also the largest social network, it makes sense to use Facebook Connect. Here are some factors to keep in mind when deploying Facebook Connect on your website:

- **Trusted authentication:** Facebook Connect uses Facebook's trusted authentication method. This means that your website (when you're using Facebook Connect) can use Facebook's authentication method without having to ask users to register.

- **Real identity:** Facebook users are represented with their real names and identities when you use Facebook Connect. This can be both good and bad. Some users may not want that.

- **Friend linking:** Linking established on Facebook is carried through to the external websites. You can show a consumer which of his friends already have accounts on your website via Facebook Connect.

- **Dynamic privacy:** The privacy settings that your customers set on Facebook carry through with them to your website. This includes changes to photographs, friends, and what information is visible.

- **Social distribution:** Actions taken by consumers on your website can be easily pushed back to Facebook or to their friends via their News Feed, requests, and other notifications.

For all the conversations (both here and online) about Facebook social plug-ins, it's important to note that it isn't the only game in town. Google, MySpace, Six Apart, and a few other companies have banded together to provide an alternative to Facebook social plug-ins. You can use Google Friend Connect to accomplish many of the same objectives. While Google Friend Connect doesn't bring your social graph directly from Facebook or another social network, it does let you invite users from them. Because it doesn't require any programming on your end (unlike Facebook social plug-ins, which do require a significant amount of programming effort), it's a popular alternative for smaller companies. It takes care of the authentication, basic social functionality such as commenting and ratings, and also includes polls, events, and member gadgets. These are all very easily installed.

Just because you don't have to invest huge sums of money in developing and nurturing your own online community, doesn't mean that you *should* develop your own online community. It may be a better option in some cases — but not always. After all, bringing a social graph to your website enables consumers to interact with their friends on your website. But it doesn't let them interact as easily with other customers about your products.

Tips and Tricks for Website SMM

Follow these steps to enhance your website's social media potential. Many of these tips and tricks may seem small, but time and again, we've seen them directly impact how a potential customer views a brand on a website. Keep in mind that some of these tips may require significant organizational change to bring them to life.

Aggregating information for your consumer

Social media has empowered consumers to form stronger opinions and express them more broadly. More people are blogging, commenting, and rating than ever before. Approximately 120,000 blogs are created every day. These contributors provide a rich base of knowledge for other consumers to use while making a purchasing decision. Consumers who tap into these blogs know more about your brand than you probably do. Rather than trying to control the message, serve as the hub and the aggregator of all information regarding the brand. Let your website become the amphitheater for the conversation. Even if the conversation is negative, you win over the long term, as Chevy did with its Tahoe campaign. The user-generated advertisement contest resulted in 629,000 visits to the website, and Tahoe sales took off.

Articulating product benefits better

A recent study (2011) by Lightspeed Research as reported by eConsultancy, showed how important customer reviews are to the purchase of a product. They found that between one and three bad reviews would deter 67 percent of the survey sample from purchasing a product. Also, 72 percent said they searched for product reviews on shopping websites prior to making a purchase.

That's social influence at play. So what can you do about it? Recognize that your consumers are informed, and make sure you sell a strong product, articulating its benefits in a more easily understood manner. You'll create happier customers who'll then do the marketing for you as others will want to identify with them through similar purchasing behavior.

Amplifying the favorite business stories

So you can't control the message anymore. Your consumers would rather listen to each other than to you. But you still have messages that you want to disseminate. You can do that by shaping, influencing, and amplifying business stories that play to your brand's strengths.

Just because your consumers are more interested in talking to each other, it doesn't mean you don't have a voice at all. According to the 2011 Technorati State of the Blogosphere Report, 64 percent of corporate bloggers and 73 percent of entrepreneurs surveyed say they are blogging more because it has proven to be valuable for promoting their business and also valuable to their profession. So publish your favorite business stories as widely as possible and also direct consumers to the individuals or groups already predisposed to your products.

Aligning your organization into multiple, authentic voices

Social influence marketing is about providing the space for consumers to influence each other during the purchase process. As a brand, you want them to positively influence each other. Do this by aligning your entire organization into a network of multiple, authentic voices. Don't leave customer interactions to the sales and marketing teams. Empower other internal constituents across the organization to serve as brand ambassadors, maybe via blogs. They'll talk about your brand in their own voices to their own communities. They may not be totally on message, but they'll be authentic — and they'll have a strong, positive influence. Trust them. See Chapter 5 for more information on SMM voices.

Chapter 16

Becoming an Authentic and Engaged Advertiser

*I*n earlier chapters, we briefly touch on social advertising and how it can play an important role in your marketing efforts. We also allude to paid and earned media in the context of the different marketing opportunities on social platforms. We also introduce appvertising.

In this chapter, we go into each of those topics in significantly more detail. Knowing how they can help you achieve your SMM objectives is critical as you become a more authentic and engaged social media advertiser. But that's not all; it's also important to leverage SMM efforts with offline marketing efforts, whether it be through television or any other form of media. We discuss that, too, in this chapter.

Social Advertising: A Potential Online Advertising Game Changer

Online display advertising has been in a steady decline recently, with fewer people clicking and interacting with those advertisements everywhere. For the most part, the industry has responded by making the display advertisements more immersive, with rollover states, forms, pull-down menus, expandable units, and streaming audio and video clips all built within them.

Those incremental innovations help grab users' attention and provide a decent return on investment (ROI) for the advertisers. But social advertisements, which infuse social content and a user's *social graph* (mapping of the person's friends) directly into the ad unit, promise to make display advertisements far more interactive, engaging, and better performing than other forms of display advertisements that have come before.

The Interactive Advertising Bureau defines a social ad as "an online ad that incorporates user interactions that the consumer has agreed to display and be shared. The resulting ad displays these interactions along with the user's persona (picture and/or name) within the ad content." This definition serves as a good starting point but can be expanded to also include user-generated content.

To explain this in layman's terms, imagine seeing a display advertisement on a website like CNN.com or NYTimes.com and uploading a photograph to it. Or you could see tweets (Twitter messages) by other people appear within it, and you could respond with comments or tweets of your own. Or imagine you're browsing Facebook, and you see a display banner that includes a photograph of a friend with a movie recommendation. Those are all social advertisements because they're either infused with social graph data or with user-generated content. In this second example, only people who know your friend will see that advertisement.

Displaying advertisements on social networks

Every year, Internet pundits predict the demise of online display advertising. They prophesize that consumers will stop looking at banner ads, and as a result, the multibillion-dollar industry will die a sudden death. And each year, the statistics prove them wrong. In fact, according to Grabstats.com, online display advertising grew 15.8 percent in 2010. Marketers continue to invest in display advertising, and with good reason. Year after year, display advertisements produce results, especially for direct-response campaigns, where the dollar investments in display advertisements is traced directly to customer acquisition. Even in down economies like the one we're going through at the time of this book's publication, companies still use display advertising to reach prospective customers. The amount they spend on display advertising may decrease, but it's still a core component in their media mix simply because those advertisements prove to be worth their investments.

But one type of online display advertising has never really worked well and continues to provide dismal click-through rates: display advertising on social networks. The reason is simple: People click display advertisements less when they're in a social environment engaging with their friends. You've probably seen display ads on social platforms like MySpace and Facebook. They do exist, but they don't perform well.

Why are these social advertisements such a big deal? Because all of a sudden, display banners that were getting little attention, especially on social networks, now can carry actual, real-time messages from other consumers. Rather than depending on fancy creative images to influence your customers to make a purchasing decision, you can allow customers to influence each other in the display banners. And rather than consumers seeing just static quotes from other consumers (after all, customer quotes aren't new in advertising), the consumers can respond to those messages with questions, comments, or endorsements of their own within your advertisement.

From being a medium through which to push a message, the display banner suddenly becomes a location for conversations where consumers can influence each other. The display banner becomes a tool in your social media marketing toolkit. That's powerful. This matters more than ever because as Forrester Senior Vice President Idea Development Josh Bernoff said, "People don't want to talk about products; they want to talk about their passions or their problems and solutions." Let them use those banner ads to carry on those conversations and influence each other in meaningful ways.

Appvertisements and How They Can Work for You

Another recent innovation in the online advertising space is appvertisements, which bridge the worlds of advertising and applications. (You get the word *appvertising* when you combine the first part of the word *application* with the last part of the word *advertising*.) These appvertisements are small *applications* (programs) that reside within social networks and tap into people's social graphs. They provide direct entertainment or educational, social interactivity, or utilitarian value to consumers who install them.

When these appvertisements provide value, consumers are typically comfortable with the sponsored branding that comes part and parcel with them. The appvertisements are successful when they have the following attributes: emotional, engaging, social, and simple. We discuss these attributes in the sections that follow.

As you consider building and launching appvertisements on a social platform like Facebook, consider these numbers: The most popular appvertisements average 140,000 installations during their first month, according to Buddy Media Research. Users spend considerably more time interacting with these appvertisements than they do with any traditional display banner ads. These applications are extremely easy to build and can be personalized based on a user's profile data. For more information on identifying someone to build your appvertisements, see Chapter 17. Here are the attributes that make an appvertisement successful.

Emotional

Appvertisements are typically fun and engaging. They solicit a response from consumers and encourage deeper participation. For example, Chase Bank created a Million Dollar Sweepstakes for their Freedom card. Participants had to buy all their purchases with the Freedom card. This appvertisement resided within Facebook, and by the time this chapter was written, a million-dollar winner had just been crowned. The value of this app to Chase was that people were spurred on to use their card for every purchase. Figure 16-1 shows the sweepstakes winner.

Engaging

For appvertisements to succeed, they must continuously engage users. They should be designed to encourage repeat use and sharing of the appvertisement. DirectTV has developed an app called Snowballs of Flurry that allows you to log in and play against your friends who also like Direct TV. It encourages you to engage with their community.

Figure 16-1:
Chase
Freedom
Million
Dollar
Sweepstakes.

Social

The most popular appvertisements are the ones that are deeply social. These are the appvertisements that encourage social interaction with others or enable users to share a side of themselves with their social circles. A good example is the TripAdvisor Cities I've Visited travel map, shown in Figure 16-2. Upon installing the application, users can mark on a map the cities they've visited, the cities they want to visit, and the cities that they're planning to visit. They can also invite friends to recommend cities for them, and users can compare their cities to those of their friends and exchange notes about the comparisons.

Figure 16-2: The Cities I've Visited travel map.

Simple

Probably the most important attribute of successful appvertisements is that they're typically very simple applications. You shouldn't try to build Microsoft Office into your appvertisement. Users are more likely to adopt apps that are simple, straightforward, and focused on doing more with less. If you install the Travel Channel Kidnap!, Bud Light Check Your Dudeness, and the TripAdvisor Cities I've Visited appvertisements, you'll notice that they're all very simply designed, quick to learn, and easy to use.

Getting Your Appvertisement Noticed

Building appvertisements is only half the battle. As with anything else designed and built for the social web, in order for it to gain traction, you must focus on getting users to adopt the appvertisement and install it on their profile pages on their favorite social platform. That can be very challenging, especially with new appvertisements being launched every single day.

You can get your appvertisements to your consumers in two ways: joining an appvertisement network or *seeding* (building) the appvertisement yourself.

Joining an appvertisement network

Existing appvertisement networks can be very helpful. These appvertisement networks promote new appvertisements on what is called the *canvas pages* of existing appvertisements. Companies that have built and deployed appvertisements in large quantities charge for the promotion of new appvertisements, typically on a per-installation basis.

Here are some appvertisement networks:

- ✔ Gigya (www.gigya.com), shown in Figure 16-3
- ✔ RockYou (www.rockyou.com)
- ✔ Kit Digital (www.kitd.com)
- ✔ Buddy Media (www.buddymedia.com)

Many of these also build your appvertisements for you.

As each appvertisement network functions differently, both in terms of how you can join the network and how much it will charge you for the promotion of your appvertisement, it's best to shop around when choosing the right one. These should all be factors in determining which platform you go with:

- ✔ Visit their websites.
- ✔ Find out how much they charge per installation.
- ✔ Research the *reach* of their networks. (Do they cover all the social platforms?)
- ✔ Understand how robust their analytics systems are.

Keep in mind that some appvertisement networks may be stronger in specific social platforms versus other ones, and you should factor that into your decision based on where most of your prospective customers are spending their time.

Joining a network isn't required, but it does serve as the simplest, quickest way to promote an appvertisement.

Figure 16-3:
The Gigya
appver-
tisement
network.

Seeding your appvertisement

The other alternative is to manually seed the appvertisement yourself, making sure that it has enough social features to encourage people to share it with others. This typically means manual effort and invariably has a cost of its own.

When you're seeding the appvertisement, you'll want to pay particular attention to the screen shots included, whether it's submitted to all the appvertisement directories, the timing of the release (choose the time in the day when most of your target audience logs in to Facebook, for example), how you invite users to install the appvertisement, and link exchange programs. Also, don't forget to set up a Facebook fan page for the application and encourage user feedback through it.

The most important tool in your arsenal of seeding appvertisements is letting users spread the word about your appvertisement for you. You do this by letting them invite their friends and making sure that the appvertisement requires the participation of your users and their friends. You also want to build in a notification system so that you have an excuse to remind your users about the appvertisement. These notifications can, for example, tell your user's friends when your user breaks an existing high score record or notify them when a friend is actually online and playing.

Use the feed functionality built into Facebook to build awareness and repeat use for your appvertisement. How you seed the appvertisement depends on the social platform where you're launching it. Each social platform has its own idiosyncrasies that make the concept of seeding the appvertisement slightly different from the next platform.

Follow these basic steps when you're seeding your appvertisement.

1. **Create the appvertisement, and make sure that sharing functionality is built into the appvertisement.**

   Developers that create this type of advertisement include Avenue Social (`www.avenuesocial.com`) and SocialCubix (`www.socialcubix.com`).

2. **Launch the appvertisement on your targeted social network by first having it published and approved in the social network appvertisement directory.**

   Each social network has a different policy regarding publishing appvertisements.

3. **When the appvertisement appears in the appvertisement directory, install the appvertisement on your profile page, and encourage your co-workers, friends, and family to install it on theirs, too.**

4. **Install the appvertisement on your company social network profile or page, and announce the appvertisement via Twitter and other social platforms.**

5. **Alert social influencers with whom you have an existing relationship about the launch of the appvertisement, and explain why it may be of value to them and their audiences.**

6. **Start using the appvertisement on a regular basis, and use any built-in notification system to remind other users about the appvertisement.**

Making Paid and Earned Media Work Together

Earned media — editorial, radio, or television coverage of an event or product that you don't have to pay for — has its roots in the public relations world. Earned media is usually free publicity through promotional and marketing efforts outside advertising. Public relations professionals have mastered the art of getting their clients earned media at a cost significantly lower than buying the media attention through paid advertisements or promotions of one form or another.

With the social media revolution, earned media has taken on a new dimension. Your brand no longer has to depend on the mainstream media to earn attention among its consumers. Your brand can also earn that attention directly by interacting and engaging with its consumers and their influencers across the social web. All of a sudden, earned media means engaging with consumers on social platforms from Twitter and Facebook to YouTube. If you can earn your consumer's attention directly, why bother with the mainstream press? And for that matter, why bother with paid media either? In fact, journalists, too, look towards the social web for story ideas. According to research published by Brodeur and Marketwire and highlighted on Marketing Pilgrim (www.marketingpilgrim.com), more than 75 percent of reporters see blogs as helpful in giving them story ideas, with 70 percent checking a blog list on a regular basis.

Working harder to gain attention

In the early days of the social media phenomenon, brands that engaged in direct conversations with their customers and their influencers automatically gained prominence. After all, what they were doing was revolutionary. The first time a user got a response from a customer service agent via Twitter must have been quite a seismic moment. Similarly, the first time a chief executive officer of a Fortune 1000 company started blogging, it drew a lot of media coverage and won him praise among his customers. Comcast and Zappos have developed a reputation for phenomenal customer service through Twitter; Figure 16-4 shows the Zappos Twitter feed. They were among the first to leverage Twitter strategically for customer service, and anyone who follows them isn't going to get the same kind of attention that they did. Today, Comcast has several employees including local Comcast teams, like Comcast New Mexico (https://twitter.com/#!/ComcastNM), who are dedicated to Twitter customer service. All they do every day is address customer service issues via Twitter. (See http://twitter.com/comcastcares.)

The days of participating in the social web to simply earn attention are over. Your brands must still earn attention as you absolutely need to, but doing so has gotten harder — and it requires more of your time. Every other brand is doing what you're doing online.

So the question is, how can your brand earn the trust and attention of consumers online in a meaningful sense? This is where paid and earned media needs to work together. We discuss this in the section that follows.

The most important myth about earned media is this: It isn't, as many people believe, free media. You still have to work for it. In fact, it takes a lot more effort to earn media than buy media. The difference is that earning media requires time and effort and changing your company from within, while paid media is about buying online advertisements. Earned media requires you to devote time to monitoring conversations, building relationships, and engaging with influencers online.

Figure 16-4:
The official
Zappos
Twitter feed.

Making paid media jump-start earned media initiatives

So how do earned and paid media work together in this socially-driven digital world? In earlier chapters, including Chapter 7, we discuss paid media and earned media opportunities on various social platforms. We also discussed when to use what technique. Here, we explore how paid media can support earned media efforts.

At the most basic level, you can use paid media to jump-start your earned media endeavors. Grabbing your customers' attention and initiating dialogue with them can be hard. All your competitors are trying to do exactly what you're hoping to do, after all. It can be difficult to break through the noise. The sections that follow highlight some specific ways in which paid media can support earned media.

An analysis by Razorfish highlights that it's important to analyze the value of paid media in relation to the value of *incremental reach* (users pass it on) and the value of the endorsement effect (*badging,* or a user promoting a brand via an image on his profile, and so on). The latter two can be jump-started by the first. The point is that when you use paid media to jump-start earned media effort, you must analyze the value of all components to assess the total value of the campaign and how the components support each other.

Build awareness

Paid media is most valuable for building awareness among consumers about a product, service, or promotion. If you're beginning to engage with customers on a social platform or in a hosted online community, an effective way to build awareness for those experiences is to create awareness via paid media across the Internet. Most of your consumers may not know that you're interacting with others on a social platform and providing product sneak peeks, offering discounts, or answering customer service queries. You can build that awareness by using paid media. This paid media can be in the form of advertisements on mainstream websites or social advertisements on the social platforms.

Jump-start engagement

Another effective use of paid media is to jump-start appvertisement installations. As we mention earlier in the chapter, your appvertisement is only as successful as the number of installations that it has. Getting people to install your appvertisement virally can be difficult. Promoting the appvertisement through an ad network that guarantees installations is one way to gain traction for it, although some may argue that the quality of the download may be less when you're using an ad network that guarantees the downloads. You can also use paid media to jump-start other forms of social engagement, like activity around a YouTube channel or a Facebook fan page.

Promote interaction

You may have already developed a thriving community and could be looking to increase engagement with a new audience segment. One way to do this is to use paid media to profile community members and highlight the value that the community provides.

For example, Intuit has a very successful QuickBooks Live Community (as shown in Figure 16-5), where customers help each other solve problems. Today, 70 percent of customer service–related issues are resolved with other users answering questions. One accountant has posted more than 5,600 answers. Intuit now has the opportunity to promote the Live Community to prospective customers as a benefit of buying their software. That can be done through paid media.

Win friends and influence

If you want to engage with your customers in a more meaningful way, but don't have the resources, skills, or permission to do so, use paid strategies. For example, American Express hosts a popular business site called OPEN Forum. The site pays experts like übermarketer Guy Kawasaki to blog on various topics, which cultivates discussion among the readers. The conversations triggered on the OPEN Forum percolate to other parts of the Internet, rapidly giving American Express additional exposure. American Express builds its reputation as a company providing valuable advice to its customers, the expert bloggers get a larger audience, the customers get the information, and each post builds brand awareness for the AmEx brand.

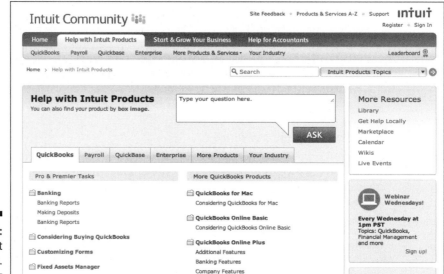

Figure 16-5:
The Intuit
Community.

Tips and tricks for campaigns

When launching and running online campaigns, you can sometimes forget to make sure that your paid and earned media efforts work well together. Your earned media efforts can save you precious dollars and enhance the paid media campaign.

Here are some tips to consider when launching an online media campaign:

✔ **Ask for earned media recommendations.**

When you ask your agency to provide recommendations for a media campaign, ask them to also provide earned media recommendations at the same time. There is no reason why they shouldn't.

✔ **Request a social advertising component.**

Always ask your agency to include a social advertising component to the campaign, and push them to explain how you can use the social advertising to jump-start earned media efforts.

✔ **Survey the landscape.**

Look at your presence on various social platforms when you're about to launch a campaign. Is there anything that you can do to amplify the affects of the campaign?

✔ **Design the campaign to be inherently social.**

Ask more of the participants in your campaign and offer more in return. For instance, direct them to your presence on a social platform — where you encourage them to friend, fan, or follow you — instead of directing them to a microsite.

✔ **Promote your brand on social networks.**

Use your social influence on the platforms to highlight the campaign, and use places like Twitter to answer queries, amplify the coverage, and share tidbits about it.

✔ **Establish a fan page.**

Create a permanent home for the campaign, which allows deeper social interaction. It'll strengthen relationships with your customers and help you on the search engine optimization (SEO) front, too. Or use your social network presence as that home.

✔ **Set influence goals, and evaluate how well you meet them.**

Make an explicit secondary goal of the campaign to increase your followers on Twitter, your fans on Facebook, and your friends on YouTube. With that goal, your creative team will bring more synergistic ideas to the table.

✔ **Don't forget the metrics.**

Measure all digital interactions with your customers, and especially find out how they reach your microsite or your website. Determine how many people were driven from paid versus earned media strategies and how many came from the social platforms. We talk about how to measure a campaign in Chapter 19.

✔ **Identify and reach out to the social influencers.**

Do it as soon as you launch the campaign; maybe they can help promote it for you. Show them the creative. Provide them something in return.

✔ **Offer some sort of reward to influencers who participate.**

Before you launch the campaign, think through whether you can provide consumers who engage with you more deeply on the social platforms with anything. They'll reward your generosity with creating buzz that will nicely complement the paid media campaign.

Making SMM Work with TV

Research published 2011 by Nielsen showed that consumers who viewed an appvertisement by Campbell's Soup was more likely to remember the brand Campbell's than those who viewed a TV ad.

Some traditional advertisers believe that nothing can replace television to build awareness for a brand. These advertisers scoff at the notion of digital advertising displacing television advertising. Asking marketers to choose between the two is a false choice. Each form of advertising has its place, and each one can complement the other effectively to meet the objectives of the marketing campaign. In the following sections, we outline two scenarios of how digital SMM campaigns can effectively complement a television campaign.

Social media has created a perfect storm in the advertising world, which results in new advertising units, like social ads and the rise of earned media, working in conjunction with paid media. And the technological innovations in live streaming is changing the nature of television online, leading to a whole new set of marketing implications for traditional TV advertisers.

Awareness through TV, engagement via the Internet

The reach of television is still insurmountable for any other marketing channel. Television advertising provides awareness for a brand, a product, or a new campaign better than other techniques. But television is most effectively used when it serves to build awareness and drive consumers to more deeply engage with a brand on other channels, like the Internet.

Take the Levi's 501 *Project Runway* Challenge, for example. Levi's 501 sponsored the reality television series *Project Runway,* in which up-and-coming fashion designers compete against each other in a string of design challenges for a big prize.

Levi's sponsored the TV show to build awareness for its jeans among young women, a target customer that had eluded the brand. Levi's also created a *Project Runway* design challenge of its own on a specially built website. On this website, users were asked to submit their own clothing designs for a competition. Other users voted on the submissions, a panel of celebrity judges weighed in, and a winner was chosen. The online program was promoted extensively through paid media across the Internet and through the television advertisements that aired around the TV version of *Project Runway.*

Thousands of consumers submitted their designs for this online challenge, with many more visiting the website to critique the designs and vote for their favorites. The television advertisements built awareness for the online competition; paid media online promoted it across the Internet; and consumers engaged with the brand more deeply on the website by submitting designs, rating others, and discussing them. It was the perfect success story, with television advertisements working in conjunction with a social influence marketing program to meet the brand's objectives. And yes, during the period of the campaign, sales to their target audience jumped.

Awareness, engagement, and conversion with television

Over the last ten years, as digital advertising has gained in prominence, a slew of traditional marketers have bemoaned the attention that the digital space has been getting. Digital marketers have been too proudly explaining how important their form of marketing is because it's more measurable, more quantifiable, and more results-driven than other forms of marketing. This tension has created a false divide between television and digital. That's all about to change.

Television is fundamentally going digital itself, in a way that none of us could have imagined a few years ago. The infrastructure that drives television — the content distribution models, the content formats, and the advertising opportunities — are all changing. And what's more, the lines between television and the Internet are blurring. Market research shows that consumers increasingly multitask. They don't just surf the Internet while watching television; they talk to each other online while watching television. And online television sites in the form of websites like YouTube, Hulu, and Joost have built-in chat and discussion forum functionality.

The face of television has gone digital, with major cable networks beginning to stream live broadcasts online. This means that as television goes digital, marketers have the opportunity to get the same advertising benefits from television they've always gotten, but with some of the unique attributes of digital such as the measurability, social capability, and interactivity.

Measuring the effectiveness of TV and the second screen

Today, if you have a subscription to a cable/satellite channel like HBO or Cinemax, you can see episodes of all your favorite shows on your iPhone, iPad, or Android device. The same can be said for some broadcast channels that supply advertising along with their content. This is called a *second screen* experience, referring to your mobile device interacting with social media in addition to your TV set.

With the feedback that can be obtained from the watching community on social media, advertisers are very excited about the depth of information they can obtain. Never before have executives been able to get such direct comments during a TV season. They have gone so far as to make changes to upcoming episodes based on comments about likes and dislikes.

Companies that help advertisers mine sentiments about TV from the web include

- ✔ Bluefin Labs (`http://bluefinlabs.com`), shown in Figure 16-6
- ✔ Radian6 (`www.radian6.com/`)
- ✔ General Sentiment (`www.generalsentiment.com`)

Figure 16-6:
Bluefin Labs
home page.

Chapter 17

Building an SMM Mobile Campaign

*P*eople use all kinds of social media to share experiences and create, refresh, develop, and maintain relationships. Consumers use full-fledged communities like Facebook, as well as blogs, comment forms, and the like to speak their minds and be heard.

As we outline in Chapter 1, social media marketing is about employing social media and social influencers to achieve the marketing and business needs of an organization. Using mobile devices like cellphones and other handheld devices in social influence marketing helps you leverage their many capabilities to engage your prospects and customers with your brand. It enables these same people to communicate with each other and share their individual experiences with your brand, products, and services.

In this chapter, you find out how the mobile phone is rapidly becoming the most pervasive communication, entertainment, and social media channel out there, with a future filled with possibilities. You get a feel for what consumers are doing with their phones and the factors that affect their use.

We explain how you can use mobile search, branded applications, and mobile-enhanced traditional and new media to engage consumers within a marketing and social media context. Finally, we discuss how you can leverage the convergence of social media and the mobile channel to benefit your business not just tomorrow, but also today!

Looking at Consumer Trends in Mobile

The mobile phone has become a key fixture in the lives of nearly everyone in the United States and, increasingly so, around the world. According to the leading research firms like comScore and Nielsen, 80 percent of the U.S. population has a mobile phone, which is more than 232 million people. In August, 2011, the comScore MobiLens service reported that the use of

- ✔ Twitter was up via mobile 75 percent from 2010 to 2011
- ✔ LinkedIn was up 69 percent from 2010 to 2011
- ✔ Facebook was up 50 percent from 2010 to 2011

Why the craze? Well, the mobile phone brings value; changes lives; and is changing the way we communicate, socialize, and conduct commerce.

A telephone and much more

For the majority, the mobile phone is quickly becoming more than a simple tool for making and receiving phone calls. Sure, you can still make phone calls with them, but for many of us, the mobile phone has become a portal to the world and a multipath channel for the world to reach us.

Today's mobile phones are newspapers, maps, books, magazines, cameras, radios, stores, game consoles, video and music players, calculators, calendars, address books, stereos, TVs, movie theaters, and concert halls. And this is just the beginning. In addition to making and receiving calls on mobile phones, people are using them to

- ✔ Access news and information
- ✔ Check up on the latest celebrity gossip
- ✔ Check the weather
- ✔ Look up addresses and find directions
- ✔ Buy products, images, ringtones — and even pizza
- ✔ Receive the latest coupons and promotional discounts from their favorite stores
- ✔ Play games
- ✔ Listen to music and watch movies
- ✔ Respond to their favorite brand's mobile messages
- ✔ Participate with and support political candidates

✔ Donate money to their favorite charities

✔ Socialize with friends and marketers

✔ Update friends and family on their locations and activities

This list is just the tip of the iceberg. Every day, consumers are doing more and more with their mobile phones, and you can create new and innovative campaigns that fit in with those uses.

The key to successful consumer engagement, especially in the social media context, is to combine both information delivery and exchange with entertainment — in other words, focus on "infotainment" services.

The release and adoption of smarter phones

No doubt about it, phones are getting smarter. Take the Wayback machine to 1983 (the Wayback was the time-travel machine in the old *The Rocky and Bullwinkle Show*), and you'd see innovative and/or fashion-conscious road warriors carrying around a mobile phone shaped like bricks and weighing a whopping 30 ounces or more. For all its heft, the grandfather of mobile devices could do only two things: make and receive calls.

Today is a different story. You can find thousands of mobile phones that come in all shapes and sizes. True, many phones are still dedicated for the single purpose of making phone calls, but these devices are smaller, have longer battery lives, and provide clearer calls. However, increasingly, phones are getting *smarter*, meaning that they're capable of doing more. Basically, they're mini (and in many cases not-so-mini) computers. This new class of phone is referred to as a *smartphone*.

Here are the categories of phones:

✔ **Regular phones:** These are lightweight, dedicated devices for making and receiving phone calls and text messages and sometimes for performing rudimentary data service, such as accessing the Internet via mobile browsers (on what's called the mobile Internet). The Motorola Razr, for example, is a popular phone.

✔ **Smartphones:** These are full-featured, multipurpose, high-bandwidth, networked, multimodal, interactive information, communication, entertainment, and commerce solutions. Some of the more popular smartphones include the Apple iPhone, phones running the Google Android operating system, and the BlackBerry from Research In Motion. Juniper Research predicts that 23 percent of all mobile handsets sold by 2013 will be smartphones.

✔ **Wireless-enabled devices:** These devices aren't phones, but each has some form of wireless connectivity — either through Wi-Fi or an embedded wireless access card. The Apple iPad, iPod touch, Sony PlayStation 4, Amazon Kindle, and various flavors of tablets are among the most popular wireless-enabled devices as this book goes to print. With Internet access, these devices naturally support interactive marketing.

More and more people are adopting smartphones and the requisite data plans to send text messages, acquire Internet connectivity, and enjoy related value-added services. That means you should consider making your SMM campaigns mobile device-friendly. Also, keep in mind that the percent of the overall population that uses smartphones today could be a much larger percentage of your target audience.

To learn more about the thousands of mobile devices that are out there (we're not kidding; there are that many), check out DeviceAtlas at `www.deviceatlas.com`. (See Figure 17-1.)

Even though the iPhone is capturing the lion's share of the press, today it accounts for only 25 percent of the smartphone market. Android has 33 percent of the U.S. market, and RIM has 29 percent.

Figure 17-1:
The myriad
of mobile
devices:
DeviceAtlas.

We're shutting off our landlines

In many countries, the mobile phone is the primary means of communication. In the United States, according to an August 2011 FCC report, almost 25 percent of Americans live in homes with wireless-only connections. Among those aged 25 to 29 more than 50 percent only use mobile phones. In addition, in the United States,

voice is no longer the primary communication channel on the mobile phone. According to Nielsen Mobile, as of October 2008, the average mobile subscriber in the United States sent 357 text messages, compared to using 204 voice minutes.

Understanding the Many Paths within the Mobile Channel

It's easy to look at a mobile phone and think, "It's just a phone." But it really isn't *just* a phone anymore. Sure, you can make calls with it and engage in social practices, just like the old landline party line phones. However, the telephone capability is just the tip of the iceberg. Today's mobile devices are much more than what most people expect. In fact, for many people, these devices are the primary method of personal communication, social interaction, and even commerce.

Figure 17-2 illustrates the many paths you can use to reach the mobile phone.

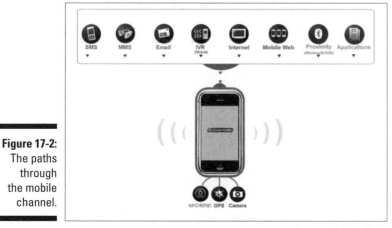

Figure 17-2:
The paths through the mobile channel.

Courtesy of iLoop Mobile, Inc.

The term used to interact with consumers through all these paths is *mobile channel.* The mobile channel refers to the collection of companies and systems, wireless networks, mobile phones, application providers, marketers, and so on that make it possible for you to interact with an individual audience member directly through a mobile phone or wireless-enabled device. Each of these paths — SMS, MMS, e-mail, voice and IVR (integrated voice response), Internet, mobile web, proximity, and applications — is unique.

Keep in mind what media scholar Marshall McLuhan taught us in 1964: "The medium is the message." Each of these paths changes how your message is received and accepted. In the social media context, this is important because if your message isn't accepted, it certainly won't be talked about and shared.

The paths are

- ✔ **SMS:** This is short message service, also commonly known as *text messaging.* A text message is comprised of 160 or fewer letters, characters, and numbers delivered through the mobile channel. You can send longer messages (called Concatenated SMS) by linking the messages together. SMS is ideal for the sharing and exchange of contextually relevant, timely bits of information — including a brief message to a friend, celebrity gossip, details on your latest sale, impulse impressions, and thoughts on a product or service. In the social media context, SMS is popular with Twitter because people update their accounts (tweet) and/or receive alerts via SMS, even though SMS is just one very small part of the Twitter experience. Keep in mind, though, that SMS is permission-based. If you're a marketer trying to reach customers via SMS, they need to have given you permission to market to them.

- ✔ **MMS:** This stands for multimedia messaging service, which is a unique protocol for exchanging digital content, such as videos, pictures, and audio via mobile phones. The term *MMS* is often generically used for all forms of digital content, including ringtones, images, video, and so on, even if the delivery doesn't follow the proper MMS protocol; more often than not, this content is sent via the Internet rather than through MMS. MMS works well with a SMM campaign where you're inviting customers to share their own pictures and videos with each other.

- ✔ **E-mail:** Traditionally, e-mail has been delivered to a mobile device, such as a BlackBerry or Palm Treo, through a special e-mail service connected to the device. Now, regular e-mail can be delivered through mobile applications (often built in by the wireless carriers or mobile phone manufacturers) or through the mobile Web. Newer phones, such as iPhones, Androids, and devices such as the iPod touch, deliver and render HTML e-mails, as opposed to the text-only versions of old. For the most part, e-mail is rarely used in marketing specifically to reach mobile devices, due to the difficulty to target a user and know the type of device she's using to read her e-mail.

✔ **Voice:** This takes the form of talking with a live person working in a call center, who in turn may trigger mobile data services as a response to the call. Voice can also refer to an interactive voice response (IVR), or automated attendant, system where your audience can interact with your service through various system prompts and menus, such as, "Say or press 1 to tell us what you think of the service." The greatest opportunity here is with social media marketing campaigns that start online and invite users to have special customized voice messages sent to their friends on their mobile phones. For example, the mobile campaign for the movie *Snakes on a Plane* encouraged participants to create customized voice messages for their friends. When the receivers answered the calls, they heard a message, in the voice of the actor Samuel L. Jackson, about the movie. The message also said that their friends (you could include any name) wanted them to watch the movie together. It appeared as if Samuel L. Jackson was telling them this. This widely successful campaign resulted in more than 4 million calls being placed between friends during the promotional period.

✔ **Internet:** Many mobile devices can connect to the Internet for a wide range of data-enabled services, including the mobile web, applications, location-based services that tell you about special discounts or recommend restaurants around you, content services like streaming video (for example, Mobile TV or MLB games), as well as mobile-carrier-managed portals, such as Verizon V CAST.

✔ **Mobile web:** Mobile web refers to the experience of browsing the Internet via the mobile phone — for example, going to the Facebook website on your phone and posting a status update. You can do this using either the web browsers built into many of the smartphones to visit mobile versions of websites (or in the case of the iPhone, you can actually see the regular website) or by using specially created applications that connect you to specific websites or web services. For example, the Facebook iPhone application is extremely popular.

✔ **Proximity spectrum (Bluetooth/Wi-Fi):** This refers to the short-range Bluetooth radio channel and Wi-Fi network capability for connecting to the Internet. Think of *proximity spectrum* as technologies that let you connect your mobile device with others close to you. Typically, Bluetooth is used to connect phones with wireless headsets and related periphery devices, but you can also use it to deliver content to the mobile phone, as you can with Wi-Fi technology. Bluetooth plays a role in social media at live events where you can send content to the phone and encourage users to share it, whereas Wi-Fi plays a huge role in that it provides the data network connectivity for mobile Internet, Internet, and application services.

✔ **Applications:** These are software utilities and services downloaded to mobile phones, and they take many forms. Some are unique to the particular platform they're deployed for, such as the Apple iPhone, Google Android, Research In Motion's BlackBerry, the Palm Pre, Nokia Symbian, and Microsoft's line of phones. Applications are incredible ways to interact with social media programs, due to their ease of use and integration into the features of the phone.

Keeping in Mind Mobile Phone Capabilities

There are many paths through the mobile devices to engage and interact with members of your community, as we discuss in the preceding section. Phones today increasingly have a wide range of enabling technologies, including cameras, location detection, and motion and touch sensors to enhance the experience.

It's a snap: Using the camera

Most mobile phones today come with a camera. For this reason, Nokia, the world's leading phone manufacturer, is one of the leading camera manufacturers and distributors as well. A consumer can use the camera in her phone to opt into a mobile marketing campaign by taking a picture of an ad in a magazine, a bar code, a physical product (such as a DVD or soda can), or herself and then use it in the social media context to contribute content to the community.

Consumers are finding that camera phones are easier to use than a standalone camera. And social network applications make it easier to upload photos directly from a phone's camera than downloading images from a traditional digital camera to a computer and then uploading them to the community site. Most social platforms, like Twitter, Facebook, and Flickr, allow you to take photographs on your mobile phone and easily e-mail them to the service.

An interesting use of mobile cameras that is emerging is with customers taking photographs of products with the phones, sharing them directly on Facebook, and asking their friends for feedback on whether they should buy the products.

Location, location, location

Location information is a very powerful tool, and it's one of the unique features of the mobile phone. When mobile subscribers are out and about, they *usually* know where they are, but their phones *always* know. Location information can make your programs more contextually relevant to a user's location, and you get those details, depending on the phone, from the user, the service network, global positioning and network triangulation technologies, Wi-Fi networks, and a wide range of other technical alchemy.

All you need to know is that you can use location to make your programs more contextually relevant with the user and the community. For example, you could run a special SMM campaign targeted toward people who are in a three-mile radius of your flagship store, encouraging them to visit and get an additional discount if they bring a friend into the store with them. (See more about this type of deal in Chapter 16.)

Location-based mobile campaigns can appear as an invasion of privacy. If they're not permission based or aren't explained clearly, they can come across as Big Brother–like efforts. If you're planning a SMM campaign with location-aware elements, we recommend targeting it toward audiences who are already comfortable with location-aware services and advertising.

Near-field communications and RFID

Although RFID and NFC technologies are far from mainstream at this point, some phones are equipped with them. These systems — radio frequency identification (RFID) and near-field communication (NFC) — are similar in concept to Bluetooth in that they're both short-range communication systems, but they have unique identification and commerce capabilities.

In Germany, for example, NFC-enabled phones are used to purchase train tickets. A user simply hovers the phone near an NFC reader, and the reader charges her linked billing account (to a credit card, for instance) for the purchase of the ticket.

RFID chips can be used to identify you and can even personalize signs as you walk by. (Did you see the scene in *Minority Report* in which Tom Cruise walks by a sign and the sign talks to him? That's what I'm talking about.)

Phone interaction

It just takes a tap, a shake, a swipe, or a swing to interact with many of the newer phones coming out on the market. The most recognizable phone on the market leveraging this motion and gesture technology today is the iPhone, but many other phones have it or soon will. The motion- and gesture-sensing capabilities of these phones improves their usability and convenience.

For instance, on the iPhone, you can make pinching motions on a picture or mobile website to zoom in and out on the screen. The iPhone 4S has a feature called Siri that allows you to make verbal requests to the phone. With some games, you can tap with one finger, two fingers, three, or more, and the number of fingers you use determines what happens. You can even given commands by shaking or tilting the device.

One of my favorite applications that leverages the shake feature is Urbanspoon, which requires you to shake the device, starting a series of jackpot wheels to spin. The application recommends restaurants near you — very cool. See Figure 17-3.

In a social media context, you can have all sorts of fun playing with these input and interaction methods and determining how to use them in your social media program.

Figure 17-3:
Urbanspoon
on the
iPhone.

The iPhone isn't the first mobile device, however, to use these types of applications. The early Palm devices were the first ones to come out with gestures as a means of user interface shortcuts and data entry.

Next-generation mobile services and beyond

If you think mobile networks and devices are going to stop innovating . . . well, don't hold your breath. The horizon holds many exciting developments. Some of the key drivers are increased network bandwidth, longer battery life (including batteries that charge from ambient radio waves), higher-resolution screens, faster processors, and more. Companies are even working on making their processes greener.

Just think of what you could do with faster data speeds on the phone. Today, 3G networks are the norm. (3G is the term commonly used for third-generation mobile networks. The first generation, or 1G, began in the early 1980s; the second generation, or 2G, emerged in the 1990s; and 3G was formed in the late 1990s.) With each successive generation, mobile network capabilities and data transfer and network speeds increased. 4G networks, with data-transfer speeds reaching 100 Mbps (megabits per second), allow you to do full-motion video conferencing and video exchange on phones and other mobile devices. This has a big impact on mobile devices' roles in social media.

Fitting Mobile into Your Social Media Practices

As a marketer, it's your job to communicate, deliver, and exchange value with your audience, and the practice of doing those things with and through mobile devices is referred to as *mobile marketing*. Mobile marketing isn't mystical; neither does it fall outside the practice of traditional marketing. The definition of *mobile marketing* is straightforward: marketing on or with a mobile device such as a mobile phone.

Mobile marketing also includes the following:

✔ **Communicating:** Imparting information and news about your offerings and related activities to your audience members: customers, clients, partners, prospects, leads, employees, advisors, investors, the press, and all the other people and organizations that play a role in your business, as well as society at large. Communicating spreads the word about what your organization does and the value it has to offer.

You probably use any number of traditional and new-media channels (TV, radio, print, live events, outdoor media, point-of-sale displays in stores, the Internet, e-mail, telemarketing, social media, and so on) to communicate indirectly or directly with members of your audience. *Direct marketing communication* occurs when you initiate contact directly with individual members of your audience, as in the case of sending e-mails or initiating phone calls. Direct marketing communication also occurs when a customer visits your broadband or mobile Internet website. *Indirect marketing communication* happens when you advertise or present some other form of promotional message through mass-media channels (such as TV, radio, or print) to expose members of your audience to your communication, but you leave it up to individual audience members to initiate direct contact with you.

✔ **Delivering:** Providing your products or services and exceptional customer service to members of your audience.

✔ **Exchanging:** Swapping value (which we define later in this list). Often, you exchange your goods and services for money, but you can determine for yourself what to take in exchange.

✔ **Offerings:** The products and services produced by your organization.

✔ **Value:** A sense of worth. People value something when they perceive that the item's worth exceeds what it costs them to obtain, consume, or use.

✔ **Mobile-enhanced traditional and new-media channels:** Marketers rely heavily on traditional marketing channels (including television) and new media channels (including websites) to build awareness among members of their audience and promote their offerings. Adding *mobile-enhanced* to the mix simply means that you're marketing to people who are accessing the media in those channels from cellphones, smartphones, and other wireless devices.

In addition, a *mobile marketing call to action* is a set of instructions promoted in the media that shows someone how to use his phone or mobile terminal to participate in a mobile marketing program. For example, one mobile call to action might be "Text SONC to 20222 to donate $5 to support Special Olympics Northern California Athletes. You donation will be billed to your mobile phone bill, and 100 percent of the proceeds is received by the charity."

Defining mobile marketing and its place within the social media context

As we mention in the previous section, there are two forms of mobile marketing: direct and indirect.

✔ **Direct mobile marketing:** Refers to the practice of reaching out and engaging individual members of your audience via their mobile phones. It also includes individuals reaching out and engaging with you in your marketing campaigns.

You can proactively engage consumers, — that is, text-message and/or call them — if they've given you explicit permission to do so. If you don't have permission, you can't directly reach out to consumers.

✔ **Indirect mobile marketing:** Because mobile marketing requires that individual customers give you permission to interact with them on their mobile phones, you can use indirect mobile marketing to expose people to your offerings and invite them to give you permission to contact them directly. Therefore, indirect mobile marketing is the practice of enhancing your traditional and new-media programs (TV, radio, print, outdoor media, Internet, e-mail, voice, and so on) by inviting individual members of your audience to pull out a phone or mobile device and respond to your mobile call to action. On television, for example, your call to action may ask viewers to text a keyword to a short code to cast a vote. (Think about the TV show *The X Factor,* where the audience votes on Twitter or Facebook.) Or you may ask participants to fill out a form on the web or on the mobile Internet, giving their mobile phone number to participate in the program.

Uniting mobile marketing with social media

The mobile aspects of social media marketing occur within both direct and indirect mobile marketing contexts. As a marketer, you can directly engage your audience either by having them reach out to you or vice versa.

Within the indirect context, you can interlace mobile marketing within your traditional and new media channels — including your website, magazine ads, and so on — by adding mobile calls to action. For example, you may

✔ **Offer a text alert service.**

You can send participants updates on your programs in text messages. Create a form on your website, where you ask participants to enter their mobile phone numbers and opt in to receiving text messages from you. Or you may invite them to join by asking them to text a specific code to a phone number that you've set up to receive these messages.

If you would like to collect more data on your customers than their mobile phone numbers (their preferences, for example), use the web form for opt-in, including fields for the additional data you need, and add the customers to your database. However, be aware that asking for such information may limit participation in the program because people may not want to fill out the form or provide much personal information.

✔ **Ask for feedback or content.**

Have participants take pictures with their mobile phones and send them to the community. Or you can ask them to contribute their ideas about the name for your next product, or give a shout-out to a friend.

✔ **Remind participants to share.**

Encourage users to share rewards from a program, such as a coupon offer, with their friends.

Community engagement is all about stimulating interaction between you and members of your audience, as well as among community members. You want them talking to each other. Mobile devices are perfect for this aspect of the social community; you can take advantage of this connectivity and the ability to share experiences whenever and wherever community members want to.

Group decision-making

Group decision-making in mobile marketing is just what it sounds like: using the aspects of mobile to stimulate interactions with groups. Mobile allows people to participate in group settings wherever they are, which makes the membership of the group even larger and more diverse than ever before.

Think about something as simple as planning a party. Using a mobile phone, you can invite all of your friends in your address book with a few button presses using a text message. Then you can ask your friends what food they would like to bring to the party, and keep a running tally of guests who plan to attend. Additional messages can go to those who haven't replied, and soon, you have a full menu ready to go. Next, you can ask everyone to bring music. And a few button presses later, the evening shapes up nicely.

One use of mobile in group situations is to orchestrate flash mobs. A *flash mob* is a large group that suddenly appears and disappears in a specific location, with viral marketing as the main driver of the mob. In the past, e-mail was the primary way to let large groups of people know about the event, but SMS is even more effective with this spur-of-the-moment type of activity.

- On September 8, 2011, Flash Mob of America and National Geographic Kids joined with First Lady Michelle Obama to create a world record for the most people doing jumping jacks together. They gathered 300,265 people on the White House south lawn to do jumping jacks, breaking the record.

- On December 30, 2010, a flash mob showed up at the Prudential Center in Boston, Massachusetts. The proceedings concluded with a planned wedding ceremony that included a flower girl and hundreds of shoppers looking on.

Sometimes done for marketing and public relations, and sometimes done as spur-of-the-moment engagement, flash mobs can be very effective at drawing attention. And mobile marketing can play a large role, allowing in-the-moment communications across large groups of people.

You don't always know what will capture people's attention. When it works, it could be very effective. The idea could be great, but it could still fizzle.

Supporting a cause

Cause marketing is the cooperative use of marketing strategy by a for-profit business and a nonprofit organization for mutual benefit. The business gets to align itself with the value of the nonprofit organization, and the nonprofit organization gets the opportunity to draw attention to its activities and possibly recruit new volunteers and donors.

The mobile channel is ideal for capturing charitable donations. You can mobile-enhance any social media marketing program and put a call to action in this marketing to elicit a response from your audience. In the case of mobile charitable donation programs, the response you're looking for is a financial contribution. For example, the Direct Marketing Educational Foundation (DMEF), a foundation dedicated to educating future marketers, raised money by encouraging sponsors to donate via text message. See Figure 17-4 for the call to action featured on the DMEF website (www. directworks.org).

The most effective of these channels for charitable donations is SMS because mobile subscribers can participate without registering for a service or using a credit card; the donation can go straight to a subscriber's mobile phone bill, with 100 percent of the donation being passed to the participating charity. The full amount can be donated to the charity because the person who donates pays the phone transaction fee and the ads are usually donated by the ad server company.

Figure 17-4: DMEF supporting the direct marketing community through SMS.

Changing the world with your fingertips

Jim Manis, one of the mobile industry's most influential players, founded the Mobile Giving Foundation (MGF) after the sale of his company m-Qube to VeriSign in 2007. Manis and the team at MGF set up a program in which MGF-certified charities, partners, and participating carriers can organize charitable-donation programs using premium short messaging services or PSMS as the means of capturing mobile subscribers' donations. As in any PSMS program, you promote the call to action; people respond to it and donate, and nearly 100 percent of the donation makes its way to the MGF-certified charity.

A 501(c)(3) or related charity can contact the MGF to go through the certification process and use the mobile channel to raise money. A company that wants to make a difference and be socially responsible can use the mobile channel to promote an MGF-certified program. For more information, visit www. mobilegiving.org.

Building Your Own Mobile-Enabled Communities

Building a mobile-enabled social community isn't as hard as you may think. You can leverage existing social media platforms or build the mobile capability right into your existing interactive marketing channels, like your website and mobile Internet site.

Leveraging existing online communities

People are already using Facebook and other social networking sites on their phones today, and they find it easy to accomplish certain tasks, such as uploading photos or posting updates. Some people even prefer to use their mobile phone; it may be much easier to get them to send in a picture from their phone then asking them to go home, find the picture on their computer, and upload it to the community.

As a marketer, you can leverage and use existing social community sites and invite your community to keep in touch with you and follow you. Each community site has varying levels of sophistication and capability for mobile accessibility. Two of the most popular are Facebook and Twitter.

Facebook

Facebook (www.facebook.com) is one of the world's leading social networking communities. Marketers, like you, are increasingly creating Facebook pages for their companies and marketing campaigns so that their community can follow them and keep up to date. Facebook has these existing mobile capabilities that you can leverage:

- ✔ **Keep your Facebook community updated from your phone.**

  You first have to register your phone with your Facebook page. (Go to your Facebook page's mobile settings by selecting Edit Page.) You can then configure your page so that you can update it by sending text messages.

- ✔ **Keep your community in sync with you via mobile.**

  Ask users in all your marketing media to register on your group or fan page to receive text alerts of your status updates, downloading the Facebook application onto their phones, and following you, or visiting you via the Facebook mobile website, http://m.facebook.com.

Twitter

Twitter (www.twitter.com) is an increasingly popular social networking service that supports microblogging, which is the journaling of your activities in 140-character-or-less messages. Twitter is considered the SMS service for the web and has attracted millions of followers.

Twitter isn't just for consumers. Companies are increasingly using it to share their community information. You can create a Twitter account for free and start *tweeting* (the term used for posting to the service). You can then invite people to follow you so that they can receive updates via e-mail, on the web, on the mobile web, and even via SMS. To have people follow you via SMS, invite them to text "follow *username*" to the Twitter short code 40404.

Other social media communities

Countless other social media communities are out there — some general (MySpace), some target niche segments (LinkedIn, Eons, Gather, Glee.com, Disaboom, Think.MTV, and MyBatanga), and the numerous social media utilities (YouTube, Flickr, Scribd, Eventful, Evite, and others). Some of these already have mobile capabilities, and you can extend others to support your mobile programs. You'll need to do some research to find out who is supporting what and determine how you can best leverage mobile-based marketing on what competitors are doing (or not doing).

If you decide to build your own social media program through the mobile web, use your competitive research to ensure that you're creating something unique and then make sure that the concept is true to your brand.

Creating your own social offerings: applications and widgets galore

You may also want to offer value to members of your audience by creating your own social media offerings or something altogether unique. The mobile space is still new, and there's plenty of opportunity to create something that hasn't been done before.

You can deploy these services over and through any of the mobile paths, such as SMS, mobile Internet, and downloadable applications. For example, with SMS, you can recruit opinions and comments, blogs, and more. The key is to consider the content format and the most appropriate path for delivering the content to mobile subscribers. Two popular and emerging social media services are applications and widgets.

Applications and widgets on the mobile front make the mobile experience come alive. Think about what makes sense for your customers and how you will make sure it is marketed successfully, and then put your imagination to work! There are any number of mobile widget providers, but you may want to check out Widgipedia (www.widgipedia.com) or some of the thousands of iPhone application developers, including iLoop Mobile (www.iloopmobile.com). *Widgets* and *applications* are phrases used interchangeably, but the best way to think about them is to consider a widget as something that sits in a web page or within another application, whereas an application can function independently.

Applications

One visit to iTunes or to one of the many sites that review applications for various phones shows you how many applications already exist. Hundreds of them, if not thousands, contain social media elements. Chat was one of first to appear, along with mobile versions of most social network sites (Facebook, LinkedIn, and so on). Here are examples of taking it to the next step:

- **Selecting a Wine For Dummies** (`http://www.zumobi.com/app_showcase`): Hey, this sounds familiar! If you are into wine, this app will help you choose the perfect one.

- **World of Goo** (`http://2dboy.com/games.php`): If you've always wanted to interact with Goo (a physics-based puzzle/construction game), here's your chance.

- **mig33** (`www.mig33.com`): Works on almost all carrier phones and allows you to share photos, stay connected with friend updates, get free IM and chat, and make cheap international calls. The application has millions of users in 200 countries.

Combining social with mobile technology allows the creativity to flow. The mobile phone provides a unique opportunity to engage with users that you can't achieve through traditional means.

Widgets

A *widget* is a small application that you can easily add to your website or to a mobile phone. Widgets can be tools or games, and they can be functional for business or just for fun. A widget typically does only one thing. Single purpose widget examples are

- Updates from eBay after auctions
- Stock quote updates
- Weather forecasts dependent on phone location
- Latest tweets from Twitter
- Simple brand-loyalty-building games, like filling the shopping cart as fast as you can to win loyalty points

You can easily enhance widgets with forms that ask people to enter their mobile phone number to get updates. You can use mobile in this context to get people to come back. For example, if they get knocked off the high score rankings, you can send them a text message to get them to come back and play some more to get their ranking back. Companies like ePrize (`www.eprize.com`), FUHU (`www.FuHu.com`), and Clearspring (`www.clearspring.com`) help you build a widget.

Adding Social Media Elements to Mobile

You should consider two additional elements while embarking on a mobile social media campaign: social graphs and search. These are important for any social media marketing program, but they're especially important in mobile ones.

Portable social graphs

*Social graph*s are the relationships that people have with each other, within a social network, an application, a site, or across the social web. Think of it as a visualization of relationships — how people connect to each other and what interests they share. But then think about the technical application of this concept. What if you knew who your customer's friends are and then provided user experiences that take advantage of that knowledge?

Facebook Connect allows Facebook data to be integrated into other websites and applications. With Facebook Connect, your customer could use a shopping application for the iPhone and then share mobile offers with their Facebook network. This would be a powerful way to recommend a product.

REMEMBER

Research shows that users are more likely to purchase products or services based on recommendations; friends and family are the most effective referrers.

Searching with mobile

Mobile search is just what the name implies. It's how you find things while on a mobile device, such as websites, people, and restaurants. It sounds like it should be simple; after all, don't all websites "show up" on your phone when you go to them? But what if you don't know the name of the site, or you're trying to find something and the mobile site address isn't what you thought it was?

Here are a few types of mobile searches:

- ✓ **Search engines:** Just like the web, search engines and portal sites have mobile versions. Sites like Google and Yahoo! are available on the mobile phone and are meant for mobile sites. One big difference is the way results are displayed. For example, when you search for restaurants in a particular city, the listings show the address and phone number (allowing you to easily click the phone number and call the restaurant).

- ✓ **Directories:** Local search and mobile directories are often available through the phone carrier. Some directory services use GPS *(global positioning)* technology to help determine where you are, and provide the right information. Directories assist users to find sites and are just like the yellow pages to the mobile web.

✔ **Recommendation services:** Not unlike technology on the Internet, mobile recommendation engines help users by providing similar or related content as their next step.

As a consumer, mobile search helps unlock the mystery and helps get the most out of your phone. As a marketer, you need to make sure that consumers can find the sites and campaigns that you work hard on. In order to be "found" by a mobile search engine, you have to look at a couple of things:

✔ **Make sure your mobile site has "good code."**

Search engines don't like messy sites that contain code errors.

Have your mobile site tested, and make sure it gets a passing grade by the code police. Two mobile site testers are `http://ready.mobi` and `http://mtld.mobi/emulator.php`.

✔ **Follow search engine optimization (SEO) best practices.**

SEO describes how to get websites to appear in search results for specific keywords. Use your most important keywords — the words that your customers use when searching for you — in your pages and your titles. Make sure that the site is accessible by using text links throughout the site. And then submit your mobile site to the mobile search engine: a simple process of going to the mobile search engine submission page and filling out the form.

You must make sure that your social mobile site is search friendly so that people can find you by phone. People may hear about an application or a fun mobile site from their friends and have to rely on a search service to find it. And your site must be searchable so that people can find each other and the elements of the application. Good user experience goes hand in hand with search friendliness.

Harnessing Mobile to Support Social Media

When considering mobile as part of a social influence marketing campaign, plan it like any marketing campaign, with a few added considerations.

✔ **Consider how you will support mobile campaigns and calls to action in other channels.**

The mobile campaign won't be successful in a vacuum — you need to market it everywhere.

✔ **Take a look at your customer list, and see if you can determine how your customers use mobile.**

Do they have iPhones or other smartphones?

✔ **Consider using a tool that can take advantage of the social graph, such as Facebook Connect or other existing social networks.**

✔ **Plan mobile applications or widgets but consider more than the iPhone.**

How can you support BlackBerry, Treo, and other smartphones with your widget or application?

✔ **Plan for user experience.**

Use usability testing to ensure that everything you develop is built with the user in mind.

✔ **Do your research first.**

Take a look at mobile usage within supporting applications (Facebook Mobile, Twitter, YouTube Mobile, MySpace Mobile), and integrate where it makes sense.

✔ **Consider using a mobile website.**

It allows users to engage with the brand and with each other.

✔ **Plan for success.**

Ensure you know what your objectives are — what do you want to get out of the relationship with people? — and ensure that you continually measure and report on your interactions.

✔ **Be relevant with your communications and with members of the community.**

Deciding When to Build a Mobile App

According to Nielsen, iPhone users download an average of 48 apps onto their device. Deciding whether your app could be among them is a tricky question. To make it easy, consider the following:

✔ **You can reach your target market.**

One important question to ask yourself is whether your target market is using mobile and is on the platform(s) you are targeting. This is critical to your success. You need to be sure that your audience is present to consider your app. In other words, fish where the fish are. Does your audience use an iPhone or Android? Do they spend much time on mobile devices? Answer these questions to your satisfaction before you go any further.

✔ **You have established goals.**

Like any good plan, it starts with goals. Understand what you want to accomplish by creating this app. Make sure you're not creating it just because your competitors have one. If it doesn't meet your company's needs, it's a waste of time and money.

✔ **You can demonstrate monetization potential or other value.**

Your app should solve a customer problem and provide real value. Apps aren't the novelty they once were. Your audience won't use it just because it's available. Also determine whether the app has value to advertisers. If it's appropriate, you may be able to entice some of your advertisers to be on your mobile app. According to a Forester Research report from March 2011 called "Mobile App Internet Recasts the Software and Services Landscape," apps will be a $38 billion industry by the year 2015. Lots of advertisers will be interested in jumping in.

✔ **You have the resources and the budget to make it happen.**

This one should be obvious, but often gets obscured in the excitement to build an app. If you don't have internal staff to create it, you'll need to outsource it. That requires a budget. Also, make sure your IT group has evaluated the linkage required between your e-commerce solution on the web. If you are selling a product that the customer needs to link to, you don't want to create a mess because they don't work together.

✔ **Your content reserves are available, and new content is being created.**

No one wants a mobile brochure. If you don't have good content and the promise of more on a regular basis, don't think it will magically create itself.

✔ **You have considered a mobile website.**

Is your website set up for mobile? This may be all you need. Consider the question carefully. It fully depends on what actions you want your customer to take and what platform fits them best.

✔ **You have a plan to get in front of your customer with your app.**

In May of 2011, *Wired* magazine reported that there were more than half a million apps in the Apple App Store. Meet your competition. You have to capture the attention of people who are dazzled every day by new, exciting apps. If you don't have a plan to help your customers discover yours, don't assume anyone will ever find it. You'll need to do more than just announce it.

Chapter 18

Energizing Your Employees for Social Media Marketing

. . . .

In This Chapter

▶ Connecting employees with social tools

▶ Using prediction markets to pick winners

▶ Making decisions collaboratively

. . . .

*U*ntil the beginning part of this decade, enterprise software looked and felt very different from the software that was designed for consumers. Enterprise software helped businesses manage customer relationships, handle knowledge management, communicate internally, and handle company operations. It focused on addressing the needs of IT managers more than the employees who were the users of the software. Emphasis was put on security, compliance, system control, interoperability, and maintenance — and strangely less on what employees wanted or needed. The fact that the software buyers (the IT managers) weren't the users (the employees) was largely to blame for this state of affairs. And then something changed.

When employees went home in the evenings, the software that they were using for their personal lives (web-based or otherwise) was progressively a lot better designed and easier to use. And more than that, the software allowed them to contribute content, share, comment, and connect with each other. Savvy technology companies realized that there was an opportunity to make enterprise software more like consumer software and social-oriented websites to better meet the needs of companies.

Steadily, these consumer-centric solutions gained traction in the corporate world, as employees started to discover that they could find free (or nearly free) and easy-to-use tools on the Internet. They could install these tools on their machines or access them online to do their jobs better. This consumerization of enterprise software forced IT managers to reevaluate how they chose software and how strict their security policies were. And with that, the Enterprise 2.0 transformation was born.

In this chapter, we discuss how you can practice social media marketing within your own company by encouraging collaboration, knowledge sharing, and communication. We also discuss the different tools that you can use to help you in this endeavor. After all, if you want your customers to influence each other about your brand and product, you might want to start by figuring out how you can encourage employees to positively influence each other as well.

We include this chapter in the book because if you plan to engage with consumers across the Internet and practice social media marketing, you had better be practicing those philosophies in your own backyard, too. It's one of the best ways to learn about social media marketing — to practice those philosophies internally within your organization.

Encouraging Your Employees to Collaborate

Enterprise 2.0 is the use of social software platforms within companies, or between companies and their partners or customers, according to Andrew McAfee, a Harvard Business School professor who coined the term. These software platforms borrow design philosophies, features, and even technology standards from the websites and web software that pervade the Internet.

Every day, more companies install these social software platforms because they want their employees to collaborate, communicate, share, and organize into communities of interest the way they do in their personal lives. There's no reason why your employees shouldn't use software built on these consumer-oriented design philosophies, with the collaboration layer built into the core — software like wikis, blogs, discussion forums, and microblogging solutions.

The best way to understand what web tools work for your employees is to ask them about the websites they visit and the web tools that they use in their personal lives. How they use consumer websites can give you hints at how they want to adopt enterprise tools.

The following sections include some recommendations for how you can get your employees to collaborate and socially influence each other in positive ways. These practices are a direct mirror of how you can engage with social influencers, too.

Employees always compete with each other for promotions, bonuses, and better career opportunities. That will never change, and it will always affect their willingness to collaborate and work with each other. As you encourage employees to socially influence each other, be aware of any insecurities they have.

Energizing employees: It's nothing new

This isn't the first time that energizing employees for social influence and knowledge sharing has been discussed. Debates in the knowledge management community on how best to get employees to collaborate date back to the early 1990s. For a long time, companies saw the Holy Grail of knowledge management as the ability to capture everything that was in an employee's head in a database so that if the employee were to leave the company, it wouldn't suffer.

This thinking evolved to the realization that no firm can truly capture the experiences and knowledge in an employee's brain, and by the time it did so (if that were even possible!), the information or knowledge is stale. Since then, the focus has shifted to energizing employees to collaborate, exchange information, and motivate one another to increase innovation and employee productivity.

Rewarding teams

Most companies are organized to reward individual performance and promote the rising stars more quickly than other employees. If you want to foster a collaborative environment where employees learn from each other, share their knowledge generously, and participate in social platforms geared toward harnessing the collective intelligence, think carefully about how you reward performance. You might be well served by putting more emphasis on team versus individual performance.

Treating everyone equally

Employees usually thrive on competition. That's a good thing. But employees who feel left out of the loop or feel that they aren't seen as critical to the organization are less likely to give their time and brain power for the community. Be sure that you treat every employee equally if you truly want to foster collaboration and the free exchange of information among your employees. They'll speak only if you give them ample opportunities and encouragement to do so. You need to let them speak on their own terms, too whether that be through the technologies that they prefer, the locations of their choice (team meetings, suggestion boxes, or one-on-one meetings), or with the mentors that they seek out.

Trusting your employees

Just as it's imperative for you to trust consumers and let them share ownership of your brand, so, too, must you trust your employees to converse, communicate, and collaborate with each other respectfully and productively. If you don't trust your employees, they won't trust you, and they definitely won't want to give their time to furthering the objectives of the organization. This matters most when you're trying to energize them for social influence: It requires a commitment and not just a job description to accomplish.

Creating the right culture

The right office culture is imperative if you want your employees to engage with one another in conversations, be transparent about what they don't know, and be willing to listen and learn from their peers, including the younger or more junior ones. Your culture needs to be one of humility and openness, and one that allows initiative without punishing people too harshly for mistakes. The way you need to behave in the social web to engage with your customers in a meaningful way applies to the way you must engage with your employees, too. And it all starts with culture.

Placing a premium on groups with a purpose

A key ingredient to energizing employees for social influence is to put the right mix of employees in a room (real or virtual) together to brainstorm, innovate, or accomplish a specific task. Bring an eclectic mix of employees together and ask them to collaborate on a specific task at hand. Their diverse skills and personalities result in unique results and can lay the foundation for a more collaborative work environment.

Collaborating in a work environment is very different from collaborating in one's personal life. You need clearly defined objectives for people to rally around; otherwise, valuable company time may be wasted.

Avoiding excessive snooping

We're always amazed to learn about companies that peek into their employees' e-mail accounts and watch what websites they visit. If you want to create a culture of social interaction where people in different offices or even countries come together and share their insights and learn from one another online, you need to make them feel that they're not being watched, tracked, or evaluated every step of the way. Treat them with the respect that you give your bosses, and they'll deliver amazing work. Whatever you do, don't snoop around. You'll lose their trust, respect, and commitment.

Picking Social Software for Social Influence

A myriad range of social software companies provides solutions for businesses. These vary from free software as a service (SaaS) solutions that you can rent for a few dollars per month to enterprise-grade solutions that cost hundreds of thousands of dollars and have been retooled for the social world. Finding the right solution for your company as you create an environment that energizes employees for social influence can be confusing, but here are the four classes of software and web solutions to consider.

Enterprise software

If you belong to a large organization, you probably don't control what software you get to use. In these instances, you should try to influence your IT department to buy emergent social software or enterprise software upgrades that include social functionality that can either be plugged into your enterprise environment or run independently:

- **Microsoft SharePoint** (`http://sharepoint.microsoft.com`; see Figure 18-1) is probably the most popular collaboration software in companies today and integrates with Microsoft Office and other Microsoft products very easily.

- **SAP** (`www.sap.com`) is deployed across large enterprises as it handles industrial grade business operations, customer management, financial, and HR needs very well.

- **IBM** (`www.ibm.com`), with its web sphere portal, is another great option; it's easy to build custom applications on it that can be delivered through a portal environment.

- **Telligent** (`http://telligent.com`) is known for its rich community functionality (its Community server product) and how it integrates with the rest of a company's IT infrastructure.

Every day, these enterprise-grade collaboration platforms add more social features to their application suites. Most have web-based interfaces, too.

Emergent enterprise social software

Emergent enterprise social software products are built from the ground up to be collaboration tools, leveraging the design philosophies, needs, and requirements of everyday people. They borrow from the likes of Facebook, Wikipedia, Twitter, and YouTube but add an enterprise flavor that makes them powerful. They are becoming established players:

✔ **Confluence** (www.atlassian.com/software/confluence)

✔ **Socialtext** (www.socialtext.com)

✔ **NewsGator** (www.newsgator.com; see Figure 18-2)

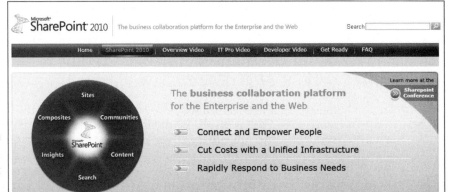

Figure 18-1:
Microsoft
SharePoint.

Figure 18-2:
NewsGator's
home page.

These solutions plug into existing corporate software environments and work with the enterprise software effectively. Because the companies who provide enterprise social software understand the needs of big business, they're usually compliant with the security requirements of most IT departments. The software is delivered shrink-wrapped or in some cases as a software as a service model. (With the software as a service model, you don't buy software but lease it on a monthly basis over the Internet.)

Small-scale social software

Smaller, significantly cheaper solutions that work nicely for small business environments are categorized as small-scale social software. Free or nearly free applications are

- **Google's Application Suite** (www.google.com/apps) integrates nicely with Google mail. The Google application suite is mostly free and shares the same user experience of Google search. So if you like the search product, you'll like this.

- **Zoho** (www.zoho.com; see Figure 18-3) is similar to the Google Application Suite but far richer in functionality. It is also web-based and includes several related tools, such as project management and a customer relationship management software.

Figure 18-3:
Zoho's
online suite.

Other strong companies to look at include

- **Traction Software** (www.tractionsoftware.com) is feature-rich and combines the best of blogging with a wiki environment. Traction Software isn't free and, for some users, can appear complex, but it's a great solution for knowledge management.

- **TeamWork Live** (www.teamworklive.com) is a simple application that's grounded in project management philosophy. As a result, it's designed to make it very easy for you to create your own project site, share it with a select group of people, and collaborate around it. It can be used throughout your organization.

- **37signals** (www.37signals.com) takes a different approach in that it has a distinct set of specific web tools that can help you conduct your business. From a project management application to a tool that tracks leads, it accomplishes a very specific need.

Consumer social software

We'd be remiss if we didn't mention the fact that you can also use consumer-oriented social platforms for your business collaboration needs. Whether it's LinkedIn (www.linkedin.com) (see Chapter 11), Plaxo (www.plaxo.com), Ning (www.ning.com), shown in Figure 18-4, SlideShare (www.slideshare.net), or even Facebook (www.facebook.com), they're all capable of handling private groups who upload and share files and discussions.

Some of these platforms may be more secure than others (especially with third-party tools and plug-ins overlaid on top of them), but they're all options for collaborating among employees nevertheless. In the case of LinkedIn, its third-party plug-ins let you share presentations, publish news, run polls, and collaborate on documents, all from within LinkedIn and with people in your social graph.

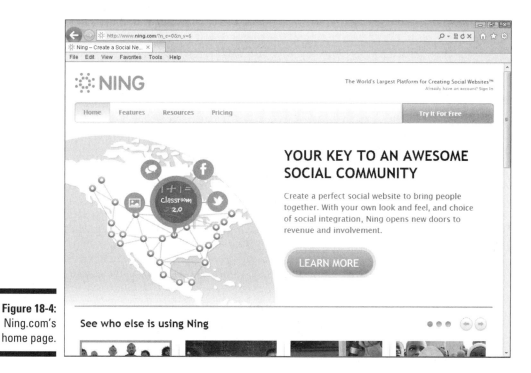

Figure 18-4:
Ning.com's
home page.

Using Prediction Markets to Pick Winners

We've seen some people define *prediction markets* as speculative markets created for the purposes of making predictions. Sounds simple, doesn't it? Assets are created with financial values, and the current market prices can be interpreted as a prediction of the probability of the event or the expected value of the parameter.

Here's what that really means: You can use your employees or your customers — and business partners, too, for that matter — to help you make better decisions. And the way you do it is by setting up a fake stock market–type environment using prediction market software where each participant is given a set amount to invest in different options (whatever you're trying to decide on). How much people invest in an option drives up its price or keeps it low. When you have hundreds and thousands of people participating and placing their bets, you get a clear sense of what the community believes to be the strongest option. Think of it as calculated social influence where the influencers are asked to put their money where their mouth is.

Companies around the world use prediction markets to make decisions. These can be strategic business decisions, such as where to locate a manufacturing plant, or simpler decisions, such as which television advertisement to run. The social influence of the community is automatically factored into the price of each option, providing very tangible guidance on what the community thinks has the greatest chance of success. HP, for example, uses prediction markets to predict workstation computer sales. In six out of eight times, the results from the prediction market were more accurate than internal corporate forecasts. Probably one of the very first prediction markets was by the University of Iowa Tippie College of Business. Called the Iowa Electronics Markets (IEM), it's been accurately predicting political election results since 1988 with only 1.33 percent error rate in voter totals.

As you look at your own company and how you can tap into the collective intelligence of your employees, think about using prediction markets. Not only will you get better advice, but you also get a more deeply engaged community of employees participating and feeling that their voices are being heard within the organization. When they're participating in prediction markets internally, they'll probably want to test the same concepts on customers and business partners, too. Your customers will feel more engaged with your company when they become a part of the decision-making process around products and services. It is a win-win situation from whatever perspective that you look.

Prediction markets require participation. This might seem obvious, but you should keep in mind that you need a committed number of participants to make it work and gain collective intelligence. When you establish a prediction market within your organization, make sure the question being posed has resonance and meaning with a large enough community of employees so that you get the maximum participation.

The same goes for external-based prediction markets. Customers aren't spending their time waiting for you to engage with them in prediction markets to help you make better business decisions for them. Be sure to incentivize them to participate, and make sure you're asking meaningful questions. Remember that these prediction markets can nicely serve to jump-start your community efforts, whether they're internal communities or external ones!

Here are a few of the prediction market software solutions that you can use for your prediction market needs:

- ✔ Intrade (www.intrade.com). Figure 18-5 shows the Intrade home page.
- ✔ Inkling (www.inklingmarkets.com).
- ✔ Lumenogic (www.lumenogic.com).

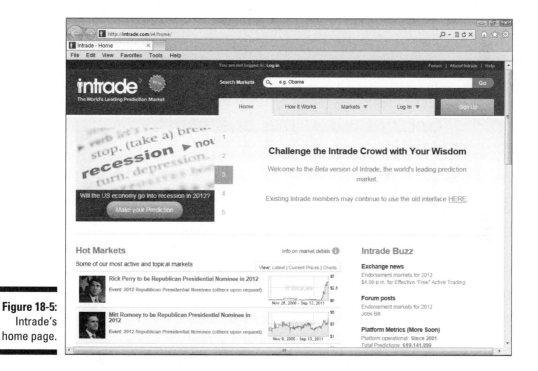

Figure 18-5: Intrade's home page.

Rethinking Intranet

Historically, an *intranet* was defined as an employee-only web-based network for communication, collaboration, self-service, knowledge management, and business decision-making. Most intranets were never designed to allow or encourage social influence, even though they're the ideal platforms for furthering collaboration and knowledge sharing within your company.

Many of the intranets were originally *top-down* (management-controlled), rigid, inflexible, and uninviting experiences that served the needs of the Corporate Communications and Human Resources departments but not anyone else. They were used to communicate messages from CEOs and senior management, distribute company announcements, and provide human resources and finance self-service forms to employees.

Intranets slowly evolved to include basic collaboration features and the ability to create and manage department-level pages; they also grew to include key performance indicator dashboards for senior executives. But still for the most part, these intranets were static, top-down, rigid tools that by their very nature discouraged collaboration and social influencing.

For your intranet to go social and truly encourage collaboration and social influence to take place, you must adapt it to enable clear communication, collaboration, navigation, search, accessibility, and more. We give you some tips on optimizing your intranet in the sections that follow.

Getting rid of the buzzwords

When you design your intranet, move away from the business and technical jargon that you may have used to describe the intranet or label features on it. Don't use words like *portals, knowledge management, digital dashboards, taxonomies, enterprise collaboration,* and *codification.* Use more inspiring language, words employees can relate to, in all your communications. In other words, humanize the intranet through language but also through the design.

For example, the original intranet at Shiv's company was called "Mom 3000," largely because, like a mother, it had all the answers to questions that employees had. Because it was so advanced, the "3000" was added to it. Needless to say, the employees all loved the intranet and grew attached to it not just because of all its features but because of its personality.

Don't try to control too much

Most intranet managers know now that collaboration functionality is essential for the success of any intranet. But many still launch those collaboration tools with overly restrictive controls. Whether it's wiki functionality or group and department pages, make the default setting on all pieces of functionality open to everyone.

Let there be more effort in password-protecting something than in opening it to the community. By default, let everyone view and edit every page on the intranet unless something has specifically been designated as confidential. And while you're at it, don't dictate how and with what tools your employees should collaborate; let them make those decisions.

Surfacing the connections

Instead of focusing only on publishing information and providing business applications to the employees, look for ways to connect people to one another. Let the intranet reveal strong and weak ties between people and create communities based on the information and collaboration needs of employees.

Make it as easy as possible for the employees by building functionality into the intranet so that people who have shared interests and objectives are linked to each other automatically. This doesn't mean publishing organizational charts but quite the opposite — having the *intranet* tell people who else within the organization has similar interests or objectives and encouraging them. The Google employee intranet, Moma, approached this by having each employee's goals and objectives visible on the intranet right next to contact information. That way, an employee would know whether their proposed conversation or project recommendation would be of high or low interest to the other employee even before contacting him.

Taking search social

Intranet managers generally believe — and rightly so — that search is the killer application (in a good way) of their intranet. They also recognize that search is extremely difficult to get right, primarily because employees expect the search to work as well as Google or Bing, even though the intranet search budget is miniscule compared to how much those companies invest in search.

One way to mitigate this is by incorporating social features into the search experience and by combining it with the telephone directory. When you prioritize search results based on what other users find to be useful and link the results with the specific users who find the results valuable, the perception of search increases dramatically because people in an organization are typically interested in the same content that others find useful. And very often, they have deeper questions beyond the content — and are always seeking people who can answer those questions. All the major enterprise search vendors, like Endeca (`www.endeca.com`) and Apache Lucene (`lucene.apache.org`), offer some form of social search.

Allowing alternate access

Critical to the success of any intranet today — and even more so if it's one that needs to spur collaboration — is the ability to provide multiple ramps into the intranet. You must build functionality so that employees can install a desktop widget that serves as a mini-window that's easily accessible to the intranet, updating them on who has posted what and making it extremely easy to upload content and share it themselves.

Similarly, it's important to build a mobile version of your intranet so that employees can get updates on their smartphones and iPads about new information published and collaboration spaces that they are participating in. Notifications are extremely important tools that further collaboration and social influence. Each time someone submits something to a collaboration space, the other members should be notified (if they so choose).

One company that gives you the mobile technology that you can incorporate into your intranet is Good at www.good.com; see Figure 18-6.

Figure 18-6: One example of a mobile intranet provider (Good).

Promoting the value of historical record

Wikipedia (shown in Figure 18-7) has done an immense amount to teach the value of a historical record. Whether your intranet has wiki functionality (the ability for anyone to format and edit the page), definitely make sure that the pages have *roll-back functionality* (the ability to see previous versions of the page).

Figure 18-7:
Wikipedia,
the mother
of all wikis.

With roll-back functionality (or *version control,* as some people call it), employees can always look at previous versions of pages. Or in the case of discussion areas, employees can view earlier collaboration, which often provides great insight as time passes. But more than that, the transparency that comes with having rollback functionality builds trust and openness in a way that no top-down communication can.

Giving your intranet a pulse

Intranet managers can learn a lot from the social web. Probably the most important lesson is for you to give your intranet a pulse. To fuel those social connections and encourage employees to collaborate with each other on the intranet, you must make sure that the intranet provides the ongoing motivations for people to collaborate.

The most important way to do this is by showcasing the pulse of the intranet. Think of it as a Twitter-like pulse, which shows all the intranet-related activities of a person's social graph in a streaming list. It encourages the employee to return frequently to the intranet and learn how others are using it. But most important, it encourages the employee to respond to the activities of others on the intranet. The streaming pulse should include documents uploaded, comments made, searches conducted, groups joined, discussions initiated, and the like. It should also include the ability for users to publish status updates and comment on the updates of others. Practically all the Enterprise 2.0 software vendors offer this functionality out of the box.

Making the goal to destructure and deorganize

What is often a company's greatest strength is also its greatest weakness, and that is its organizational structure that enables resources of all kinds to work harmoniously to enable the company to achieve its objectives. But it also means that employees have to be fragmented and divided into teams and departments that in time have difficulty working and communicating with each other.

The social intranet is one where the intranet helps to break down those organizational barriers. It also encourages people to make decisions and collaborate free of positional bias. To encourage collaboration and the natural social influence that usually takes place, encourage destructuring, and build online communities of employees where people are encouraged to be honest, transparent, and willing to declare what influences their points of view. With that in place, you'll be well on the path to having an intranet that truly energizes employees and allows for the social influence to take place most naturally.

Giving employees other choices

Irrespective of how well you design your intranet, there will always be employees who'll want to use some external products or websites for their collaboration needs. Some may even want to stick to sharing documents over e-mail and using a file server.

That's fine. Don't force them to migrate to your intranet. Ideally, people should gravitate toward it if it is indeed the best solution. If not, let people use what they want. It's far more important that they collaborate and influence one another than it is for them to use the intranet. Let them make that choice.

Chapter 19

Applying Metrics to the SMM Realm

*T*here's a common myth that social media marketing isn't really measurable. Many a consultant has said that you can't measure the value of a conversation. They believe that measuring a phenomenon is always difficult, especially when you're still figuring out how to market in it.

The truth is that social media marketing is as measurable as any other form of marketing. It wasn't the case two years ago — but that's quickly changing. Today, there are tools, techniques, and mechanisms to measure social influence marketing. These are broader brand metrics, which may not be as measurable as a direct-response marketer may like.

There are also specific campaign- or program-oriented metrics that you can capture, analyze, and map to other performance indicators. These may be in the category of a YouTube campaign, an online community effort, a pass-along widget, a blogger outreach program, or a viral video campaign.

It's all well and good to capture metrics about your social media marketing efforts, whether they're broader brand metrics or specific ones around social media marketing campaigns. It's also extremely important to marry these metrics with your other marketing metrics and see how they correlate. For example, it's no use having lots of widget installations if they have no correlation with brand awareness, favorability, or actual sales. As a result, the most important challenge in social media marketing is not measuring it, but correlating the data to broader business objectives. Therefore, when you put your social media marketing metrics in place, think about how you can use them to determine whether you met your marketing objectives and also how you want to interpret them in the context of the rest of your marketing and business objectives. Otherwise, you'll just be capturing meaningless data.

Taking a Core Measure of Social Media Marketing

In this section, we start by suggesting a core brand-oriented metric — the single metric that you must map your social media marketing objectives against. And not just that. You must map your brand against this metric on an ongoing basis. We call it the social media marketing score, or the SMM score. It's inspired by the Net Promoter Score, which asks customers, regarding the specific product or service, the question "How likely are you to recommend the product to a colleague or a friend?" It then subtracts the number of detractors from the number of promoters to give a single Net Promoter Score. You'll notice that although the Net Promoter Score is fundamentally a loyalty metric, the SMM score is a brand-health metric, but based on customer interactions, too.

As you look at the SMM score, keep in mind that the industry is still in the throes of determining the best holistic metric. Check out the Social Media Advertising Consortium (`www.smac.org`) for more information on this subject.

The SMM score is designed to be a pivotal measure that recognizes the participatory nature of branding and, more directly, your brand's health compared to all of your direct competitors in the social web. Think of the SMM score as the blood pressure for your brand in the social web. It'll tell you how you're doing but not why or what to do about anything that might be going wrong. Those questions are answered when you dig deeper into understanding the factors that contribute to the SMM score.

You calculate the SMM score based on these two critical attributes:

- ✔ The total share of consumer conversations that your brand has online. This is fundamentally about reach — the volume of conversations surrounding your brand.

- ✔ The degree to which consumers like, dislike, or have no opinion of your brand when they talk to each other about you. It's centered around impact or consumer sentiment.

These two attributes combined make up the SMM score. This combination of measures is important because it isn't enough that your brand has a very large share of consumer conversations, especially if most of those conversations are negative in nature. That does more harm than good to your brand. It's important that you adjust the volume of the conversations for the sentiment surrounding your brand.

You should track the SMM score for each brand on an ongoing basis as the brand launches campaigns, brings new products to market, activates influencers, and engages with customers across the social web. Be sure to track your SMM score before your campaigns so that you can always benchmark your score against a baseline.

Here's the formula for calculating the SMM score for your brand, relative to its competitors:

```
SMM score = net sentiment for the brand , net sentiment for the industry
```

The components of the formula are as follows:

```
Net sentiment for the brand = (positive + neutral conversations - negative
                conversations) , total conversations for the brand
Net sentiment for the industry = (positive + neutral conversations — negative
                conversations) , total conversations for the industry
```

Note four important factors about the SMM score:

- ✔ **This is a relative score versus your competitors.**

  The competitors you choose to include in the calculations directly impact your SMM score. So the SMM score is primarily a relative measurement.

- ✔ **The SMM score combines positive and neutral sentiment.**

  An argument can be made for using only positive sentiment and ignoring neutral sentiment. The SMM score includes neutral sentiment, too, because any mention of your brand helps your brand awareness (as long as it isn't negative). And therefore, you should factor it into the score.

- ✔ **The sourcing and quality of the data that you use to compute the SMM score may directly affect the total scores.**

  The data that you use to compute your SMM score comes from the conversational monitoring firms that we discuss in earlier chapters. These companies, including Visible Technologies (www.visible technologies.com; see Figure 19-1), Cymfony (www.cymfony.com), Nielsen BuzzMetrics (www.nielsen-online.com/products_buzz. jsp?section=pro_buzz), Lithium (www.lithium.com), and others count the total number of conversations pertaining to your brand (usually using brand mentions as a way to make the calculation) and then, through a technological system, add sentiment (positive, neutral, and negative) to each conversational instance.

✔ **Some monitoring vendors let you capture mixed conversations, too.**

These are conversations that include both positive and negative sentiment within them. If you're capturing mixed sentiment for your brand, use those numbers for the denominator (total brand or total industry) calculations, but don't use them for the numerator. Mixed conversations, by definition, can't reliably be ascertained as helping the brand and, therefore, can't be included with positive or neutral conversations in the numerator.

Figure 19-1:
Visible
Technologies.

The data you get from a monitoring firm may not always be good. These technology vendors are getting better and better every day in capturing all the conversations that are happening across the social web and running those conversations against their sentiment engines. But they don't capture the sum of all the social media conversations. However, most of the large vendors grab data from all the blogs, forums, microblogging solutions, and community sites online. They account for the majority of the conversations happening online and, in that, serve as a good measure.

To give you a perspective on how SMM scoring works, Table 19-1 shows an example of SMM scores developed with historical data from the auto industry. There were 2,106,523 social media conversations concerning five brands in the auto industry in the last six months of 2008. The brands included were Ford, Honda, Toyota, Nissan, and GM. The table shows their share of voice, net sentiment, and their SMM scores.

Table 19-1	Auto Industry SMM Scores		
Company	*Share of Voice*	*Net Sentiment*	*SMM Score*
Honda	29.6%	81%	30
Ford	31.8%	78%	31
GM	5.8%	73%	5
Nissan	14.5%	80%	15
Toyota	18.1%	80%	18

What's interesting is how share of voice and net sentiment both impact the SMM score. Toyota's share of voice is larger than Nissan's, which contributes to its higher SMM score, for example. Ford, which faced similar challenges to GM in the last half of 2008, has a much higher SMM score. This may be because in the last year they've invested a lot more in managing their brand in social media. Although GM was early in experimenting with social media, with a CEO blog and a UGC (User Generated Content) campaign, its handling of the bailout may have hurt its reputation in the social web. With all the changes that have taken place in the auto industry since 2008, these numbers would look quite different today.

So what do you do with the SMM score? You track it against all your marketing activities to determine how they're impacting your brand in the social web. As you track your SMM score over time, you should be able to answer questions like these:

- What impact does advertising in all the different media have on a SMM score?

- How does a SMM score affect overall brand affinity and purchasing decisions for your brand over time?

- What does it take to put a program in place to manage one's SMM score effectively? Can you do so in a cost-effective manner?

- How does your SMM score differ based on specific topics of conversations?

Along with actual metrics based on customer behavior, you can use heuristic (or expert) evaluations to ascertain how your brand is doing in the social web in relation to its direct competitors. Wetpaint and The Altimeter Group came together to establish a heuristic framework for ranking the world's most engaging brands. Topping the list of most engaging brands were Starbucks, Dell, eBay, Google, and Microsoft.

Considering Influencer-Specific Metrics

It isn't enough to calculate your SMM score on an ongoing basis. That's a very important measure — it's your brand health in the social web — but it isn't the only measure. You need to measure how your brand stacks up against the influencers whom you care about, the platforms on which you participate, and for the campaigns that you run.

As discussed in Chapter 1, there are three types of influencers surrounding your customers: expert, referent, and positional influencers. You need to know how many of the influencers in each of these categories are favorably inclined toward your brand and are, as a result, favorably influencing your customers.

This is no easy task, and the truth is that determining and measuring the favorability of influencers toward your brand is an imperfect science. It simply hasn't been figured out yet. But here are some tips for measurement surrounding specific types of influencers:

- ✔ **Expert influencers:** After you identify them, track their press mentions, blog posts, Twitter streams, Facebook comments, and discussion forum responses to determine how favorably or unfavorably they talk about your brand. Many of the conversational monitoring vendors provide tools that help you identify these influencers and track their favorability toward you.

- ✔ **Referent influencers:** Technology companies like RapLeaf (www. rapleaf.com; see Figure 19-2) can help you identify your referent influencers on the specific social platforms by anonymously analyzing the profiles of people for mentions of your industry category or your brand specifically. They then map these to a meta-social graph and can tell you how many people within your demographic and target audience have high networks, influence other people significantly, and talk about your category or brand favorably.

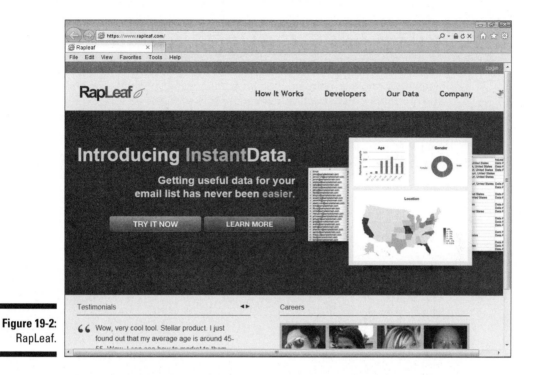

Figure 19-2:
RapLeaf.

✔ **Positional influencers:** Other vendors, like Clearspring (www.clear spring.com) and Gigya (www.gigya.com), do the tracking for you by capturing how people download widgets that they see on their friends' blogs and add them to their own pages. This helps identify both positional and referent influencers. For example, Razorfish (Shiv's former employer) patented an incremental action tag solution that tracks how social media applications (widgets, applications, viral media, and so on) are downloaded and passed along.

After you identify the influencers and you're tracking their favorability toward your brand, the next question is whether they're actually influencing significant conversations across the social web and pushing people to your website or to buy your product. That's not easy to measure, but the industry is moving in that direction.

Fundamentally, with your social influencers, irrespective of the type, you want to understand who they are, where they're participating, with whom they're participating, what topics they're interested in, and how much they're sharing.

Evaluating Each Platform's Metrics

Different social platforms have different mechanisms for measurement. For each major social platform, you must know what you can measure and what the numbers you get actually mean. In this section, we look at the major social platforms and discuss the forms of measurement on each one of them.

Measurement components fall into four "buckets." Each time you launch a social media marketing program, try to check off measurement objectives against these four criteria, as defined by Sometrics (www.sometrics.com; see Figure 19-3), one of the leading in-game payments provider.

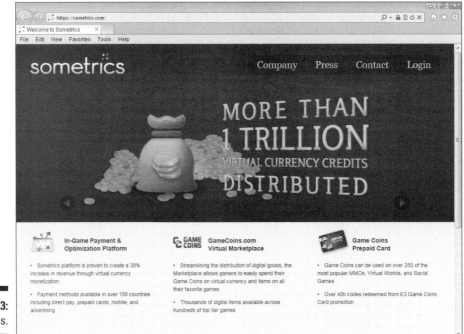

Figure 19-3:
Sometrics.

Here are the four buckets:

- ✔ **Traffic:** Includes impressions, unique users, and basic engagement, including page views per visit.

- ✔ **Demographics:** Covers the basics of who is visiting or interacting with your brand. It typically includes age, gender, income, education, and location.

✔ **Sociographics:** Captures your customers' friends and their relative importance, based on their interests and where they lie in your customers' social graphs.

✔ **Social actions:** Includes the actual social activity undertaken by your customers when they interact with you on the social platform — the specifics of what they do.

TIP

For every metric that you track for your brand on the different social platforms, try to capture the same metrics for your direct competitors. It's extremely important to know how their Facebook fan pages, YouTube channels, Twitter accounts, and MySpace profiles engage people in contrast to your own presence on the social networks.

Facebook

Your brand probably has a fan page on Facebook. You may even have done some advertising on Facebook. (See Chapter 7 for more about Facebook.) So now you want to learn about how to engage those fans more successfully. You can do that by going to fan-page-related metrics called Facebook Insights. You can find these metrics by going to your Facebook page, clicking Edit Info, and choosing View Insights. Remember that you need to be designated as a page administrator to see the Edit Info link.

Once you have chosen View Insights, a dashboard page opens with a variety of overview metrics. You will also see three subtabs show up on the left side underneath the Insights tab. They represent more detailed reports for three key areas — Fans, Reach and Talking About This.

Following is a look at the dashboard report and then we drill down to the three subreports:

✔ **Dashboard report:** The dashboard report gives you an overview of what Facebook considers to be four key overall metrics. It also shows you the percentage the number is moving up or down. This gives you an at-a-glance look at how that metric is progressing.

The key metrics are

• **Total Likes:** All the people who have liked your page during the timeframe of the report.

• **Friends of Fans:** The number of friends that your total number of friends has.

• **People Talking About This:** The total number of people who are engaged with your content.

• **Weekly Total Reach:** The number of people who have come in contact with your content in any way.

Next, we look at the three subtab reports:

✔ **Fans:** If you have a fan page on Facebook, the most basic measure is the number of fans. These are the Facebook users who have specifically chosen to align themselves with your brand. The number of fans largely represents how popular your brand is on Facebook. This is important because you can blast messages to all your fans. Along with number of fans, the average growth of fans is an important metric, too.

For example, one of the most popular fan pages on Facebook is the Disney fan page for *Toy Story 3;* see Figure 19-4. With more than 24 million Likes on their page, they are a success story. Keep in mind, however, that even though Disney is a top Facebook fan page, many small businesses have achieved marketing success with even just 1,000 fans.

Figure 19-4: The Facebook page for Disney's *Toy Story 3.*

✔ **Reach:** Reach literally refers to how many people you reached with the content you have on your page. These are people who are aware of your brand. They could be fans or nonfans who become aware of you via one of their friends. In this section, you see statistics including age, gender, and location of your fans; how you reached them, either through organic or paid ads or virally; unique users by frequency; and external referrers (where your traffic came from).

✔ **Talking About This:** This measure tells you how many people are interacting with your content by discussing it or sharing it with others. This includes comments, Wall posts, Likes, and other interactions generated by each post. This data includes a breakdown of the age, gender, and location of the people talking about you and how people are talking about you (for example, Liking your page or attending an event).

To learn more about Facebook Insights, Facebook has posted a 20-minute video tutorial at `www.learnpageinsights.com`.

Outside the fan pages, Facebook applications allow you to capture a lot of important metrics. Building a Facebook application is like building a website: You need to define the strategy; brainstorm the concept; and then, with the help of a designer and a developer, actually build it before submitting the application to Facebook for approval so that it can appear in its directory and be made available to all users. If you've built a Facebook application and have it running on your fan page or on the profile pages of Facebook users, you can capture data about the number of users who have

✔ Added your application tab

✔ Added your application profile box to their profiles

✔ Added your application information section

✔ Bookmarked your application

✔ Subscribed to your application e-mails

You can also capture a variety of metrics for user activity involving your Facebook applications. These include the number of

✔ Active users during the past 7 days.

✔ Active users during the past 30 days.

✔ Canvas page views. (The *canvas page* is the main page for your application.)

✔ Unique canvas page viewers.

And then, if you're more technically minded, here are some more technical metrics:

✔ Number of API (application programming interface) calls made

✔ Number of unique users on whose behalf your application made API calls

✔ Average HTTP request time for canvas pages

As you can see, a lot of activity on Facebook can be measured. What matters most, though, is how those measurements support your business. It's no use measuring a lot of different things on Facebook if it doesn't help your business. Also, metrics aren't useful if you don't know what to do with them. As a result, before you start a social media marketing program on Facebook, think carefully about what you're trying to accomplish and which metrics are most appropriate for that purpose. And then start the measuring. In fact, this guideline applies to any form of measurement on all the social platforms.

AppData (www.appdata.com) tracks the most popular Facebook applications on a daily basis. You can also view which developers are responsible for the most popular applications. As of August 2011, some of the most popular applications include CityVille, Empires & Allies, Texas HoldEm Poker, and FarmVille. The developers with the most installations of their applications are Zynga, Microsoft, Mensing, Electronic Arts, and Wooga.

YouTube and video clips

With the launch of YouTube Insight (www.youtube.com/my_videos_insight), you have access to more data on the clips you publish and who views them. YouTube Insight gives you the following statistics about your users and clips:

- ✔ **Views:** First and foremost, you can see the total number of views charted out by week. This is the same data that public users can see. The tool also shows you the number of unique views and the number of views by location (country or state). This can tell you if the people watching your clips are actually in your target market.

- ✔ **Discovery:** This data tells you how people found your videos. This is valuable because if you know the journey that viewers have taken to get to you, you can try to strengthen that path so that that more people will find you.

- ✔ **Demographics:** This categorizes the data by age, telling you what percentage of the views came from users in specific age groups, such as 25–34-year-olds.

- ✔ **Community:** This gives you information about the people who have interacted with your YouTube clips. This includes commenting, ratings, and favoriting counts.

- ✔ **Subscribers:** This data tells you about the churn of your channel viewers — how they came and when they left. The unit measures are time and geographic region.

✔ **Hot Spots:** This is an interesting measure that requires a good bit of viewing data. If you don't have a large amount, you won't be able to use it. Essentially, it measures whether your video holds the audience's interest. Are they watching it all the way through? Do they stop it halfway? It's not enough to know how many people watch it. You want to know how it impacts them.

You can also export these statistics from YouTube Insights to a spreadsheet to easily keep track of your stats from month to month.

You can also narrow these statistics by video or by geographic region. This is extremely helpful because it can tell you, for example, how much higher your Japanese viewers rated a video clip as compared to ratings from your American viewers.

However, these metrics from YouTube are sometimes not enough to get an accurate picture. In that case, it helps to have more metrics, and fortunately, analytics companies like TubeMogul (`www.tubemogul.com`; see Figure 19-5) can provide those.

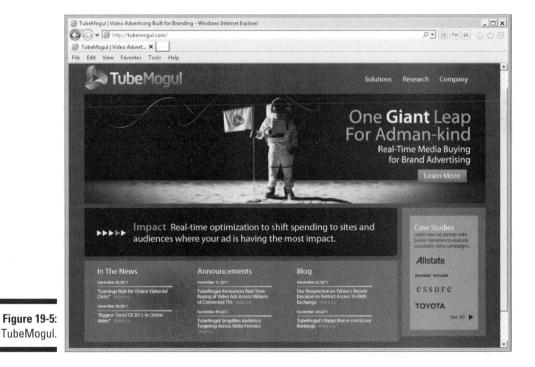

Figure 19-5:
TubeMogul.

Here are some of the analytics that companies like TubeMogul can provide if you use their services to upload and distribute video clips across the social web:

- ✔ **E-mail and embed reports:** Tells you the number of times your video clip has been e-mailed to someone or embedded on a blog or a website.

- ✔ **Link intelligence:** Gives you insight into who is linking to your video clips. The data includes information about links on both blogs and traditional websites.

- ✔ **Aggregation of data:** Lets you view aggregate statistics on several video clips at a time. For example, you can access aggregate data on clips that all belong to a single campaign.

Also, depending on whether you're using a video site with Adobe Flash, you can also track viewed minutes, viewer attention, per-stream quality, syndication tracking, and player tracking.

Twitter

Because Twitter has an open API (application programming interface), you can measure a lot more on Twitter than elsewhere. This is largely because developers have built dozens and dozens of analytic tools on top of Twitter. All of these can help you understand the reach and frequency of the 140-character tweets.

As with the blogosphere, you can learn a lot about the number of people who get your tweets, how many are retweeted, and which influencers help you the most. But there's something you need to keep in mind: What you can't find out is who those actual people are who are reading the tweets — their demographics, psychographics, and behaviors. In other words, don't expect to get from Twitter the same level of detail around your customers that you do when you run banner campaigns across the Internet. This may change in time, but as we're writing this book, those numbers aren't as accessible.

Here's what you can find out from Twitter:

- ✔ **Brand mentions:** The first and most basic metric for Twitter is knowing how your brand is mentioned and with what frequency on Twitter. Twitter Search (http://search.twitter.com, as shown in Figure 19-6) lets you scan all published tweets for mentions of your brand. Twitter Search can also help with understanding the volume of tweets about your brand.

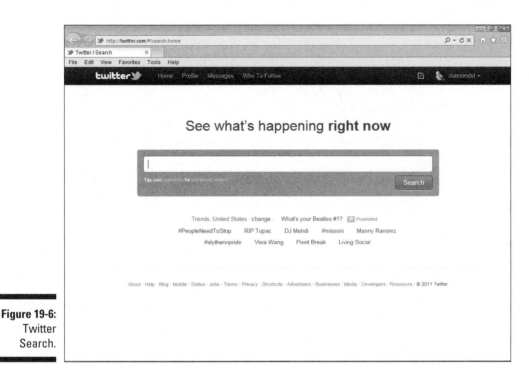

Figure 19-6:
Twitter
Search.

✔ **Influence:** You can measure influence in Twitter more directly than in any other social platform. With tools like Twitalyzer (www.twitalyzer.com), you can measure the reach, velocity, and social capital of anyone on Twitter, including your own brand. Tweet Grader (http://tweet.grader.com/) also computes a username's relative ranking compared to other users on Twitter. Another Twitter influence measuring tool is TweetLevel (http://tweetlevel.edelman.com), created by Edelman Digital. It analyzes a tweeter's influence, popularity, engagement, and trust.

✔ **Pass-alongs and click-throughs:** Knowing how much your influencers tweet about you is very important to track as well. The best way to do this is by continuously scanning the list of tweets that mention your brand or your username specifically. This helps you understand how much you're being retweeted. Dashboards like TweetDeck (www.tweetdeck.com; see Figure 19-7) (now a part of Twitter) can make this tracking much easier because they allow you to list multiple search terms and see all your replies (basically, tweets that reference your username) in one place. You can also connect across other networks like Facebook, MySpace, LinkedIn, foursquare, and Google Buzz.

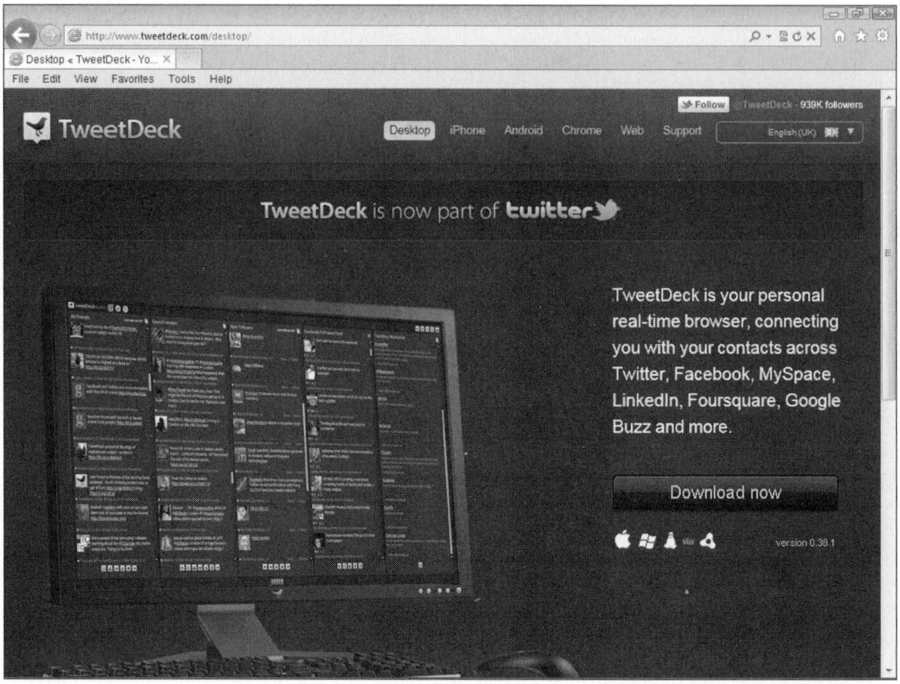

Figure 19-7:
TweetDeck.

In addition to tracking tweets that have been passed along, you may want to understand how many tweets have resulted in clicks to your website. This is where services like bitly (`http://bitly.com/`; see Figure 19-8) and Tweetburner (`http://www.tweetburner.com`) come into the picture. You can shorten website addresses using these services for your tweets. But the greatest benefit is that when you do so, you can track the exact number of people who clicked the link in your tweet over time. For example, if you're promoting a special discount, you can tweet about that discount and include a link to the page on your website using bitly. You can see, on an hourly basis, the number of people who actually click the link in your tweet. That way, you can determine the number of clicks and the number of people who took advantage of the discount.

Another loosely related factor to consider with Twitter and your website: It's important to track the number of visitors coming to your website from Twitter. This is helpful to understand from a lead-generation perspective. Knowing how many people are coming to your website from Twitter versus from search engine or display banner campaigns can and should influence how much effort you put into your Twitter marketing efforts.

Figure 19-8:
bitly.

The Twitter API is very flexible, allowing new developers to quickly build new Twitter applications. So by the time you read this chapter, there may be a new Twitter analytics tool out on the market, which is why we recommend always searching the web for new Twitter applications or using a Twitter directory like the Twitter Fan Wiki (`twitter.pbworks.com/Apps`).

The blogosphere

Don't ignore the blogosphere. Outside Facebook, most online conversations happen within the blogosphere. Measuring the influence and reach of your brand across the blogosophere can be tricky, though. Millions and millions of blogs are published every day with billions of posts published. Does a brand mention on a specific blog matter? How do you know which posts matters over which others? You can use Google Blog Search (`www.google.com/blogsearch`) to get an understanding about who is talking about you in real time.

Here are some metrics that you can and should capture from the blogosphere. These build on the core metrics of unique visitors, page views, and return rates:

- Number of brand mentions versus your competitors
- Ratio of comments and *trackbacks* (a method of counting of other bloggers that reference your post) to posts on your own blogs
- Frequency of posts and comments on your blog and your competitors' blogs
- Technorati ranking of blogs that mention your brand
- Technorati ranking of your blog and your competitors'
- Total number of conversations (unique visitors to all sites talking about your brand)
- Total number of times that the post has been tweeted or retweeted, saved to Digg, tagged in Delicious, and discussed on FriendFeed

Widgets and social applications

Outside applications that reside within Facebook, you should measure the impact of your social media widgets and applications elsewhere on the Internet. Here are some of the key metrics to consider, as introduced by the Social Media Working Group of the IAB (Interactive Advertising Bureau):

- **Installs:** Simply the number of people who have installed your application.
- **Active users:** The number of total users interacting with your application over a day, week, or month. Some applications lose significant activity in time, so watch this metric carefully.
- **Audience profile:** Demographics of the people who are interacting with your widget. This may need to be self-reported, depending on where you install the widget.
- **Unique user reach:** The percentage of users who have installed the application among the total audience of social media users.
- **Growth:** The average number of increase in users within a specific time frame (between two dates).
- **Influence:** The average number of friends among users who have installed the application. This is a relatively less meaningful metric.
- **Application/widget installs:** The number of widget installs that a user has on her profile. This matters because more installs typically may mean lower interactions with your widget.

 ✔ **Active users/widgets in the wild:** The number of people using the widgets on a regular basis.

 ✔ **Longevity/life cycle:** Another key metric that tracks how long a widget or application stays installed by a user before he uninstalls it.

Needless to say, when examining these metrics, always try to understand how the metrics you capture relate to actual sales. Sometimes the link may be easy, but in other cases, especially if you do not have large numbers, drawing the correlation between metrics maybe difficult.

Another way to understand brand health in the social web is to search status updates on both Twitter and Facebook. For example, if your brand has 30,000 fans, you can search to see if any of your fans are discussing your brand in their own status updates.

Website community metrics

If you're evolving your own website for social media marketing, you may require new metrics to understand how successful you are. Rather than just measure how many people are visiting your website and where they're coming from, you're going to need to look at what exactly they're doing on your website and how they're interacting with each other. Whether you're using community software from a vendor like Lithium (www.lithium. com) or Pluck (www.pluck.com), or have installed customer reviews from Bazaarvoice (www.bazaarvoice.com) or PowerReviews (www.power reviews.com), the following metrics are important to consider:

 ✔ **Traffic:** The number of people visiting the community pages of your website is the first core metric. *Community pages* here means the discussion pages as well as the pages where you have customer reviews and ratings.

 ✔ **Members:** The next-most-important metric is the number of members of your community pages. These are the number of people who have registered so that they can publish content or share reviews. It's important to track whether the pace of people registering increases or decreases in time. You'll also want to understand who your most prolific contributors are and who have the most influence.

 ✔ **Interactivity:** The number of people who participate in a specific conversation, the number of replies, and the frequency with which they do so is very important. For example, how quickly on average someone replies to a conversation thread and the number of participants engaged in the conversation serve as guides to the health of your community.

✔ **Civility:** Another important metric to manage is how civil the conversations in your community are. Whether the community discusses health care or something simpler, such as digital cameras, how much people show that they trust and respect each other through the conversations is important. This can be ascertained by examining the language used, the tone of the conversation, and the way people express disagreement.

✔ **Content:** And last but not least, no community can be measured without establishing metrics around the actual content. To understand your community better, you'll need to understand which pieces of content are the most popular, traffic-generating, and valued over time. You'll also want to understand what type of content is published and shared the most, and whether that sharing is done on your website or to the social platforms.

Other metrics to consider

As you examine metrics on the major social platforms and analyze your SMM score, be sure to account for activity on the other social platforms. You'll want to track the following information about them:

✔ How much your brand and its associated websites are bookmarked on sites like Delicious (www.delicious.com) and Flickr (www.flickr.com)

✔ Alexa (www.alexa.com), Compete (www.compete.com), and Quantcast (www.quantcast.com) rankings

✔ Brand mentions in discussion forums and on other community websites, like Cafe Mom and the microblogging service FriendFeed (www.friendfeed.com)

✔ The number of friends and brand mentions on other social network sites that may have a larger presence in certain regions of the United States or in other countries around the world, including

- Bebo (www.bebo.com)

- ASMALLWORLD (www.asmallworld.net)

- Flixster (www.flixster.com)

- hi5 (www.hi5.com)

- Meetup (www.meetup.com/)

- LiveJournal (www.livejournal.com)

- MySpace (www.myspace.com)

- Xanga (www.xanga.com)

- orkut (www.orkut.com)

Chapter 20

Understanding Social Media Governance and Tools

· ·

· ·

*T*here's no doubt that social media is going to have a pervasive influence on marketing in the future; arguably, it already does. It is touching every dimension of marketing. In large organizations, it is resulting in new types of collaboration, processes, policies, and governance structures.

But what's more, SMM is starting to influence corporations in substantive ways beyond the realm of marketing and into public relations, sales, customer service (or consumer relations), and legal. Having strong social media governance and tools is more important than ever.

Recognizing How SMM Impacts Other Company Functions

Early in the book, we discuss SMM as it relates to brand marketing and direct response. We also frame social media marketing in the context of customer service and real-time marketing. In this chapter, we look at how social media marketing touches some of these other corporate functions and then review good governance practices. After that, we discuss the different governance models.

Public relations

Marketing and public relations have a symbiotic relationship, and in some organizations, public relations rolls up into the marketing organization. Both groups have important roles to play in the world of social media, but they come at it from different places.

Fundamentally, the marketing function owns the relationship with the consumers and is the steward of the brands. With the relationships often being formed and nurtured in the social media space, it becomes critical for the marketing function to lead all social media marketing efforts. This means that the following activities are typically led by the marketing team:

- ✔ Defining the brand's social voice
- ✔ Managing the social media platform pages
- ✔ Owning and driving social calendar activities
- ✔ Running social media campaigns across social media
- ✔ Planning and buying all social media advertising
- ✔ Coordinating all community management efforts

However, public relations has a critical role to play too. They manage relationships with the media, who in turn heavily influence consumer perception. Often, the mainstream media treats the social media space as distribution for its stories. Furthermore, the most successful and largest social influencers online often behave like media companies too. As a result, the place at which marketing and public relations come together in social media marketing is where influencer management takes place. When it comes to social media influencer management, both the marketers and the PR professionals have valuable and important roles to play. It is in this area that tight collaboration is required.

The following activities are typically led by the PR team:

- ✔ Leading all mainstream media relationships
- ✔ Driving core communication plans with outbound PR efforts
- ✔ Running all communication crisis management efforts
- ✔ Jointly managing social influencer relationships

Consumer relations

For a long time, consumer relations/customer service didn't have much of a connection with marketing on a daily basis. But that has started to change as marketing and consumer relations activities often happen within minutes of each other on the social media brand pages (whether the brands want that to happen or not).

A good example is that in any given moment on a brand page in Facebook, one consumer may be expressing his love for the brand and talking about fun brand activities while another may be complaining about a defective product. In such a scenario, who manages what? There are no set rules, and they vary by industry. Typically, the first line of response to a consumer is the social media marketing team because they serve as the voice of the brand on the platform. If the situation demands a serious response very quickly or is an issue that escalates suddenly, it is handed off to consumer relations.

Although these divisions of labor are easy to write up in a process document, the truth is that when it comes to customer queries, the social media marketers and the consumer relations professionals need to collaborate and partner very closely. Each group brings different skills and experiences to the table, and it largely doesn't matter who actually is posting what — rather, it is most important for that collaboration between the two functions. The same applies to marketing and public relations. That's where a stronger governance model comes into play. The volume of messages in the consumer relations realm versus more general marketing conversations drives how tight that collaboration needs to be.

Sales

If SMM were quite literally and narrowly about marketing, it wouldn't be half as interesting to companies as it is today. What makes it special is that within the domain of SMM, you have facets of consumer relations, public relations, and sales, too. As discussed earlier in the book, offering sales and discounts for customers serves as a very strong incentive to Like a brand on Facebook or follow it on Twitter. In fact, some companies have special Twitter accounts through which they push out exclusive sales.

Following are three notable examples:

- ✔ **@DellOutlet:** They serve up deals on Dell computer products.
- ✔ **@JetBlueCheeps:** They publish airfare and vacation discounts.
- ✔ **@Amazondeals:** They push discounts on its whole catalog.

In each of these three examples, the brand set up a separate Twitter account through which to push the deals. When that happens, it is easiest for the page to be managed directly by the sales organization. However, it often makes sense to promote the deals via the core Facebook and Twitter pages of the brand. In that case, the publishing should be managed by the same social media coordinators in the marketing organization who are responsible for the page.

Another, more complex scenario is when the brand has ecommerce enabled on its Facebook page. There's no doubt that in such a scenario, the page needs to be managed by the ecommerce team or a digital team that may (or may not) sit in the marketing department. But here too, the management of the community and the social voice of the brand should be driven through one team and one social media marketer, so tight coordination is required.

Legal

The people who are the most worried about social media are often the folks on the legal teams. They get concerned about how whether something that is published can violate someone else's copyright or may make the company liable in some form. The legal teams are definitely justified in their fear, and although there are no potentially overlapping responsibilities between the legal team and the social media marketers, it is important to set up clear guardrails covering what can and cannot be published on the social media platforms. In scenarios that don't conform to those guidelines, the social media marketers should meet with the legal teams to discuss the exceptions.

Having the legal teams review every single response and every single comment published may not be realistic. But as long as the proper guard rails, escalation strategies, and processes are in place, the legal teams should be comfortable with social media marketers publishing content on a regular basis without direct approvals. The guidelines, however, probably need to vary dramatically from industry to industry. In some more regulated industries, approvals of every piece of content might be a necessary evil.

Introducing Social Media Governance Models

Every organization requires social media governance. Whether large or small, if you are a company using social media, you require governance models in place. Just the hypercollaboration required to succeed (as witnessed by the topics discussed previously) necessitates strong governance models between both marketing and other functions and within marketing too.

This gets increasingly complex when you have global and local marketing teams and also marketing teams broken up by product lines.

Following are the key governance models to consider:

✔ **Centralized governance:** In a centralized social media governance model, one team is responsible for SMM and drives the daily management of the brand outposts on the various social platforms. This group also drives influencer management in partnership with the PR teams. They loop in legal, consumer relations, sales, and other department representatives as needed. This model is effective in smaller organizations or companies that aren't geographically distributed or do not have a significant number of product lines.

✔ **Hub-and-spoke governance:** In the hub-and-spoke model, you have both global and local social media marketing teams. Each team is responsible for a core set of activities. Accounts that are more global in nature are managed by the global team, whereas those that are local are managed locally. As more brands move to social media management platforms like Buddy Media and Vitrue, the need to have both global and local teams (with different permission policies, roles, and responsibilities) gets increasingly important. Clear differentiation in roles and responsibilities with specific process documents and tone and voice guidelines are necessary to make this model a success. For example, a given tab on a Facebook page may have global elements to it (managed by the global team) and local content zones that the local teams publish to regularly.

✔ **Distributed governance:** In a distributed governance structure, there's a very small or a nonexistent centralized SMM team. Each product line or geographic territory has its own social media teams and its own corresponding social media profiles. Coordination happens more informally between the different markets by sharing social media calendars, redistributing content, and tone and voice guideline, but little else is shared. Each geographic region or each product line chooses how best to approach SMM and does it in its own fashion with its own philosophies tools and processes.

✔ **Extreme distributed governance:** This model has practically no coordination between different marketing teams responsible for social media across different geographies and product lines. This approach is not recommended because it can result in the same brand being represented in different ways in different countries or even simply on multiple brand pages. This quickly results in confusion for the customers. Without even minimal coordination, influencer management becomes challenging because the same influencer maybe hearing different messages about the same brands from two different people in one organization.

Some organizations also put committees or councils in place to encourage

- Greater cross-functional collaboration
- The establishment of social media policies and guidelines
- The facilitation of group decision-making
- Conflict resolution
- Crisis management

Depending upon the size of your organization, how your company is structured and whether organic, spontaneous collaboration takes place or not, this may be a valuable structure to put in place.

Social media policies and guidelines

Every organization needs strong social media policies and guidelines. The policies are best defined as articulating what employees can and cannot do. They are often used to drive what can be published and by whom on a social media platform (when representing the brand) and what procedure you should go through to get to that publishing.

Guidelines, in contrast, are typically defined as best practices covering how to participate in social media as a brand or as an employee representing the company. In the guidelines, you typically see recommendations, examples, guardrails and best practices. Organizations large or small need to practice social media marketing effectively.

The major components of a social media policy typically include the following:

- ✔ Guidelines for identifying oneself as an employee of the company
- ✔ Confidentiality clauses — what you are free to publish and what you shouldn't
- ✔ Respect and privacy rights components pertaining to others that you may talk about
- ✔ Legal components and liabilities — often just expressing that the opinions are your own can help
- ✔ Rules for participation on social media platforms during work hours and beyond
- ✔ Best practice examples of how to engage — especially on company social media pages

You can write a social media policy document in many different ways. Every organization is different, and you need to have something that's suitable to your organization's needs, philosophies, value system, and culture. However, it helps to look at other social media policies. Social Media Governance (www.socialmediagovernance.com) is a strong resource for advice, templates, and examples of social media policies.

Social media policies need to be living documents. As the Internet evolves and social media platforms change, you need to update your company's social media policies to keep pace with that change. As a result, be sure to revisit your social media policies on a regular basis to determine that they are up-to-date and reflect the current needs of your company.

Tips and tricks for social media governance

Moving to effective social media governance is a journey that requires continuous iteration, planning, replanning, and structural tweaking. Following are some tips and tricks that can help you institute stronger social media governance in your organization quickly:

- ✔ **Define its purpose.**

    Social media governance is one of those initiatives that can quickly become a lot bigger or broader than it's supposed to be. When it gets larger, it often gets unwieldy. As a result, when starting out to establish social media governance, begin by defining its purpose, scope, and connection points to other governance structures in your organization. List the specific channels, employee groups, and scenarios that will be covered under the governance model.

✓ **Develop strong processes and practices.**

No governance model or policy and guidelines will be effective without robust processes and practices put in place early on. As soon as you define the purpose, start thinking about the right processes and practices for your organization. This is probably different for every organization. The best way to get this right is to see what types of processes have been successful for other initiatives in the organization.

✓ **Keep policies and guidelines concise.**

As discussed earlier in the chapter, policies and guidelines are extremely important. However, it is easy to get carried away and make them long and cumbersome. In their first iterations, try to keep these as concise and simple as possible. If your employees don't understand the simple versions, they will be more intimidated by something complex and long.

✓ **Establish ongoing training and education.**

Establishing governance models, processes, policies, and guidelines are all important. But they're only as good as their rate of adoption. That's why putting training and education processes in place is extremely important. Sometimes the training may need to be just a series of webinars or online classes. In other instances, periodic electronic communication or in-person "lunch and learn"s can be more helpful. Use whatever approach has worked for other similar initiatives in your organization.

✓ **Do continuity planning.**

In lots of large organizations, a person is never in one job for a very long time. You may be charged with developing and implementing a governance model today, but you may be in another job a year from now. Therefore, it's key to identify people in the governance structure who know enough about the model and the practices to be able to take over from you if your role changes.

✓ **Keep legal departments involved.**

Some participants in the social media governance model may feel that the Legal department may only need to be peripherally involved. With the FTC (Federal Trade Commission) and other governmental organizations playing a stronger and stronger role in defining social media policies for companies, legal departments need to be actively involved. Stakeholders with vested interests should also be included. Don't leave them out.

Dealing with a Social Media Crisis

Sooner or later, you will be hit by a social media crisis. As a brand, you may do something that angers your community. Something may happen to one of your products or services that results in a sudden, sharp backlash from people across the social media ecosystem. If and when this happens, knowing how to respond in the first 24 hours and the first week is absolutely critical. Companies have saved or lost many millions of dollars simply by how they responded to a crisis. Don't make the mistakes that others have.

If you are hit by a social media crisis, the following are key steps to take immediately:

1. **Bring together an emergency response team.**

   Usually a combination of marketers, consumer relations professionals, PR teams, product managers, and consultants — a core emergency response team should be identified, established, and empowered to make all decisions regarding the crisis.

2. **Listen to the community.**

   Using the social media tools discussed in the earlier chapters, try to understand the extent of the backlash and whether it is increasing or decreasing over time. Also, pay particular attention to the complaints and whether there's uniformity from different people. Also try to understand whether the crisis has geographic boundaries or is limited to a certain set of people who share demographic traits. Try to unearth whether they are new customers, existing customers, or neither.

3. **Identify and solve the problem.**

   There's no better way to deal with a social media crisis than by addressing the problem that is at the heart of the crisis. Devote extra energy and resources to understanding what the problem is, why people are complaining, and what the potential remedies may be. This may seem obvious, but many a company in the midst of a crisis has focused a little too much on protecting its reputation than on truly understanding and solving the root source of the crisis.

4. **Create lists of key influencers, and research their positions.**

   There's no way that a social media crisis can be contained without the participation of key influencers in the online space. It is important to create lists of these influencers — some of whom may be aligned with your brand and your position in the crisis and some against. Regardless of their opinions, you need to know who is most influential on the subject. Determine who may be able to tip the scales and help with your message.

5. **Respond frequently and with transparency.**

   Even if you do not have a response to the crisis and are still trying to understand what is going on, respond to the community. It is critical to show that you are hearing their complaints and to explain that you are seeking solutions. A social media crisis demands hypertransparency. If you do not operate with that frame of mind, you're certain to turn off even more people than you have with the core issue.

6. **Be open to having the community influence and define the outcomes.**

   In a social media crisis, many people respond by being even more guarded, closed, and corporate in their approach to all communications. Although a crisis may indeed be a tricky time, it doesn't mean that you should create additional distance between you and your customers. Instead, depending upon the nature of the crisis, ask the community for ideas on how best to shape the outcomes. Sometimes, they may be the ones that will be best able to provide answers.

Chapter 21

Moving Towards Real-Time Marketing

*I*magine for a moment that you're a consumer standing in front of one of the many billboards in Times Square. Chances are that you're staring at a billboard that was months in the making. The original consumer insights that drove the advertising campaign were probably researched at least eight months earlier. The core creative idea for the campaign that the billboard along with other advertising represents was probably conceived at least four or five months ago. And the specific billboard itself was probably designed no less than two months earlier, with the media being finally bought within the last month or two.

Does something about this image strike you as odd? Well, it should. As a consumer, you're being asked to favorably respond to a message on a billboard that has little immediate relevance to your life in the very moment that you're staring at it. In fact, the insights that drove the creative on the billboard may not have any immediate applicability to who you are as a consumer either. The billboard that you're staring at could well be stale. That's why real-time marketing is so important.

Introducing Real-Time Marketing

Real-time marketing is the antithesis to the Times Square billboard scenario. Imagine if the billboard could reflect consumer insights, creative, and execution that were all driven to respond to who you are, what you're thinking, and pop culture in the world at that *very given moment.* In other words, real-time marketing is all about going from strategy and consumer insights to creative and advertising in a matter of minutes or hours instead of a matter of months or even years, as is sometimes the case.

This is arguably a complex, seemingly unrealistic concept. Until the advent of social media and real-time buying, it seemed a pipe dream. But that has changed with the increased digitization of the entire media ecosystem. For the first time ever, we can now get real-time consumer insights as they are formed by consumers. We can design creative experiences responding to those insights and even run them in digital media locations — all in a matter of minutes. In the future, too, as television sets get continuous Internet connections (often referred to as addressable TV), the creative, once produced, will be changeable in near real time too.

But to make real-time marketing practical for your business, you need to understand its core components. They are the following:

- ✔ Real-time insights
- ✔ Real-time response
- ✔ Real-time engagement studios
- ✔ Real-time co-creation
- ✔ Real-time distribution
- ✔ Real-time engagement

Each of these components is discussed below, and they all are built on the foundational principles of SMM, except now, with real-time marketing, the principles and practices of social media marketing are brought into real time and are taken to an even broader and more dynamic scale than before. In this chapter, we discuss each of these core concepts to illustrate how.

Real-time insights

More than 200 million tweets are sent by consumers around the world on a daily basis. Add to that the billions of comments on Facebook, conversations on public discussion boards, and blog posts written every day. All of a sudden, marketers have a rich trove of data to analyze. They use it to infer consumer interests, tastes, and preferences. Some of this data may be more accessible than others. What's certain is that there's so much new data, often with both time and location stamps (meaning you know the time and place where the message was posted), that it simply cannot be ignored.

This data is used to draw deep longitudinal insights about consumers, but it can also be used to infer immediate, actionable short-term insights and consumer preferences. For example, do you know what the most popular show on television is this week? You can tell, not by the number of people who watched the show, but instead by the number of people who talk about it. Of course, the fact that a show fits into a specific social media demographic also plays a part. Similarly, do you know which artist's music is being talked about the most online in this very moment or whether one pop culture event is more significant than another? You can capture real-time insights about your consumers in three ways. The first is more prescriptive in nature, whereas the second is more observational. The third is completely technologically driven. They are as follows:

- **Prescriptive real-time insights:** If you know three or four different events taking place on a given day but cannot guess which will be the most important to your consumers, you can use social media to determine which is the most important. You can analyze the volume and type of conversation around each on that day. Here's an example:

  Between September 16 and 22, 2011, four major pop culture events took place in the world. Leading up to that, it was difficult to tell which would be the most important and be of greatest interest to a set of consumers. Those four events were Prince Harry's birthday, a Manchester United/Barcelona football game, an India-versus-England cricket match, and the finals of *Dancing with the Stars*. For a pop culture brand, knowing which of these for events would matter the most to consumers is critical.

  By watching consumer conversations around these four events and comparing them to each other as the day unfolded, it became quickly apparent that the soccer game was most talked about. The smartest brands would have then marketed against the football game. That's capturing real-time insights. Similarly, you can choose to track the real-time conversations on other topics, whether they are specific sports, athletes, celebrities, or movies to track their daily popularity.

- **Descriptive real-time insights:** Several different tools and technologies in the marketplace can tell you which conversational topics are trending as the most important. Following these on a regular basis can you help you determine what your consumers are thinking about and what's considered topical, of deep interest, or simply hot for them in that given time. Knowing this information can help you alter your advertising messaging, how you engage with those consumers on social media platforms, and potentially influence which products you choose to push as well.

  Probably the easiest way to gather these real-time insights is by looking at the Trending Topics list on Twitter. This list tells you what topics are being talked about the most in any given moment by Twitter users. You can then further narrow down the list to see what are the most popular conversation topics for a particular city or country. Other services built on top of Twitter help you easily sort through the most popular music, movies, sports events, and other pop culture activities. Some examples of this are TweetMeme `http://tweetmeme.com/`; Twazzup `www.twazzup.com/`, and Trendistic `http://trendistic.indextank.com/`.

In a similar fashion, Google Trends helps you draw real-time insights with similar geographic filters by analyzing the comparative popularity of different search terms. Yahoo! does something similar too. All these tools help you understand what consumers are thinking and engaging with in any given moment of time.

✔ Technologically driven real-time insights: The third way to get to real-time insights is by using technological tools that analyze conversations on mass scale for you and also review the popularity of keyword search terms in Google and Facebook advertising. Based on the cost of those keyword terms, these tools can tell you what topics matter most to consumers and what are most likely to elicit a response from them. Taykey (`www.taykey.com`) and Adaptly (`adaptly.com/`) are two such tools that can help you with this analysis.

Real-time response

The next concept in real-time marketing is real-time response. This is the type of response that's typically covered in any social media marketing effort. It is the response that you do through the social media channels in as timely and culturally relevant a fashion as you can. It's an organic response, through the voice of the brand, and it's targeted as much as possible to consumers that care.

But there is one fundamental difference between real-time response and the more traditional SMM initiatives that you may undertake. Real-time responses are organic responses through the lens of real-time marketing insights. So, for example, if you sold soccer shoes, and you knew that the Manchester United/Barcelona soccer game was the most-talked-about thing on September 16, 2011, on that very day, you'd use that cultural event to start conversations across Twitter, Facebook, and other social channels with your key consumers. Because you can target different consumers by location on Facebook, you would probably target specific conversation types for the Manchester United Fans and different ones for the Barcelona fans.

This is a real-time response. You are joining popular online conversations that matter to specific customers of yours in specific locations in an extremely timely, culturally relevant fashion. They are all built off real-time insights in ways that add value to the conversation. The critical difference between real-time response and traditional SMM is that instead of depending on a predefined calendar for your communications, you are responding to real-time insights and happenings in the real world.

Real-time engagement studios

Real-time response, by its very nature, is a more text-based response mechanism that typically happens on Twitter, Facebook, or one of the niche social networks. But responding in those ways can be limiting for your brand and may not fully capture the essence of your brand or the story that you're trying to tell your consumers.

This is where engagement studios come into the picture. The best way to think of an engagement studio is as a mini-agency that sits within your own company. This matters more and more because when you capture a real-time insight (or, more specifically, real-time content; see example below), to really create marketing value from it, you need to be able to mash it up extremely quickly. To do that, you either need a studio or an agency that can turn around creative in a very short amount of time. Engagement studios are one way for this to happen.

So how do you use an engagement studio? Imagine you're a marketing manager at PepsiCo, and you're enjoying a lazy day off from work. You're walking down Fifth Avenue in Manhattan, and it's a beautiful, sunny day. You're on top of the world. Imagine then that you see Lady Gaga walking toward you. But better still, imagine that she has a Pepsi in her hand and is sipping it. You take out your camera and quickly take a short video of her drinking the Pepsi. Now imagine you're able to send this back to Pepsi's headquarters, where, in an engagement studio, the video is edited, cleaned up, and made ready for national TV. That's the power of having an engagement studio.

Real-time co-creation

The next concept in the real-time marketing framework is real-time co-creation. There's no use doing real-time insights or real-time response, or even creating compelling content, if it doesn't have a real-time co-creation dimension to it. Real-time co-creation is all about bringing consumer feedback into the marketing process. Co-creation is an iterative process that improves content by exposing it to feedback and revision by both customers and the company.

This is extremely important with real-time marketing. You're doing so much so quickly that it is easy to miss the right vibe and cause your brand irreparable harm in your rush to get something out. The only way to mitigate that is with real-time co-creation efforts. Real-time co-creation efforts can be done in a variety of different ways. The following are some options:

- ✓ **Digital ad creative testing:** If you are running paid digital advertising on Google or a platform like Facebook or Twitter, you can optimize the creative very quickly based on how well it performs. In fact, often, the ad serving system automatically optimizes the creative for you.

  For example, suppose that you're running advertising and want to test three different versions of ad copy. You can run all three, and depending on how each performs (the number of clicks each version gets), the ad serving solution shows the one that's doing the best. You can use this format to test ad creative that is run in other locations too.

- ✓ **Seeding with a private community:** Many brands launch and run private online communities where they ask consumers for feedback on production innovations, marketing efforts, and future business plans. If you're creating a piece of content (whether for SMM or elsewhere), you can first run it in your private community and solicit feedback before using it on a much larger public scale.

- ✓ **Tapping into individual content creators:** Another alternative is to tap into content creators directly to help create your marketing communications. Companies like CrowdContent (www.crowdcontent.com) source content creators from their huge community of writers. It happens very quickly, with the greatest benefit being that you're using their community to help find the right content creator instead of vetting someone on your own. Another company that can help in this space is Maker Studios (http://makerstudios.com), which does something similar for video content.

Real-time distribution

The vision of real-time marketing can only truly come to life if you have a real-time distribution system in place. There's no use gathering powerful insights, creating powerful content, and testing it with consumers if you cannot then distribute it on mass scale. As we say in the "Real-time response" section earlier in this chapter, the first step is in launching and running the responses through the organic social media channels.

However, there are other ways in which to distribute the content, experiences, and various forms of communication. Following are some of the key forms of distribution to consider for your real-time marketing content:

✔ **Social media platforms:** This is probably the easiest way to distribute your real-time content, but it is important to start with your own social media channels. Why? Because it is critical to first meet the needs and provide early access to advocates of your brand. They're typically the ones that follow you on Twitter or have Liked you on Facebook. This first takes the shape of organic engagement on the social media platforms, but beyond that occurs through paid social media engagement.

✔ **Websites:** It is sometimes easy to forget but your own website is an important content distribution channel. Contrary to all the public hype, people do still visit product websites. If you have it structured in a meaningful way, the website can serve as a great place to engage your consumers in real time.

✔ **Digital advertising:** Arguably, the quickest way to get mass reach for your real-time marketing efforts is by leveraging the scale of digital advertising. Increasingly, you can buy digital advertising on a real-time basis and swap creative in and out in the moment. You can even put social media content (a Twitter feed, for example) into the display advertising. Digital advertising is an important arrow in the quiver of your real-time marketing efforts.

✔ **E-mail programs:** Your e-mail programs can serve as an important real-time marketing distribution engine for your real-time marketing efforts. Don't shy away from using these effectively. In fact, even with the rise of social media, e-mail continues to be a complementary means of communication. The challenge is making it work effectively without over-burdening your consumers.

✔ **Packaging:** If you sell a product that is available at retail, the packaging is a form of media. Whether it is QR codes (a quick response code, which, when scanned by a mobile phone, retrieves a URL with information) or image recognition technology, you can now make your product a media access point. Upon scanning the package, the consumer is given access to the content that can be updated in real time.

All the previously listed options can be activated in a matter of minutes. In the future, even television advertising will be adjusted and optimized on a real-time basis, driven by real-time marketing insights and creative needs. What's more, for the first time ever, the real-time marketing efforts can be done on mass scale: a scale that historically was limited to traditional marketing efforts only.

Real-time engagement

After you've tapped into your consumer's real-time insights, co-created real-time experiences, and triggered the engagement with them, the last key piece is real-time engagement. This is arguably the hardest to do in a scalable way. Expect to have fewer consumers engage meaningfully with you when you move beyond pushing content or experiences to them and ask them to participate in an ongoing basis.

Real-time engagement can take many different shapes. For example, it can focus on building and nurturing daily engagement with your consumers through Facebook, Twitter, or Google+. After you've triggered consumer engagement driven by real-time insights, you can then use that as an opportunity to engage with them on a more regular basis. What follows are some tips and tricks to consider for real-time engagement:

- **Make paid, owned, and social media work together.**

  Sometimes the best forms of real-time engagement are the ones that use the reach of paid media, harmoniously coupled with the deep engagement of social and owned media.

- **Don't limit yourself to the web; think about mobile too.**

  Whether it is via foursquare or some other service, real-time engagement can be fueled through location-based services. It can take the shape of real-world scavenger hunts, tips at special locations, and physical-world reward systems.

- **Partner with media companies that practice real-time marketing.**

  Some media talk to consumers every single day through television and the Internet. You can partner with them to find ways to engage with consumers on a daily basis.

- **Harness Twitter Trending Topics to engage in real-time.**

  There's nothing stopping you from participating in conversations that are trending on Twitter. Determine meaningful ways to join and contribute to those conversations, and use promoted tweets to strategically amplify your own engagement efforts.

Organizing for Real-Time Marketing

Practicing real-time marketing successfully requires an interdisciplinary team coming together and partnering extremely closely. Just because you need to move really quickly doesn't mean you shouldn't do so in a very collaborative, inclusive fashion.

In large companies, real-time marketing teams typically include representatives from brand strategy, social media marketing, legal, media, public relations, and consumer relations functions. In small companies, the SMM team typically carries the responsibilities for real-time marketing and operates with predefined guidelines and processes.

The most challenging piece of real-time marketing is knowing which consumer trends to market against and which ones to avoid. There's no doubt that some trends will be much more relevant to your brand and your specific consumers than others. However, discovering which those are only comes in time by testing and viewing the responses.

To help jump start your real-time marketing efforts, take the following steps:

- **Create a list of key topics.** You cannot participate in every consumer trend or pop culture moment. But by creating a list of priority topics that are of interest to your consumers and matter to your brand, you'll know which trends to prioritize over others when things start popping. For example, if you're a shoe company, tapping into a real-time trend around running will be far more important than one about reality TV shows.

- **Put aside some media dollars for paid advertising.** Create a small bucket of advertising dollars to support your real-time marketing efforts. Use these dollars to amplify any real-time marketing activity against the trends and topics that matter most to your consumers.

- **Pay attention to trends as they're popping.** Trends are most valuable if you are able to ride their growth and exposure to more and more people. Keep an eye on trends that are just starting to pop; they may be more valuable and cheaper to market against than a trend that has already hit the mainstream.

- **Listen to key influencers in your space.** Sometimes the best way to discover a trend that matters to your customers and your business is by watching what key influencers in your space are talking about. Often, they're the ones who talk about them first and take trends mainstream.

- **Start small and test and learn.** Real-time marketing is new, and getting it right in ways that match the scale and budget of your brand can be difficult. The only way to practice real-time marketing successfully is to test different tactics, observe how they perform, and then build to bigger and bigger programs from there.

Taking TV into Real-Time Marketing

Approximately 60 percent of people watching television have a laptop, a mobile phone, or a tablet computer open in front of them. In fact, iPads are used the most when people are watching television. Here are some tips for taking TV into real-time marketing if your brand runs TV advertising:

- **Utilize traditional buttons.**

    The ends of television ads that include calls to action for the brand are called *buttons.* Be sure to include your Facebook URL or your Twitter handle in them at the end.

✔ **Make sure to track conversations.**

If you are advertising on television, typically for the show you are advertising against, there are lots of online conversations going on. Think about buying Twitter search terms against those conversations so that your message is amplified. You can then craft your Twitter communications to be contextually relevant to the show and anything else happening in the media ecosystem in that moment.

✔ **Make dynamic calls to action.**

Depending on what you're advertising, you can benefit from more dynamic buttons in your TV advertising. For example, if you know the advertisement is going to run during the Grammys, your call to action at the end of the ad can be about going online and seeing which artist is the most talked-about. That way it is more real-time, relevant, and contextual.

✔ **Treat the TV ad as a piece of a broader narrative.**

It is easy to forget, but television advertising can be an important part of a broader narrative of a brand that's centered in real-time digital engagement. As you plan your TV advertising, think about what else may be happening in the world on the day it runs and what types of conversations consumers will have online in that moment. Factor that into your planning.

Part V
The Part of Tens

The 5th Wave   By Rich Tennant

"Here's an idea. Why don't you start a social network for doofuses who think they know how to set a broken leg, but don't."

In this part . . .

Chapter 22 lists ten key SMM best practices that you must absolutely pay attention to. Chapter 23 includes ten common mistakes — mistakes made by the best of us who have been practicing SMM for quite a while. Chapter 24 lists ten must-read blogs that will keep you updated with the world of SMM and digital marketing more broadly. Finally, Chapter 25 lists the top ten online SMM tools to try.

Chapter 22

Ten SMM Best Practices

....

Social media marketing efforts may fail for a lot of reasons. And not surprisingly, hundreds if not thousands of articles online are about why certain SMM efforts failed. Strangely, there's a lot less discussion about what succeeds and why. We certainly don't have all the answers, but what we do know is that by following these ten best practices, your chances of success are much greater.

Open Up Your Brand to Your Consumers, and Let Them Evolve It

This is difficult for many marketers. You've probably spent money and time building your brand only to have someone telling you to let go of it. This may sound absurd. The truth is that the more you let your consumers internalize your brand, talk about it in their own language, and manifest your story in their own way, the more success you will have with your SMM efforts.

Letting your consumers evolve your brand doesn't mean you're losing control of it completely. How you let consumers evolve your brand must be done in a fashion that is in sync with your company values, what your customers expect of you, the industry you operate in, and the appropriateness for your brand. But that doesn't mean you shouldn't let go at all. Brands that hold onto too much mystique run the risk of appearing cold, distant, and alienating. Those risks are accentuated now with the social web, so be careful, even if you're Chanel or Louis Vuitton.

Develop a SMM Voice without Silencing Other Voices That Support Your Brand

Surprisingly, for every brand that's fearful about opening up to consumers, just as many go to the other extreme and inadvertently silence external voices. Your SMM voice is fundamentally about having a mechanism to talk to your consumers in a language and style that they understand. It's a voice to talk to them in a more humane and personal manner.

You shouldn't use your SMM voice to speak the loudest and most exclusively about your brand. Nor should you use it to silence your critics in a heavy-handed manner. To develop a strong SMM voice is to develop strong listening skills, a thick skin, and a nuanced understanding of how to respond to the fuming blogger, for example, without turning him off completely. You want to extend your reach and influence through others. Don't try to do so by being the loudest or by becoming deaf. No one likes a bully.

Respond to Everything, Even If It Means You're Up All Night

For all the hype about social media, one important, sobering fact remains: It takes an immense amount of work. Listening in on conversations, even with monitoring tools, is an exhaustive, time-consuming exercise. Responding and participating in those conversations can take the wind out of your sails and ruin many a weekend, if not a marriage. Arguably, many people think that social media marketing isn't scalable because the larger your company is, the more expensive it gets to participate.

But that's the wrong way to think about social media marketing. Your consumers are talking about you every day across many different channels and platforms. Their attention has become a lot more fragmented, and they're much more impatient, too. The only option is to work harder for their attention and their dollars. If you have to set expectations around the timeliness of your participation, do so, but definitely don't ignore them. For example, a two-day delay in response hurt the Motrin brand immeasurably when customers felt that Johnson & Johnson wasn't hearing their concerns about a Motrin TV advertisement. Those marketers at J&J thought they were ahead of the game by responding on Sunday evening, but that, too, was too late. To assist in managing responses, you need to build relationships online with influencers before you need them. That way, they can do some of the work for you while you go offline.

Think Beyond the Obvious, and Use SMM to Evolve Your Business

To assume that social influence is just about marketing is to take a narrow view of it. The way your consumers communicate, share information, collaborate, entertain, get entertained, work, and do anything has fundamentally changed. People are influencing each other in new ways all the time and using social technologies to change their lives.

As a marketer in an organization, it's important to recognize that SMM can do more than just help you reach your consumers better. You can learn from your consumers by harnessing their insights about your products and brands; you can change how you conduct customer service or launch new products; and you can change how you interact with your own employees, shareholders, business partners, and external constituents. You can even use it to redefine your core products. Don't miss the opportunity to leverage SMM concepts for every part of your business.

Focus Not Just on Social Media, but Also on Social Influencers

It's easy to lose sight of your social influencers amid the buzz about social media. There's no question that social platforms like Twitter, Facebook, LinkedIn, and YouTube are hugely popular, and they're changing the way people interact with each other online and approach entertainment. But this isn't just about marketing on those social platforms. After all, consumers don't always respond to brands that dwell on them. They'd rather spend their time talking to one another. That's why it's important to focus on the social influencers, too, because they can reach the consumers for you.

It's important to focus on the social influencers because they're the ones who increasingly have the largest impact on brand affinity and purchasing decisions. They are the ones who have the most influence on your consumers. They're everywhere, and not just on the social media platforms. By ignoring these social influencers, you're ignoring your largest and most potent sales force. Look beyond the buzz of social media, and focus on the social influencers, wherever they may be, interacting with your consumers.

Structure Your Marketing Department for This Social World

Undoubtedly, the Internet and the social media revolution have changed marketing significantly. It's no longer about creating cool, creative ads and pushing messages out to customers via different channels. Nor is it just about print advertisements and in-store displays that may or may not grab the attention of your consumers. It's about a two-way conversation — online and offline — and looking holistically at how all your marketing efforts — digital or not — can work together.

And this begs the question, have you structured your marketing department appropriately for this world? You probably have interactive marketing in one corner of your department organizational chart. But can you still separate interactive marketing from the rest of marketing? Does it make sense? And along similar lines, should you silo market research from product innovation and brand and direct-response marketing when you live in a world with real-time customer feedback? It might be time for you to revisit your marketing department's organizational structure.

Take Your Organization with You, from the CEO to the Field Representative

We discuss in this book how you can apply SMM to different parts of your business and beyond the realm of marketing. We also cover strategies and tactics for making SMM work in conjunction with the other forms of marketing, whether they're digital or offline. But that isn't enough. To succeed in SMM means that you must carry your whole organization with you — everyone from the CEO down to the field representative.

SMM is fundamentally about everyday influence in all its forms and crowd-sourced innovation and product design. To embrace SMM and succeed in it requires your whole organization to orient itself toward it. Your CEO is probably one of the best spokespersons for your organization. He should be one of the people talking to your consumers in a SMM voice that they appreciate, wherever they may be spending their time online. On the other end of the spectrum, your field representatives are out there selling products. Each of them has a network of customers. They, too, are powerful SMM voices. Empower them to speak on behalf of the company to their constituents offline *and* online. Succeeding in SMM means taking everyone in your company in this direction. And a good place to start is by surveying your own employees to understand how much they're using social media today and how they feel it can be harnessed to support your business.

Conduct Many Small Tests Frequently, and Build on Each One

Without a doubt, the field of social media marketing is young. The social advertisement formats are still evolving; companies are just figuring out how to participate in the conversation; customers are discovering how powerful a voice they have online; and the technologies that allow all this to happen and be tracked are in a constant state of flux.

Knowing how to practice SMM and for what specific purposes may not always be easy. The government might have started to regulate blogger outreach programs in your industry, for example (as it recently has with the pharmaceutical companies). The only way to succeed in SMM is to conduct many small tests and build on each one. Don't try to boil the ocean all at once, and don't be frozen with paranoia either. Put a strategy in place that means many small, logical steps, each one building on the success of the previous one, deepening your relationships with the influencers and establishing yourself more deeply with your consumers. It takes longer to get where you want to, but it's a safer path to take.

Capture Every Single Piece of Data that You Can

As we discuss in Chapter 19, you can measure a lot of your social media marketing efforts. SMM is meant to support your overall marketing and business objectives, and you'll know whether it's succeeding in helping you accomplish those only if you're measuring your campaigns, initiatives, and strategies. Everything must be tied to results.

The only way to do that with rigor is to capture every single piece of data that you can about your SMM efforts. From the number of influencers activated to how many views a YouTube clip got that translated into a sale and the brand attitudinal lifts you saw based on a SMM campaign, you must capture all that data. Don't forget about capturing data that supports other parts of your business, such as a reduction in customer service calls or the amount of time it takes to bring products to market, if you've brought customers into your product innovation process. Data is everything.

Make Mistakes, but Make Every Effort to Correct Them as Well

We all learn from our mistakes, and that's a wonderful thing. But when practicing SMM, it isn't enough to learn from your mistakes — you also need to make every effort to correct them. And quickly, too. One of the many attributes that make SMM stand out from other forms of marketing is that you're engaging with your customers in real time as they interact with each other at a scale never seen before.

This means that both the good and bad of your brand (or marketing efforts) can be amplified across the Internet in no time, potentially causing either immense benefit (witness the viral effect of a funny YouTube clip) or immense damage (as Comcast experienced several years ago). This means that when you make a mistake — and you will, as everyone does — be sure to make every effort to correct it as soon as possible. Otherwise, you'll find yourself in a crisis that spins completely out of your control.

Chapter 23

Ten Common SMM Mistakes

*Y*ou may follow all the right steps with your social media marketing efforts and still fail. In fact, however frightening it may seem, you may fail completely. The reason is that you may make one of the ten common mistakes of SMM. Steer clear of the common mistakes in this chapter, and you will have a better chance at enjoying a successful social media marketing campaign.

Encroaching on Customers' Time

Many companies forget that their customers can have a limited number of conversations at once. They often gravitate to specific social platforms for coincidental reasons, but after they're on them, it's hard to move away. They become accustomed to that social environment, invest in it through their contributions, and bring their friends on board.

Any company thinking of starting a conversation with its customers must begin by asking where its customers currently spend their time, how willing they might be to move their conversations to a new location, and whether they can manage another set of conversations. If you don't think this through before you build something, you may have an empty community.

Pestering Customers Who Don't Want to Hear from You

The social web is fundamentally about people talking to each other about subjects that are of interest to them. It isn't designed to be a marketing vehicle. However, some brands naturally have permission, in a manner of speaking, to be a part of those conversations, while others may not. It's important to know whether your brand has that permission. Finding out whether your brand does have permission can be tricky, but the first step is to determine how you want to engage with your customers (what your social voice will be) and how much your customers trust your brand and are favorably inclined toward it. Then ask yourself whether your customers look to you for advice and information beyond the realm of the actual product that you sell. As you answer these questions, you'll discover whether your brand has the permission to participate.

For example, the Barbie brand celebrated its 50th anniversary in early 2009 and ran an extensive social media marketing campaign. People were excited about the anniversary and welcomed Barbie into their conversations. There was a lot of passion and nostalgia associated with the brand. It was a natural fit for social media marketing. People wanted to talk about it. But that may not always be the case. Ask yourself whether you have permission to practice SMM with your customers. In contrast to the Barbie example, a brand that has always been aloof, distant, and serious won't have the natural permission to start participating in online conversations in a personal, humorous, and light fashion. It would seem that the brand has been hijacked, and customers won't respond favorably to that. That's an example of a brand not having permission.

Choosing the Wrong SMM Voices

It's critical to choose your SMM voices carefully. Don't assign the job to an employee who lacks communication skills or passion for the social web. And don't choose someone who can't commit the time and effort that it requires to be a SMM voice. This person needs to know the social platforms like the back of her hand. She needs to be willing to invest the time to participate and respond to queries.

Companies that have chosen employees who lack authenticity as their SMM voices are rarely successful. In the case of Whole Foods Market, the CEO was blogging and commenting in discussion forums. The only problem was that he was doing it under a pseudonym and bashing his competitors. When the truth surfaced, he lost all credibility. As a result, be careful whom you choose to be your SMM voices, and train them on how to be a SMM voice. This may seem obvious, but you'll be surprised how many obvious mistakes are made around SMM voices.

Being Impatient

With SMM efforts, it can be difficult to know when it may *break out* (in other words, when your SMM effort may suddenly gain immense traction). Many a marketer has canceled an SMM effort too quickly, only to see a competitor launch something six months later that turned out to be widely successful. Be patient with your SMM effort; it may not be a runaway success on day one or day one hundred. It could take longer.

With these efforts, recognize that SMM isn't a campaign; rather, it's a commitment. Because you're working on the social web, you're marketing to customers one at a time in a personal, engaging, and conversational manner, and that doesn't always happen quickly. Your goal, always, is to get the customers to do the marketing for you. But it may take longer than you'd like. That's something to always recognize. And to do this right, when you start your SMM effort, convince your bosses that it needs to be a 6–12-month commitment at least. If they get cold feet after the second week or the second month, you mustn't let them pull the plug on the effort.

Treating SMM in Isolation

Marketers who don't integrate their SMM activities are always bound to fail. The reason is simple: You can't market to customers in a conversational, personal, and transparent manner on the social platforms but then use a different language, style, and tone elsewhere. Your SMM activities must always complement existing marketing initiatives.

So whether the rest of your marketing efforts constitute display advertising, search engines, TV advertisements, print, outdoor media, advertising on mobile phones, or just a few of the these, make sure that you're thinking about how SMM works with those other marketing efforts. Ideally, each of those marketing initiatives should tie in with the SMM ones, as SMM strategies and tactics can be promoted and extended through these other advertising formats and media, too. This especially applies to mobile, where increasingly cellphones allow for social influence in new and dynamic ways, with applications that integrate customer reviews and real-time polling for feedback.

Having Only One Approach

Another common mistake of SMM is to treat influencers the way you would treat a member of the press: showering them with attention, inviting them to exclusive launches, and peppering them with press releases. The reality is that influencers in the SMM world are different, and it's important to be aware of those nuances. Otherwise, you'll turn them off.

For example, expert influencers who share a lot in common with the mainstream media press would *still* rather not be treated like the press. They want the special attention but expect you to engage with them on their own terms, recognizing the boundaries that they operate in. Many of them now publish guidelines for marketers explaining how they want to be approached. Referent influencers have never been marketed to in the past, and they usually don't know what to expect or how best to manage expectations. And the positional influencers would much rather you not even know that they're a big influence on the customer. So when you market to the influencers, think carefully about the influencer type and how to appropriately market to them.

Thinking of SMM as a Channel

Marketers who treat SMM as a channel have the least success. The reason is that you aren't pushing the message through a channel, as you would in traditional advertising. If you use traditional advertising strategies on the social platforms, you won't get the results that you're looking for. Think of social influence marketing as truly a new form of marketing with new strategies, best practices, and rules of engagement.

Failing to Plan for the Worst

If you don't plan for the fact that you'll probably face a PR crisis at some point or other when you practice social media marketing, you'll be blindsided when it does happen. Now, not every SMM activity results in a PR crisis — most never do at all. But because you're engaging with your customers in a more direct, authentic fashion, there are risks that you may not see with traditional advertising.

The risks take two forms:

- **The actual structure of a SMM campaign:** You may ask users to do something, and they may respond to that negatively. Or a small part of the responses may be so inflammatory in nature that it may undermine the campaign or your brand.

- **Unintentionally elicit a visceral reaction:** This was the case with the infamous Motrin episode in early 2009, when moms responded extremely negatively to what they considered to be a derogatory TV advertising campaign. The campaign launched on a Saturday, and the marketers didn't notice the firestorm and respond quickly enough. Make sure that you do your scenario planning so that you know how to respond to any different crisis that may arise.

Focusing on One Large Campaign

Social media marketing is fundamentally about many little efforts that when strung together have as much impact (usually much more) as a single traditional campaign or marketing program. This means that it's always important to plan to launch several small initiatives at once, rather than run one long, mammoth one.

This matters more than ever because your customers are doing a lot of digital snacking. They hop from one platform to another, exchange notes about something in one social network, and then move on to view a video clip, and sometimes go offline for days on end. Putting all your eggs in one basket doesn't serve you well.

Forgetting to Reward Your Participants

You must incentivize, reward, and recognize the contributions of the community. This may seem obvious, but you'll be surprised how many marketers assume that consumers will participate generously without any return. Make sure you match the reward to the level of participation you demand. These rewards don't have to be monetary in nature, but if you're asking something extra of the community that surrounds your product, you'd better be willing to thank them for their contributions, reward them for their participation, and recognize how they're changing your company for the better. These rewards can be as simple as invitations to special events, discount coupons, featuring customers on your website, and sneak peeks of new products and services.

Chapter 24

Ten SMM-Related Must-Read Blogs

. . . .

A chapter with just ten must-read social media marketing blogs can't do justice to the wealth of information online that covers social influence marketing. Still, you have to start somewhere, and here are ten of our favorite blogs that help us further our own thinking in SMM. Most of these blogs appear in the *Ad Age* Power 150 marketing blogs list (which you can find at `http://adage.com/power150`), and if you're looking for other blogs to also follow, look to that list.

Web Strategy

www.web-strategist.com/blog

Jeremiah Owyang is an analyst at the Altimeter Group who lives and breathes everything he preaches every day. He's deeply passionate about social media and how you can use it to achieve your business objectives. He provides practical, thoughtful, and actionable advice for you and social media specialists. His blog usually covers topics like the state of social media, how it's changing marketing, and ways in which you can organize your marketing efforts around social media.

Jeremiah publishes frequently, and his posts are usually peppered with links to earlier posts or to external sources. His blog is always a must-read, and Shiv can attest he's also charming and engaging, both in his writing and in person.

Steve Rubel

www.steverubel.me

Another must-read blog is the Clip Report, published by Steve Rubel of Edelman PR. He's also a columnist at *AdAge*. Although Steve doesn't explicitly cover social media marketing or social media, at least half of his posts do address the topic. His posts are typically quite short, visual, and insightful. They generally fit into three categories: news tidbits (which include market statistics and expert interviews), personal reflections on social media and digital marketing, and his own practical experiences. We suggest that you definitely bookmark the Clip Report, especially if you're interested in a digital PR angle on SMM. It's worth noting that until June 2009, Steve used to blog at www.micropersuasion.com until he moved to the Clip Report format, which consolidates all of his online publishing efforts in one place.

Chris Brogan

www.chrisbrogan.com

Here's a man who truly fits the archetype of social media guru. He lives and breathes social media. We like Chris' blog for its unfiltered, passionate, and reflective commentary on how social media forces businesses — large, medium-size, and small ones — to engage with their customers differently. It's an unadulterated look at the social media space from someone who isn't working for a large company but for himself. Filled with passion and raw insight, it's definitely a good read.

Logic + Emotion

http://darmano.typepad.com

Now, this is a blog that's rather unique, for a very simple reason. It's filled with extremely compelling visualizations that explain social media concepts succinctly and powerfully. David Armano is thoughtful, analytical, and visual with every post, and he's addressed subjects like the evolution of advertising and the relationship between paid and unpaid media extremely well. He's a former agency person who helps businesses transform themselves with social technologies. As a result, his posts may be a little less marketing-oriented now, but the blog is still worth bookmarking and reading.

Conversation Agent

www.conversationagent.com

This blog has some things in common with Chris Brogan's but looks at social media more broadly. Valeria Maltoni bills herself as someone who helps businesses understand how customers and communities have changed marketing, public relations, and communications. Her posts cover her own experiences in social media and provide tips and tricks for navigating the social media world. She also analyzes current events from a social media perspective (witness her posts about the Iran election in the summer of 2009), and she interviews thought leaders in the online marketing space.

Influential Marketing Blog

http://rohitbhargava.typepad.com

This blog, authored by Rohit Bhargava, focuses on the connection points between marketing, advertising, and PR strategy. As the Ogilvy senior vice president of Global Strategy and Marketing, Rohit discusses what companies can do with social media and explains where they're succeeding and failing. His posts are thoughtful, recommendation-driven, and easy to scan. He focuses on the influence side to social influence marketing more than the others and, therefore, writes more broadly. He also speaks at industry events and discusses social media optimization on his blog like no one else can.

The WOMMA Word

http://womma.org/word

Published by the Word of Mouth Marketing Association (WOMMA), this blog discusses everything that has to do with word-of-mouth marketing, both online and offline. Because the organization is rooted in the offline world, it provides a slightly different perspective on social influence marketing than other blogs. The posts cover word-of-mouth online and offline across all the major channels, from TV and print to digital. The posts on ethics and word of mouth are especially interesting.

Advertising Age's DigitalNext

http://adage.com/digitalnext

This group blog covers everything in digital marketing, but because social media marketing is such a hot topic, more and more of its posts have a SMM orientation. Because its audience is marketers who have to worry about a lot more than just social media, it takes a more conservative, critical, and analytical take on social influence marketing.

Apophenia

www.zephoria.org/thoughts

This is the one academic blog that we're including in the list. Danah Boyd has a PhD in Information from the University of California-Berkeley and is a senior researcher at Microsoft Research; a research assistant professor in Media, Culture, and Communication at New York University; a visiting researcher at Harvard Law School; and an adjunct associate professor at the University of New South Wales.

Her research on social media, social networking (especially as it pertains to youth culture), online identities, and online communities has been incredibly important in helping everyone in the industry understand how consumers are actually immersing themselves in the social space. This is definitely another must-read blog, especially if you're trying to understand consumer motivations.

Going Social Now

www.goingsocialnow.com

Going Social Now is Shiv's blog, covering all things social media marketing. He focuses on the trends, influencers, and the roles they play, the evolving advertising formats, consumer adoption, and social technologies. He also discusses digital marketing more broadly. The blog serves as a resource for you, the reader, and includes 101 explanations, additional *For Dummies* content that didn't make it into the book, and links to even more wonderful resources beyond the ones we mention here.

Chapter 25

Ten Top SMM Tools

⋯⋯⋯⋯⋯⋯⋯⋯⋯⋯⋯⋯⋯⋯⋯⋯⋯⋯⋯⋯⋯⋯⋯⋯⋯

When you're launching a social media marketing campaign, a good first step is to measure the size of the social activity on the web. When you see the numbers of possible customers (who fit your demographics, psychographics, and technographics), you can reach using social tools, it's usually a no-brainer that a social media campaign is a good thing. Fortunately, several strong online tools show how to measure social activity on the web.

Many of these tools are free and serve as a good starting point for your research efforts. But remember, no single tool is perfect for capturing web usage. Therefore, it's always useful to use multiple sites together to get the best data. Also, looking at the relative changes in the statistics over a period of time (versus the raw numbers, which may not always be totally accurate) may be a safe approach to take. Keep this list handy when you're doing your research.

Technorati

www.technorati.com

Technorati is a leading blog search engine that indexes more than 112.8 million blogs and 250 million pieces of tagged social media. Every year, it publishes a *State of the Blogosphere* report that identifies who is blogging and how blogging fits into the larger web. In its November 2010 blogosphere report, it states that 25 percent of all bloggers are engaged in mobile blogging and that a growing number of blog posts are shared on social networks. This is helping to keep blogging as relevant as ever.

Why should you care? It helps to know how many people read blogs so that you can understand what percentage of your total customer base you'll reach via marketing on blogs.

BlogPulse

www.blogpulse.com

BlogPulse's name should be a clue as to its function — it's a blog search engine that provides trend data. It is owned by Nielsen, and its tag line is, "Discover what's hot." When you go to the home page, you find tools to search trends, view featured trends, mine conversations for trends, and review profiles of key bloggers. Some consider this tool to be more powerful than Technorati because it enables you to track trends and analyze data at a deeper level.

Google Blog Search

Blogsearch.google.com

This search engine is a strong alternative to Technorati and BlogPulse for searching blogs. As always, Google simplifies the search by presenting you with a single search box. You can find lists such as recently updated blogs. Of course, this list is outdated the minute you search it, but it gives you a good indication of the ongoing activity.

Quantcast

http://quantcast.com

Quantcast is an independent media measurement service that finds basic traffic patterns for mainstream and niche social networks. What's valuable about Quantcast? It serves up free reports on audience composition, making your job as a market researcher easier. You can find a list of the top million sites and then dig deeper to find where your audience goes online. Alternatively, you can compare sites via a search box on the home screen.

Compete

www.compete.com

Compete is a web service owned by Kantar Media that allows you to view and analyze websites' statistics. You can check out site profiles for approximately 3 million websites and determine the number of monthly visits and percentage of change month over month. Their pro version unlocks a large amount of additional data, including demographics and income. They also maintain a ranking list that is useful.

Nielsen BuzzMetrics

www.nielsen-online.com/products_buzz.jsp?section=pro_buzz

BuzzMetrics is a monitoring service for the social web. According to Jon Gibs, vice president of Media Analytics, BuzzMetrics is focusing on the social web to determine not only who is sending the message, but also who is listening to it. In that way, they can determine meaningful measurement.

comScore

www.comscore.com

comScore is a high-end web service for analyzing websites' statistics. They have a wide and deep variety of services to measure audience participation. They have a very good library of presentations and white papers that you may want to check out. They also have a data mine from which they publish infographics that are terrific to use in your own presentations.

YouTube Insights

www.youtube.com/my_videos_insight

Insights is an easy-to-use tool built into YouTube. It gives you a great summary of activity and shows you such things as demographics and popularity among competitors. To access it, you need to log in to your account or create one if you don't already have one. Look at the links across the top of the page, and choose Insights.

Boardreader

www.boardreader.com

Boardreader is a helpful tool that you can use to view and analyze activity on discussion boards. Lots of great trend and other tracking information is tucked among forums and boards and is not readily accessible from other methods. This tool makes it easy to find.

Facebook Insights

www.facebook.com/insights

Insights is a valuable Facebook tool to help make the data from Facebook trackable. Until its introduction, it was difficult to determine exactly what was happening on your "corner" of Facebook. With this suite of analytics tools, you can find data about such things as demographics and readership. Facebook developers can dive even deeper. There are two main sections — Users and Interactions — so that you can determine what actually works with your particular readers.

Index